KU-196-235

Teaching ICT

Reflective Teaching and Learning: A guide to professional issues for beginning secondary teachers

Edited by Sue Dymoke and Jennifer Harrison

Reflective practice is at the heart of effective teaching. This core text is an introduction for beginning secondary teachers on developing the art of critical reflective teaching throughout their professional work. Designed as a flexible resource, the book combines theoretical background with practical reflective activities.

Developing as a Reflective Secondary Teacher Series

These subject-specific core texts are for beginning secondary teachers following PGCE, GTP or undergraduate routes into teaching. Each book provides a comprehensive guide to beginning subject teachers, offering practical guidance to support students through their training and beyond. Most importantly, the books are designed to help students develop a more reflective and critical approach to their own practice. Key features of the series are:

- observed lessons, providing both worked examples of good practice and commentaries by the teachers themselves and other observers
- an introduction to national subject frameworks including a critical examination of the role and status of each subject
- support for beginning teachers on all aspects of subject teaching, including planning, assessment, classroom management, differentiation and teaching strategies
- a trainee-focused approach to critical and analytical reflection on practice
- a research-based section demonstrating M-level work
- a comprehensive companion website linking all subjects, featuring video clips of sample lessons, a range of support material and weblinks.

Teaching Mathematics
Paul Chambers

Teaching History
Ian Phillips

Teaching Science
Tony Liversidge, Matt Cochrane, Bernie Kerfoot and Judith Thomas

Teaching ICT
Carl Simmons and Claire Hawkins

Teaching English
Carol Evans, Alyson Midgley, Phil Rigby, Lynne Warham and Peter Woolnough

Teaching ICT

Carl Simmons and Claire Hawkins

Los Angeles | London | New Delhi
Singapore | Washington DC

© Carl Simmons and Claire Hawkins 2009

First published 2009

Apart from any fair dealing for the purposes of research or
private study, or criticism or review, as permitted under the
Copyright, Designs and Patents Act, 1988, this publication may
be reproduced, stored or transmitted in any form, or by any
means, only with the prior permission in writing of the
publishers, or in the case of reprographic reproduction, in
accordance with the terms of licences issued by the Copyright
Licensing Agency. Enquiries concerning reproduction outside
those terms should be sent to the publishers.

SAGE Publications Ltd
1 Oliver's Yard
55 City Road
London EC1Y 1SP

SAGE Publications Inc.
2455 Teller Road
Thousand Oaks, California 91320

SAGE Publications India Pvt Ltd
B 1/I 1 Mohan Cooperative Industrial Area
Mathura Road
New Delhi 110 044

SAGE Publications Asia-Pacific Pte Ltd
33 Pekin Street #02-01
Far East Square
Singapore 048763

Library of Congress Control Number: 2008942900

British Library Cataloguing in Publication data

A catalogue record for this book is available from the
British Library

ISBN 978-1-84787-253-1
ISBN 978-1-84787-254-8 (pbk)

Typeset by C&M Digitals (P) Ltd, Chennai, India
Printed in Great Britain by T. J. International, Padstow, Cornwall
Printed on paper from sustainable resources

Mixed Sources
Product group from well-managed
forests and other controlled sources
www.fsc.org Cert no. TT-COC-2082
© 1996 Forest Stewardship Council
FSC

CONTENTS

ACKNOWLEDGEMENTS

The authors would like to thank the following people for their help and support in the writing of this book:

Richard Foster and the staff and pupils at Darwen Vale High School, Lancashire for generously allowing us to film in their school.

Colin Johnson for the original artwork in Chapter 3.

Alex Savage for being so generous with his resources and ideas.
Our families, friends and colleagues for their patience, support and encouragement.

1 SO YOU WANT TO TEACH ICT?

This chapter explores:

- how the book can help you
- a philosophy of education and the development of your own philosophy of education
- the meaning of education, teaching and learning today
- the purpose of the curriculum in schools and how this is changing
- how information and communication technology (ICT) fits into the curriculum
- key people you will be working with in school ICT departments
- the future prospects of ICT in the school curriculum.

Teaching is an exciting and rewarding career. You will be working with people who have innate curiosity and love learning though creative and exciting approaches. While we know the rewards of the teaching profession, we also recognize the challenges you will face. We hope that this book will be of practical use to you when taking your first steps as a new ICT teacher.

We have both been secondary ICT teachers, teaching across the secondary age range and in further education. We are both strong believers in peer support and have gained much from our own network of peers over the years – none of us are perfect and we believe in sharing ideas and approaches to help us all become better teachers. Our own career paths have now lead us to higher education where we train people who want to become ICT teachers. The principle of sharing ideas is evident in our work with our colleagues and in how we encourage our students to engage with (their own and their pupils') teaching and learning. We hope that this book will allow us to share ideas with you to help you become an ICT teacher.

We teach people from many different backgrounds who enter the profession through a variety of routes: undergraduate degrees with recommendation for qualified teacher status (QTS) or Professional/Postgraduate Certificate of Education (PGCEs) with the possibility of gaining Master's-level credits. We recognize the unique talents, skills and personalities which each beginning ICT teacher brings to the profession, and we hope we meet the challenge of meeting such diverse audience needs. However, whichever route you are taking into teaching, your end goal remains the same: to be a successful teacher of ICT. We have tried to make this book useful for all of you.

HOW THIS BOOK CAN HELP YOU

This book is essentially practical in its nature. We aim to give you pointers to relevant research, but we do not intend becoming over-involved in exploring this (there are many books and journals which will allow you to explore relevant research in more detail). The 'What the research says' section explores an aspect of education and some of the associated research in more depth – you can use these as starting points for your own research. The approaches we explore are based on our own experience, that of our colleagues, our students and from research. This book can be used by those who are studying on undergraduate, PGCE or Graduate Teacher Programme (GTP) routes into teaching who want practical support, by those who have just completed their studies or it can provide a framework for those supporting beginning teachers. There is a companion website which offers additional materials (weblinks, video clips exemplifying issues explored in the book, additional commentary, pro formas and so on), but this book can be used as a stand-alone resource too.

I am thinking of becoming a teacher

Those who are considering becoming a teacher can use this book to gain an insight into teaching and learning approaches and the role of the ICT teacher. You will gain an insight into current issues in ICT education, what you are expected to teach, as well as the fundamentals of planning, differentiation and classroom management strategies. These areas are usually explored during interviews for teaching courses. It will also give you an overview of ICT teaching allowing you to make a more informed decision about your career path (see companion website www.sagepub.co.uk/secondary video clip, *Rewarding career*, to hear Richard talking about his teaching experience). You can use the points for reflection and further reading texts to help explore your own thoughts on teaching and learning.

I am studying on an undergraduate route into teaching

The book will give you practical help and support in the core responsibilities of an ICT teacher. It will help you to identify appropriate teaching and learning approaches for your pupils and the topics you are teaching, exploring differentiation, assessment and how to plan effectively. Throughout the book, you are asked to reflect on or investigate topics to help you to identify your own beliefs, style and the most appropriate approaches for you as an individual, developing teacher. The book also identifies relevant research which you should explore further using the weblinks and suggestions for further reading at the end of each chapter and on the companion website. The transcripts and scenarios in the chapters and the video clips on the companion website (www.sagepub.co.uk/secondary) exemplify points in the text. You should look for further examples during observations on placement and in your own practice. The points for reflection and research links (see companion website) can help you to identify a suitable topic for your dissertation for your final year.

I am studying a PGCE which includes Master's-level credits

Many of your requirements will be the same as an undergraduate, although the condensed nature of your course will see you wanting immediate answers to problems. This book can be used either as a textbook to provide the overall picture for teaching and learning in ICT, or you can dip into it to find answers to particular problems or issues you are facing at that moment in time. The transcripts and the video clips (see companion website, www.sagepub.co.uk/secondary) will help you to quickly identify how the theory discussed in the text will apply in practice. You should supplement this through your own observations and reflections during your school placements. The points for reflection, research identified in each chapter and the sample research questions on the companion website will help you to identify suitable topics for Master's-level research. We would strongly recommend that you follow up the research identified in the book and the further reading and weblinks at the end of each chapter and on the companion website.

I am on the Graduate Teacher Programme

This intensive, employment-based route into teaching will need immediate answers to classroom situations. Before you start on the programme, you may want to read the book as a textbook to give you an insight into the issues you will face over the next year of your training. You will then be able to dip into the book as and when you need to address particular issues. You should use the transcripts and video clips on the companion website to help you identify how theory translates to practice. You will need to develop reflective practice (Chapter 2) to help you identify how you are applying theory in your own classroom. You can use the points for reflection to help stimulate discussion on relevant issues with your mentor. It may also be helpful to revisit the points for reflection and research identified in the book and on the companion website if you pursue a Master's qualification at a later date.

I am an NQT

This is a busy and demanding year when it can be difficult to balance your continuing professional development with adapting to a new career. The latter chapters provide guidance on your newly qualified teacher (NQT) year, possible routes for developing and extending your professional role and for building further on the Professional Standards which you met through your training. This year should enable you to experiment with different approaches and to find your own style. The book will help you to reflect on these areas and may suggest different ways of discharging your professional role. In the future, you may opt to study for a Master's qualification. The points for reflection in the chapters, research methods and research ideas on the companion website could be revisited to guide you and provide ideas for your dissertation.

I am a mentor for beginning teachers

This book will provide you with an overview of what beginning teachers learn and some of the requirements of Master's-level courses. The book identifies points for reflection in each chapter which could be used to stimulate discussions or research ideas which you could use to help the student teacher identify and develop their thoughts for assignment work. Some student teachers will seek support from you for their assignment work. We know that many ICT teachers who studied ICT or computing at university may not have engaged in dissertation-type research before (instead completing practical projects based on systems models). There are two different models for research provided on the companion website (www.sagepub.co.uk/secondary, Chapter 2 and 10 resources) which will provide you with an insight into and framework for supporting students with this type of work. Discussion of theory in the book is supported by transcripts of classroom practice and video clips on the companion website. You could use these to help beginning teachers identify and reflect on the practice they are observing and to analyse their own practice.

PHILOSOPHY OF EDUCATION

You have decided that teaching is a potential career path for you. You may be just starting on this journey or you may already be some way along the path. It is worthwhile pausing to reflect on the beliefs and values which you are bringing to the profession and the broader context of education which may inform your own philosophy of education.

Every day we all use words and concepts which we presume convey the same perceptions and ideas to the people around us. Very infrequently do we analyse the words we are using and what we actually mean by them.

Reflection Point

Reflection Point 1.1

Consider the following words and the prompt questions.

Education

What is education? What is its purpose? When does it happen and how?

Teaching

Who is a teacher? Are teachers the only people who teach? How is teaching different from training? What makes a good teacher and why?

Learning

What is learning? How do we know that learning has happened? How do we learn best? Is learning involuntary or do we have to consciously learn?

Think about how you use these words and what you mean by them. Do you think that your perception of them is the same or different to other people's? What may cause differences in perception?

In this section, we do not aim to provide answers to these questions (as there are not necessarily any right answers to give), rather what we want is to cause you to think about them and start to examine your own views and beliefs.

Education

Our view is that education is a holistic approach to the development of an individual. It should develop their knowledge and understanding of the world around them and provide them with the skills to function in society (which includes, but not exclusively, economic contribution). This, then, is more than just teaching facts and how to apply them, rather it is to do with how an individual relates to and engages with others, the contribution they make to society, their own self-awareness, self-confidence and ability to function in the world. We would also take this further, for education and learning should surely not stop when a person leaves an educational institution (be that school, further education or university). A role of education should also be to inspire a love of learning and to develop an inquistive mind. This should not always be for economic gain, but a personal curiosity to find out more about the world around us, leading to a greater understanding of those topics which interest us. Some of this may overlap with jobs or career aspirations, but we hope that pupils leave school wanting to know more about a plethora of subjects, with a real love of learning for its own sake.

Reflection Point 1.2

What do you believe?

- Why do you think education is important?
- How did your education influence your life and why?
- Why do you want to be a teacher?

(See www.sagepub.co.uk/secondary for further prompts to help you devise a philosophy of education.)

Reflection Point

Teaching

The best teachers are those who have a real passion for their subject. They communicate their excitement to pupils and are creative and innovative in their teaching. They inspire in pupils a similar love for their subject and a desire to know more about it. A teacher is generally deemed to be someone who has been appropriately trained and who works in a school and certainly that is the interpretation we are using in this book, but is that all? When a parent teaches their child to ride a bike, to share their toys or learn their times tables, are they not acting as a teacher too? If we have a mentor at work who shows us how to do our job and helps us settle in, are they a teacher as well? If we examine these broader definitions of 'a teacher', we can see the holistic nature of teaching and educating: there are multiple factors influencing a pupil's development, with teaching and learning in school being only one of these. In fact, it could be said that every individual teaches children through their words and actions.

In the first points for reflection, we asked you to consider the difference between teaching and training. Training aims to provide a specific, usually narrow skill-set. It is often related to a particular task and the skills developed may have limited value away from that task. Teaching is about development of the whole individual, not a focus on developing a particular skill. Teachers should be concerned for the whole person, not just how that individual pupil relates to their subject area.

Learning

There are many theories of learning. During your training as a teacher, you will no doubt explore the theories of Vygotsky, Dewey, Piaget, Kolb, Gardner, Bruner and so on. You will be expected to relate these theories to your own practice and identify what it will mean for you in the classroom. The work of these theoreticians (and others) have helped us to move forward in our understanding of learning, but there are no definitive answers. Also, these theories were not always intended to be used by educationalists; they are more often related to the study of psychology and have been adapted for use by teachers.

Learning is sometimes done as an isolated activity, for instance reading a book for our own interest, but usually we learn within a social context with other people. Distance learners frequently express a feeling of isolation, are often anxious and need more additional support than those learning in a face-to-face context (McInnerney and Roberts, 2004). Perhaps this indicates that humans are more naturally adapted to learning in a social context and often in collaboration with others.

Reflection Point

Reflection Point 1.3

Consider how you learn best, perhaps focusing on something which you do or know particularly well, and consider how you learnt it. What makes that form of learning most effective for you?

Now consider a situation where learning was not effective. What made this learning experience ineffective? How could it have been improved?

What lessons can you learn from this reflection for your teaching and learning practice?

Learning with and through collaboration with others, for instance in group or paired work, can be particularly effective. Ofsted (2005b: 19) identified that in some cases teachers were not encouraging pupils to use talk sufficiently. The report states the 'importance of pupils' talk in developing both reading and writing'. In 1976 Barnes identified that our use of language (in talking and free writing) helps us to reshape our experience helping us to learn. How often do we talk through a problem to help us understand it better or to reach a solution? Talking helps us to clarify our thoughts and develop our understanding. Vygotsky theorized that those who engaged in private talk (either internally or out loud) were more able to progress in their learning and become better learners. The way we structure learning opportunities in our classrooms will influence how much is learnt and becomes embedded knowledge for pupils. It is too easy for pupils to learn a required or expected response without developing a deeper, more personal understanding of the concepts we are teaching. We want pupils to develop their own understanding and knowledge rather than simply regurgitating ours.

People have a thirst for knowledge and understanding: we want to know 'why …?'. As infants we start to develop our understanding of the world in which we live and this continues as we grow: learning is a continuous process. Sometimes we deliberately set out to learn something new; at other times we learn almost unconsciously through observing or listening, while we watch television, talk to our friends or read the newspaper. As teachers we need to exploit pupils' natural desire to learn, to utilize their learning outside school and encourage them to actively engage in the learning process and to become self-regulated, motivated, lifelong learners.

Learning is done by an individual – we cannot force them to learn no matter how hard we 'teach'! Teaching is not the same as learning, but it is sometimes perceived as being the same by beginning teachers. Most people will agree that they learn best (and improve) through hands-on practice. This means that we need to let go of teaching from the front of the room and instead provide opportunities for pupils to learn through practice. Strategies for encouraging learning in your classroom are explored throughout the book, but particularly in Chapter 4.

SHAPING THE CURRICULUM

Schools and the education system exist in a complex arena. Everyone has an opinion on what schools should do and what education should achieve: somehow these different perspectives must be reconciled. The Qualifications and Curriculum Authority (QCA) undertook extensive consultation and research before publishing the new secondary National Curriculum (QCA, 2007). The National Curriculum is structured around programmes of study for the subjects covered by the National Curriculum. ICT has a discrete programme of study which details what should be taught throughout the school years, including Key Stage 3 (Years 7–9) and Key Stage 4

(Years 10–11). Based on consultations during the National Curriculum review, the QCA identified three principal aims summarizing the ethos of the views expressed by different stakeholders (including pupils, parents, teachers and employers). These were that young people should become:

- successful learners who enjoy learning, make progress and achieve
- confident individuals who are able to lead safe, healthy and fulfilling lives
- responsible citizens who make a positive contribution to society (Waters, 2007, 2008).

When we compare the previous National Curriculum Programme of Study for ICT (DfEE, 1999) and the new one (QCA, 2007), there are no really significant changes to the content and concepts taught. There is an increased emphasis on developing the knowledge and understanding necessary to become a discriminating and capable user of ICT and e-safety is now explicitly included. In any ICT curriculum, you will find reference to databases, spreadsheets, presentation-based work (such as word processing and desktop publishing) and multimedia. The National Curriculum, though, does not explicitly mention these applications, instead addressing the capability of the user in selecting and using relevant tools appropriately and efficiently. Concepts such as fitness for purpose, audience needs, efficiency in processes, relevance and detection of bias or inaccuracy in data are all addressed. From this, you should be able to see that discrete teaching of ICT in schools is much more than a skills-based training exercise. We are teaching pupils to use ICT effectively in everyday situations.

The National Curriculum review has refined the structure of the curriculum and made it possible to deliver learning in more flexible ways. Over the next few years, schools will explore this flexibility, and the expectation is that subject areas will work more closely together to deliver a more integrated curriculum. The challenge for teachers is to see the National Curriculum as the minimum entitlement for pupils and to deliver a broader and richer curriculum in schools.

Reflection Point 1.4

Review the audit on the companion website (www.sagepub.co.uk/secondary) and consider if your subject knowledge is broad enough to address all of the topic areas raised.

What else do you think should be taught in ICT lessons? Are there other topics which inspire you which you would want to include? How might you achieve this?

ICT: PART OF THE JIGSAW

Just as ICT is permeating all aspects of our lives, it is becoming an integral part of teaching and learning in schools. There are three roles for ICT in school:

1. ICT is a discrete subject within the National Curriculum. The programme of study gives details of ICT concepts and processes which pupils should learn. These will include the underpinning theory for ICT and the development of ICT capability enabling pupils to become confident and discriminating users of ICT. It is recommended (DfES, 2002) that ICT is taught as a discrete subject for at least 60 minutes per week at Key Stage 3. At Key Stage 4, a functional skills qualification in ICT is being piloted highlighting the importance of ICT alongside English and mathematics.
2. ICT is used in other subjects as a *tool* to enhance teaching and learning. For instance, geography may use Google Earth to explore geological features of land disrupted by tectonic plate movement, or modern foreign languages may use video conferencing to converse with pupils in a school in France. These subject areas are using ICT but not directly teaching the concepts of ICT.
3. ICT is used by teachers to plan and administer lessons and their other duties. This may include using ICT to create worksheets, upload material to a virtual learning environment or using electronic mark books to analyse pupil data.

There is a clear distinction between the use of ICT and the teaching of ICT. Simply using ICT in a lesson does not necessarily provide learning opportunities for the underpinning concepts; it will not always build and develop capability. However, there are those who will argue that because ICT is *used* in other subjects that it is being *taught* through those subjects. Normally this use helps to reinforce the learning which has already taken place in an ICT lesson rather than introducing new ICT concepts. Teachers of other disciplines are, quite naturally, focused on their own subject area, not on ICT teaching. To try to explain this distinction more clearly, let us consider the teaching of English. English is read, spoken and listened to in every subject area, yet the legitimacy of teaching English as a discrete subject is never called into question (nor are we advocating that it should be). It is understood that there are other concepts and processes which require a subject specialist and dedicated curriculum time to be explored. This is the same in ICT.

The intention for the revised National Curriculum (QCA, 2007) is for more integration between the subjects. This will mean departments working more closely together to identify linkages between subjects and timing delivery of topics to enable these to coincide. Introducing cross-curricular projects which help pupils to explore the integrated themes across a range of subject areas helps de-fragment pupils' knowledge of different curriculum areas. ICT has a central role in this. There is already a requirement for all subject areas to identify and integrate ICT opportunities into their lessons. With increasing use of virtual learning environments (VLEs) and e-portfolios in school, other teachers will be seeking support and ideas from ICT teachers and staff. This presents a huge opportunity for ICT teachers, who will be able to influence the use of technology in school and be in a strong position to collaborate on developing a more flexible curriculum which supports greater use of ICT in innovative and creative ways.

Reflection Point 1.5

What role do you think the ICT department and staff should have in advising and supporting staff from other subject areas? How do you think cross-curricular projects may benefit pupils and staff? Are there any disadvantages to cross-curricular projects?

Beyond the curriculum

The curriculum for ICT is fairly busy. Usually ICT at Key Stage 3 is allocated one 60-minute lesson per week. Designing a curriculum which includes a fundamental ICT skill-set, opportunities to attain ICT capability and cross-curricular links is challenging. For instance, many pupils struggle to use the keyboard efficiently: they are frequently confused about the use of the shift key (particularly when Caps Lock gives a capital letter equally well!); they do not understand how to use or set tabs; keyboard shortcuts are a mystery. When entering Year 7, pupils may never have used a network (with shared peripherals, their own login and password and own area to save work); they may not understand setting up directory structures, naming conventions and the relevance of file extensions. The challenge for an ICT teacher is to find time to incorporate these fundamentals into the curriculum, through either integration into other topic areas or by addressing these in a separate unit at the start of the year.

Many pupils will be very familiar with social networking, gaming, storing photographs, downloading music and so on. These tend to be topics we have not traditionally taught. We may touch on copyright issues related to downloading music, and e-safety around publishing photographs and using social networking sites. Some teachers, though, are starting to exploit social networking tools (such as blogs or wikis) for educational purposes. We often assume that pupils know everything about the tools which they appear to access daily, but they frequently do not. There may be a significant number of pupils who will not have home access to a computer and may not have even used email before.

Reflection Point 1.6

Identify some ways that emerging technologies such as social networking tools, games and mobile technology could be used for educational purposes in lessons. (See weblinks for further details.)

WHO'S WHO IN ICT?

Teaching can be an isolated activity, with one teacher in front of a class of pupils, but there will be a number of people you will work with in an ICT department:

- *Head of Department* oversees the operation of the department, including curriculum development, assessment and monitoring (including pupil data) and resource management
- *your mentor* may be the Head of Department or may be another ICT teacher. They will liaise with other staff to ensure your placement meets your needs
- *ICT teachers* fall into two categories: those who are ICT specialists and those who are specialists in other curriculum areas, but also teach ICT
- *Key Stage Co-ordinators* develop the curriculum and resources for a particular key stage. They will normally do this in liaison with the Head of Department and with other teachers
- The *network manager* and *technicians* are support staff who do not normally teach. They provide ICT and network support for staff and will normally advise on the development of ICT resources for the school (not just within ICT). It is important to be on good terms with the information technology (IT) support staff as they set passwords and network permissions (essentially they can make your life easier (or otherwise) while you are on placement)
- *cross-curricular co-ordinator* will oversee the identification of ICT opportunities in other subject areas and will work to co-ordinate the delivery of related topic areas across the school curriculum. They will also work on any cross-curricular projects which are identified
- *non-ICT teachers* will book and use ICT classrooms and resources for lessons requiring those facilities
- *ICT teaching assistants* are teaching assistants who specialise in ICT and are attached to the department. They will normally support a range of pupils in ICT classes. Teaching assistants who are attached to a subject area are able to develop an expertise in that subject which can be more helpful to pupils. If a teaching assistant does not have any knowledge of ICT, this can become a barrier to support which, as the teacher, you would need to manage.

It is important that you work effectively and professionally with everyone in schools. One of the lessons in this book is that good, creative teaching and learning strategies can come from a range of sources. Be prepared to listen and learn from everyone during your time in schools.

FUTURE PROSPECTS

You are entering the teaching profession at a time of significant change (although education never seems to stand still). It is an exciting time with opportunities for people with new ideas, innovative approaches and a good knowledge of the educational potential of new technologies. The content and structure of what we teach is shifting. The changes proposed by the government's White Paper, *14–19 Education and Skills* (DfES, 2005a), written in response to the Tomlinson Report (Working Group on 14–19 Reform, 2004), are now coming to fruition. The coming years will measure the success of the renewed qualifications landscape. The new vocational pathways (including diplomas) will involve teachers in greater collaboration between various educational partners and employers. The success of qualifications like the diplomas rely heavily on the commitment and involvement of industry in pupils' education and training. Industry and other employers were the principal authors of the diplomas. This was to ensure that the skills gaps employers had identified in school leavers were addressed. The commitment from these employers, therefore, should be strong.

The pilot of the functional skills qualifications is exploring the potential of offering these as stand-alone or as an integrated element of existing qualifications. The government wants to see all pupils leaving school with knowledge of basic, core skills in literacy, numeracy and ICT. ICT is seen as a skill for life, now as important as being literate and numerate.

Change is driven either internally through needs identified by people within education or change is imposed from external sources. Many of the drivers for change appear to be from external sources, but the origin of some of these are from educationalists themselves: educational research informs government-driven change, for instance Assessment for Learning (Black and Wiliam, 1998). Teachers recognize that there are issues with teaching and learning today which need to be addressed and some of these will require a fundamental shift in the way in which teaching and learning take place. The government's *Every Child Matters* agenda (DfES, 2004b) provides us with broad aims of what we want for our children and young people. There is continuing research into teaching and learning practice, but we need innovative, creative teachers to grasp the opportunities presented through research and to develop this into good practice in our classrooms today. We all need to consider what our dreams and aspirations are for education and how we can help schools to meet these challenges.

 ## Further reading

Barrow, R. and Woods, R. (2006) *An Introduction to Philosophy of Education*. London: Routledge.

Jarvis, P. (2006) *Towards a Comprehensive Theory of Human Learning: Lifelong Learning and the Learning Society*. Vol. 1. Oxford: Routledge.

Mortimore, P. (ed.) (1999) *Understanding Pedagogy and its Impact on Learning*. London: Paul Chapman Publishing .

 ## Weblinks

Live links to each of these websites can be found on the companion website, www.sagepub.co.uk/secondary.

Futurelab support innovative ideas for using ICT creatively for teaching and learning – www.futurelab.org.uk/

James Atherton's website provides an overview of teaching and learning theories – www.learningandteaching.info/

The National Curriculum (2007) – http://curriculum.qca.org.uk/

2 CONTEMPORARY ISSUES IN ICT TEACHING

This chapter provides an overview of:

- the role of ICT in the school curriculum
- recent changes to the National Curriculum and the 14–19 curriculum
- ICT use to support the *Every Child Matters* initiative in schools
- the role of reflection in the profession and how best to engage with this process
- engaging in educational research now and in the future
- key technological changes in schools and how these could be used to support teaching and learning.

ICT is an ever-changing subject. There will always be developments within the subject that you will need to be aware of and keep up to date with. Alongside this are other changes to the environment within which we work (political, social, technological) which can also impact on the educational arena. This chapter briefly explores some of these issues. You will encounter these again in context as you read the book.

The constantly evolving landscape of ICT can be a source of anxiety as well as inspiration for ICT teachers. Many of the technologies we use in schools will have been superseded by the time our pupils enter the workforce. So, what do we teach them? The fundamental concepts of ICT do not change (although they may be refined), which provides ICT teachers with an element of stability while technologies change around us. Throughout the technological changes we still teach pupils the principles for choosing appropriate ICT for a given task, how to use a systems model and human–computer interface (HCI) principles. This should reassure teachers of ICT when the pace of technological change seems overwhelming.

ICT IN THE CURRICULUM

ICT can be seen in a number of contexts by teachers, through:

- discrete teaching of ICT
- cross-curricular use as a tool in other subjects
- use by educators to support teaching and learning, including administrative tasks.

Within this book, we are more concerned with the first of these, but you will also encounter the latter two here and throughout your teaching career.

Discrete teaching of ICT develops pupils' capability. It provides the theoretical underpinning knowledge of ICT needed to be equipped to adapt to evolving technologies. The use of ICT as a tool in other subjects is important to help consolidate ICT skills through other contexts, which is vitally important given ICT's limited curriculum time.

Cross-curricular use of ICT is encouraged by the government and monitored by the Office for Standards in Education (Ofsted), but busy teachers in other subject areas may see this as a tick-box exercise unless it is co-ordinated across departments and forms part of a strategic vision. The co-ordination role may be allocated to the ICT department, particularly as well-developed, cross-curricular use of ICT could benefit pupils' achievement in ICT. Ofsted is looking for ICT to be fully embedded in the school curriculum to the extent that it is 'an everyday aspect of pupils' learning' (Ofsted, 2005a: 1). While some schools do this well, many others still have much work to do before this becomes a reality.

Technology is recognized as a transformative tool. It is increasingly used for developing and managing schools at a strategic level, but teachers are also expected to use ICT to develop and enhance their own practice. ICT is a mandatory National Curriculum subject and it is very difficult to meet the requirements set out in the National Curriculum and the secondary frameworks through purely cross-curricular teaching. The recommended 60 minutes per week for ICT at Key Stage 3 (DfES, 2002) can be supplemented through cross-curricular reinforcement and consolidation. There are many good examples of how ICT is used effectively through other subject areas (see BECTA weblink, at the end of this chapter, for examples). The challenge for schools is the distribution and allocation of ICT resources if ICT is to become fully embedded across the curriculum.

It is likely that your own view is that all of these issues are important, but that discrete teaching should provide the foundation for ICT capability while cross-curricular delivery should help to reinforce and consolidate that capability.

CURRICULUM CHANGES

The academic year starting in 2008 has seen a number of changes come to fruition across the secondary curriculum. The most recent changes to the 14–19 curriculum were brought about by the Tomlinson Report (Working Group on 14–19 Reform, 2004) and the government's response (DfES, 2005a). This has resulted in a modification of the qualifications structure, the qualifications which are on offer and the ways in which students are able to progress through their studies. More pathways are available for vocational qualifications and new types of qualifications are available with the launch of diplomas. Diplomas are compelling education providers to collaborate further and to form consortia to ensure their success. The success of these initiatives will not be fully known until the review scheduled to commence in 2013 has been completed and the results published.

ICT has seen a range of new vocational qualifications in recent years. Some of these qualifications are flexible in meeting the requirements of different schools, whereby schools can select the units which are most appropriate to their pupils and the strengths of their department. These tend to offer a broad range of units covering traditional ICT skills (such as databases and presenting information units) as well as units which focus on more contemporary technologies, such as those connected with web development and gaming technologies. Other qualifications have more focused progression routes, but provide interesting and engaging learning for particular groups of pupils.

The changes to the 14–19 curriculum necessitated a review of the Key Stage 3 curriculum too. It is sensible to examine the foundation point of the knowledge, skills and understanding which enables pupils to progress to suitable qualifications in Key Stage 4 and beyond. We should be providing an integrated curriculum which builds on, consolidates and enhances pupils' knowledge and understanding throughout their formal education. This review resulted in some changes to the curriculum at Key Stage 3 and also to the level descriptors relevant to the Key Stage 3 age range.

We would hope that these recent reviews and changes will result in some stability of the curriculum and qualifications framework for some years to come. This would enable teachers to consolidate and develop the curriculum to meet the needs of their pupils.

PROFESSIONAL ISSUES

Teachers have an immediate and lasting impact on children and young people, which may continue to affect them throughout their lives. What you say and do guides pupils when forming opinions of the world around them and, more importantly, of themselves. Professionalism is connected with how you behave, which is influenced by your values and beliefs. It is of paramount importance that you act in a professional manner throughout your career. Your dedication to promoting effective teaching and learning, helping pupils to achieve to the best of their ability, will be underwritten by your professionalism.

Reflection Point 2.1

Think of two or three people who you feel are professional in their approach. What contributes to your view of their professionalism? Write down the characteristics of professionalism.

Identify areas where you meet these characteristics and aspects of professionalism which you need to develop further.

Reflection Point

EVERY CHILD MATTERS

Every Child Matters (DfES, 2004b) came about following the tragic death of Victoria Climbié. The aim is for services for children and young people (up to the age of 19) to become integrated to help prevent further similar tragedies. *Every Child Matters* has five central tenets to which each child is entitled:

- Be healthy
- Stay safe
- Enjoy and achieve
- Make a positive contribution
- Achieve economic well-being.

Reflection Point 2.2

Review the five central tenets of *Every Child Matters* and identify how schools and teachers can make a positive contribution to these. Identify the role of ICT in supporting these aims.

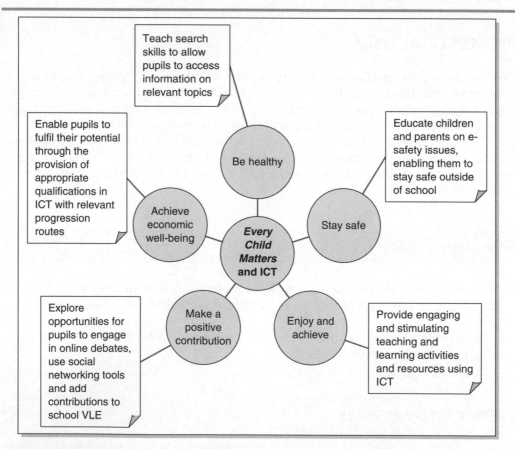

Figure 2.1 *Every Child Matters* and ICT

Figure 2.1 gives some examples of how ICT can contribute to *Every Child Matters*. It is not comprehensive, but helps you to identify some opportunities which exist. The importance of *Every Child Matters* is the step change which everyone who is involved with children and families has had to make. All agencies should now work together to achieve the aims of *Every Child Matters*, sharing information and strategies to form an integrated service provision. As a teacher you will be part of this.

REFLECTION

The Professional Standards for QTS (Training and Development Agency, 2007) now include reflection, which has not explicitly appeared in previous versions, thereby formalizing a skill which has always been important to the profession. The 2007 Standards also make reference to the importance of effectively working with those who are supporting you by acting on their feedback.

Reflection seeks to develop our understanding of a situation and to identify ways of improving it. It is a personal viewpoint in which feelings and emotions play an important part. Reflection is typically used in complex and dynamic situations, helping us to develop our understanding of the interplay of different factors and how we can better address similar situations in the future. The majority of people have to work hard at developing reflective practice; good quality reflection does not come naturally. You will need to dedicate time and effort to improve your skills in this area.

Reflection is a difficult skill to learn. It requires critical thinking skills, the ability to analyse a situation, to synthesize different views from peers, mentors and from research, and then to develop ideas to help improve your practice. It is also a cyclical process: once you have developed your ideas and put them into practice, you should naturally evaluate their success and reflect on the outcome and whether further changes are needed.

Reflection moves through a number of stages (see companion website, www.sagepub. co.uk/secondary, for transcripts with commentary and video clips demonstrating reflection). There are a number of models available which may help you to develop your reflective skills. Typically, the stages include:

1. Briefly describe what you have done or what has happened.
2. Broaden and deepen your understanding of what has happened and why through further reading and discussion.
3. Consider and analyse the situation – how it may be repeated or changed in the future.

Others may have different numbers of stages or break the stages down further, but essentially the process remains the same. Figure 2.2 provides an example of how a beginning teacher has reflected on an incident in class.

As can be seen in Figure 2.2, the reflective process is cyclical. The teacher has reflected on the incident and has identified a possible way to improve classroom practice. Once

Example: Reflective practice

I asked two pupils to demonstrate their work at the end of the lesson and for others to critically evaluate the work. A number of the comments were negatively phrased and had the potential for bullying: I needed to stop the pupils who were doing this. Overall though, the pupils enjoyed demonstrating their work and others got ideas from what they saw which suggests that it is a worthwhile activity.

Black et al. (2003: 51) state that:

'students' learning can be enriched by marking their own or one another's work, whether this be classwork, homework, test scripts or presentations to the class'.

This suggests that I should try again with pupils sharing their work, but I need to be able to avoid the potential bullying of negative comments.

Bereiter and Scardmalia (citied in Batho, 2005: 81) on modelling writing:

'The thinking that goes on in composition needs to be modelled by the teacher, who can thereby show the problem-solving and planning processes that ... pupils are often unaware of ... and so that they can benefit from observing and discussing each other's mental efforts.'

It seems to me that I may need to model the techniques for effective critical evaluation of work. Perhaps I need to produce a sample piece of work and then work through it showing the class how to critically evaluate – if I start off modelling the technique, I could then encourage the pupils to join in allowing them to practice on a 'safe' piece of work. We could draw up some rules for critical evaluation together!

Next lesson I will model critical evaluation using a sample piece of work I have created and as a class we can try to establish an evaluation criteria which pupils can use with their own and each others work.

This section shows the teacher describing the incident.

Here the teacher is drawing on research and starting to reflect on what happened.

The teacher is reflecting on how to improve classroom practice and identifying concrete solutions.

Figure 2.2   Example of reflection in practice

those changes have been implemented, further reflection on its success and any further improvements would be needed. Figure 2.3 shows the cyclical nature of reflection.

You may wish to explore some of the models available to help you reflect. We particularly find Gibbs (1988) a useful structure.

Reflection is an important skill for teachers to possess. It enables you to identify issues and formulate solutions, and it means that you should become more adept at noticing small details in your classroom which can have a big impact on your lesson. This also helps to inform other aspects of your practice including research.

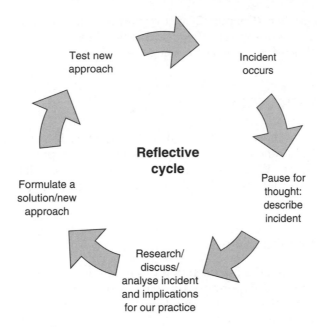

Figure 2.3   Reflective cycle

RESEARCH

As a beginning teacher, you will be making sense of a whole range of information and evidence, textbooks, lectures, government publications, Ofsted reports, journals and Internet sources. Coupled with this, you bring a whole set of experience, values and beliefs of your own to your professional practice. Research and evidence should be the lens through which you make sense of this wide range of opinions, fact and experience.

During your course, you will engage with research for your own personal development as well as for assessed aspects of your course. This will continue throughout your career and currently the expectation is that all teachers will gain a Master's-level qualification (DCSF, 2008a: 12–16). As an ICT practitioner, you may have already engaged with project work where you have used a systems approach to collect and analyse evidence – for example, conducting end-user interviews, collecting current documentation and observing workplace practices. This experience will provide a good foundation for developing some of the analytical techniques which are required for research. However, you may now be asked to engage in research which applies to education rather than ICT development and this can look very different. It is important that you have experience of a variety of research methodologies to enable you to engage effectively in research now and in the future.

There are various forms of research and methodologies and for comprehensive details on these, we would recommend consulting a book such as Cohen et al.'s (2007) book on *Research Methods in Education*. On the companion website (www.sagepub.co.uk/secondary), we present two approaches to research for your consideration. The first is the typical pattern of a research dissertation (Chapter 2 web resources) and the second explores action research (Chapter 10 web resources). If you are mentoring a student teacher, you may also find these approaches helpful when discussing research methodology.

TECHNOLOGY CHANGES

Within three years (at most), children will be using an application that has not even been imagined at the time of writing. In this section we explore the impact of new technologies in schools. We also discuss the key issues to consider in choosing classroom technology. You will find signposts to websites to help you keep up to date with educational technology.

Virtual learning environments

Over the past few years, the introduction of virtual learning environments (VLEs) in schools has increased exponentially. This is due largely to the government's e-strategy document *Harnessing Technology: Transforming Learning and Children's Services* (DfES, 2005b) which set out an action point for all pupils to have access to a personalized online learning space which may support an e-portfolio by 2007/08. A further target requires 'non-school models of learning for disaffected learners' (DfES, 2005b: 6) which could be achieved through a VLE.

The most basic use of a VLE allows teachers to post their worksheets and other resources online for pupils to access electronically, but this is not the best use of the technology. As an ICT teacher, you should be pioneering in your use of the VLE and should use it to personalize pupils' learning experiences. The VLE has certain advantages for working with pupils – while your expectation may be that pupils will use the resources in class and not access it at home, there will be a number of pupils who will want to do additional work to extend their knowledge.

The VLE can obviously be used to put differentiated resources online as well as extension work which goes towards meeting the personalization agenda (Teaching and Learning in 2020 Review Group, 2006). The temptation with a VLE is to produce linear lessons and resources which pupils work through as per a normal face-to-face class, but VLEs operate on the same principles as a website, allowing us to use hyperlinks to enrich our material and provide unique pathways through content. This is the world in which our pupils operate – except in school. The power, therefore, of the VLE for our pupils rests in two particular areas:

- the ability to provide work and resources which pupils can access in an order which helps them to develop and build their own knowledge
- the use of discussion boards to help develop their ability to collaborate, to explain and justify their decisions and assertions.

E-portfolios

Closely linked to the growth of VLEs in school is the development of e-portfolios for pupils' use. A portfolio is a depository for documents or artefacts related to an individual. They are usually a continuously growing and evolving platform for a person to exhibit their work. Ideally, the portfolio should be retained and developed throughout a person's life, enabling them to use it to meet different purposes and to provide a record of their personal journey. An e-portfolio is an electronic version of this.

E-portfolios are increasingly used for assessment purposes (see video clip: *eportfolio* on companion website, www.sagepub.co.uk/secondary). There are commercial solutions which offer a range of features, but in school you will probably use generic software, such as PowerPoint or Adobe Acrobat (to convert files to pdf) to create e-portfolios. The possibilities for e-portfolios are still being explored by educationalists. The vision is for pupils to create e-portfolios in school which can then be used throughout their life for showing their development as a learner and showcasing material for qualifications, potential employers, continuing professional development (CPD) activities and so on (Stefani et al., 2007). One of the key questions regarding e-portfolios is that of ownership and transferability. The e-portfolio needs to be hosted: who will be responsible for hosting pupils' e-portfolios once they have left school? Until this issue can be resolved, lifelong e-portfolios for pupils are unlikely to come to fruition.

E-portfolios are only one of the ways that e-assessment is permeating schools. As VLEs become more embedded in school life, there will be greater emphasis placed on the role of e-assessment. The Key Stage 3 ICT online test (QCA, 2007: 20) is an example of how online assessment can be used for formative assessment purposes during normal lessons.

Interactive whiteboards

Interactive whiteboards are no longer a new technology, but it is a technology for which the quality of use is variable: some are used as glorified data projectors, while other teachers use them in innovative and creative ways to really enhance teaching and learning. There are a number of resources for interactive whiteboards available on the web and through commercial producers. Equally, you can create your own resources (such as hide and reveal or matching exercises) which will match the learning objectives and needs of your classes and pupils. Interactive whiteboards make it easy for you (or a pupil) to annotate work, to create, save and revisit lists or spider diagrams which capture pupils' contributions, to demonstrate techniques or to dynamically respond to learning needs rather than following a linear presentation.

It is unlikely that a school will have an interactive whiteboard in every classroom, so teachers may need to consider alternatives. Depending on the teaching and learning approaches being employed, it is possible to use a wireless mouse and keyboard or a graphics tablet to allow pupils to participate interactively or to demonstrate techniques. This can reduce costs where an interactive whiteboard is not strictly necessary. Throughout the book, references are made to the use of interactive whiteboards in lessons. Notice how different teachers use the technology to support the teaching and learning activities taking place in the classroom.

Electronic voting systems

A good way of encouraging whole-class participation in your lessons is through the use of electronic voting systems. Each pupil has a hand-held device which links to the teacher's computer. The pupils are able to vote on a limited number of options and the whole-class results are immediately calculated and displayed on the screen. As well as the interactivity and immediacy which engages pupils, these systems allow the teacher to assess understanding in the class. The software records responses from each handset facilitating assessment of individuals' understanding. The teacher is also immediately able to react to correct any misconceptions or misunderstandings which are highlighted through the whole-class responses displayed on screen.

Social networking

Social networking tools have much to offer the world of education, particularly those who value social constructivist teaching methods. Unfortunately, these relatively new tools are frequently excluded by those who configure Internet access in schools. It is true that there are potential dangers to granting pupils unmonitored and undirected access to these sites in school, but by blocking them completely, their educational potential is lost and pupils' interest in ICT stagnates. Our role should not be to censor such sites, but to educate pupils in their safe use – we cannot stop pupils from accessing these sites outside school and if they are not taught how to use them safely we are neglecting our duty of care.

Wikis, podcasting and blogs can be used by teachers to disseminate resources, but can also be used effectively by pupils to create content themselves. Teachers need to consider how best to use these resources while maintaining the safety of pupils. The British Educational Communications and Technology Agency (BECTA) provide guidelines (see weblinks) on the safe use of ICT, including social networking tools. Before beginning work with classes using these tools, you should consult the BECTA guidelines and discuss relevant school policies with your mentors.

Innovating

It is not possible (or even desirable) to have all of the latest technologies in our classrooms: schools have limited budgets. It is possible, though, to use creatively the technologies we do have. Futurelab (see weblinks) is dedicated to the innovative use of technology in education. Futurelab projects include:

- *Teaching with Games* which evaluated the educational benefits of using commercial games in the classroom
- *Create-a-Scape* which uses personal digital assistants (PDAs) to interact with the local environment using sounds, video and pictures
- *Newtoon* which is a mobile gaming project which helps to teach physics.

Also investigating and leading on innovative use of ICT for educational and research purposes is the Joint Information Systems Committee (JISC). The JISC is involved with post-16 education projects and services (see weblinks).

The Professional Standards for QTS encourage teachers to innovate and to be creative. Innovative uses of technology can come from many sources and often primary schools or other subject areas have ideas which can be adapted for use in ICT.

Choosing technology for education

As with any resource you use in your classroom, the technologies you select must be fit for purpose. It is easy to become enamoured of the latest technology, but these are big investments for schools. The educational benefits of having the technologies in the classroom must be given full consideration. Curriculum Online provide a guide on their website for evaluating resources (see weblinks). It is possible to have effective teaching and learning take place with older technology, but sound pedagogy, just as it is possible for little learning to take place with new technology and poor teaching.

Reflection Point 2.3

The discussion of the technologies above suggests ways they can be used to help teaching and learning, but sometimes technology can become a barrier. Consider the advantages and disadvantages of using these (and other technologies) in the classroom.

- How do the technologies contribute to the learning taking place?
- Do they help or hinder teacher time, preparation and interaction with the pupils?
- Are there non-technological or simpler alternatives?

Observe teachers in practice – what alternatives do they use to the technology? How effective are these in comparison?

What the research says: games in education

An area of increasing interest to educationalists is the learning potential from games. Many children play video or online games from an early age. The games engage, motivate and entertain, but they also provide learning opportunities, some of which are identified by children themselves (Byron, 2008). Many people, though, express concerns about the use of games in the classroom and a teacher would need to consider the merits of using games on a pedagogic basis.

Games, of course, come in many shapes and sizes. They vary from simple multiple-choice quizzes through to massively multiplayer online games (MMOs) such as *World of Warcraft*.

(Continued)

(Continued)

Here we briefly explore some of the benefits and concerns expressed for the use of games in education.

Massively multiplayer online games appear to hold potential as they require collaboration between participants to solve problems. Steinkuehler (2008: 13) explains that 'the structure of collaboration found in many online games parallels the structure of collaboration that increasingly marks … high-end workplaces'. Gamers create a community of practice which sees new gamers being apprenticed into the community by more experienced practitioners sharing their knowledge. This mentoring is also seen where experienced gamers become involved in new experiences. The participants learn from each other, construct their own experiences and understandings. Friendships are developed online as a result of playing the games. This can be a boon when children are in isolated rural areas and cannot readily see their friends socially. Equally, for those who find it difficult to socialize face to face (for instance, those with Asperger's syndrome) this presents a different context for developing relationships which may harness their strengths (Byron, 2008: 20).

Gamers engage in significant research activity to develop appropriate strategies using a range of sources. They formulate hypotheses and share these with members of the online team. Participants justify their views by drawing on evidence from their research (Steinkuehler, 2008). Many of the skills and the underpinning knowledge and understanding gamers use can be mapped to the ICT National Curriculum (QCA, 2007).

ICT competencies are further developed through the use of a wide range of ICT technologies during research and other 'fandom' activities (materials produced by fans of the game). This helps to develop the capability of ICT users showing initiative and increasing independence expected in the National Curriculum (QCA, 2007). In addition, online games enable gamers to create their own content. Users show 'understanding and use of computational models, such as algorithms or code … represented by player-generated artifacts such as user interface modifications' (Steinkuehler, 2008: 12). We need to carefully consider how this level of competency could be achieved, harnessed and encouraged within the classroom setting.

Looking beyond ICT there are educational benefits in terms of the development of literacy. Participants develop literacy skills through reading research material, manuals and fandom resources. Some participants become creators of this material themselves (Steinkuehler, 2008). Much of the communication mechanism is through online chat, instant messaging and discussion forums developing literacy skills. The integration of these tools in and around the periphery of the games also aids the learning which takes place. Research has found that communication aids the quality of decision-making in the game, it aids reflection on the learning which has occurred, and helps users to develop mediation and leadership skills (de Freitas, 2007: 17).

Alongside the educational benefits above are the opportunity to re-engage reluctant learners and provide opportunities for pupils to learn in different ways.

Much of the research into risks associated with gaming has involved adults rather than children. The principle concern expressed is the potential for aggressive behaviour, stimulated by the content of games. While some studies have shown that this is an issue in the short term, there appears to be little research or evidence regarding long-term effects. The *Byron Review* (Byron, 2008) raises concerns related to brain and cognitive development in children. Children cognitively lack the ability to distinguish fantasy and reality. Certainly, some scenarios may provide heightened stress for children, which may impact on a child's development (Byron, 2008: 151).

Other concerns are based on the educational potential of games. There is confusion in the terminology used between game developers and educationalists (de Freitas, 2007: 10) which will need to be resolved if successful collaboration is to take place. Game designers know how to develop engaging material, while educationalists know the curriculum content. It is bringing these two aspects together which is challenging (de Freitas, 2007; Kiili, 2007). Further, it is important that they are integrated with pedagogy which ensures the learning outcomes desired are what is eventually achieved (de Freitas, 2007: 13).

Dr Tanya Byron (2008: 187) conducted a major review of the risks and potential benefits of the Internet and gaming for children which was published in 2008. She has reviewed evidence from a significant number of studies on the effects of gaming, but highlights that the majority of studies look at the effects on adults rather than children. She concludes that 'It would not be accurate to say that there is no evidence of harm but equally it is not appropriate to conclude that there is evidence of no harm' (Byron, 2008: 152). Given the potential benefits which are indicated by research, she goes on to state that she supports 'efforts to explore the opportunities for using gaming technologies for learning and development' (Byron, 2008: 187). We can be hopeful that further development in this area will be forthcoming through her recommendation that 'Government supports a dialogue between the games industry and the education sector to identify opportunities for the benefits of game-based learning to be evaluated in educational environments' (Byron, 2008: 13).

Further reading

Bell, J. (2005) *Doing your Research Project: A Guide for First-time Researchers in Education, Health and Social Science*. 4th edn. Maidenhead: Open University Press.

Byron, T. (2008) *Safer Children in a Digital World: The Report of the Byron Review*. Department for Children, Schools and Families. PP/D16(7578)/03/08/xx. (www.dfes.gov.uk/byronreview/).

Cohen, L., Manion, L. and Morrison, K. (2007) *Research Methods in Education*. 6th edn. London: Routledge.

Weblinks

Live links to each of these websites can be found on the companion website, www.sagepub.co.uk/secondary.

BECTA provides guidelines for safe use of ICT and examples of good practice – www.becta. org.uk/
Curriculum Online offer advice on evaluating resources for ICT – www.curriculumonline.gov.uk/howto/evaluatingresources.htm
Futurelab support innovative ideas for using ICT creatively for teaching and learning – www.futurelab.org.uk
JISC provide funding and support for innovative technology use to support education – www.jisc.ac.uk

3 WHAT ARE YOU EXPECTED TO TEACH IN ICT?

This chapter covers:

- transition arrangements for Key Stage 2 pupils progressing to secondary school
- curriculum organization for secondary ICT
- the changes to the National Curriculum in 2007 and 14–19 agenda
- an overview of the National Curriculum, government initiatives and other resources which can be used to aid teaching and learning of ICT
- how to develop medium-term plans (also called schemes of work) for ICT, including consideration of cross-curricular themes
- integrating assessment requirements into medium-term planning to enable all pupils to progress.

When sequencing Chapters 3 and 4 we faced a difficulty: beginning teachers are generally taught to plan lessons, and then to develop schemes of work. This order makes sense to start with, but once your planning skills start to develop, you create schemes of work first and use these to plan your lessons. We have made the decision to present the chapters in the sequential planning cycle order which you will encounter in schools and throughout your career as a teacher. Therefore, Chapter 3 covers developing schemes of work, followed by lesson planning in Chapter 4. If you are looking at this chapter after being asked to plan your first lesson, you may want to jump ahead to Chapter 4 and return later to this chapter.

KEY STAGE 2 AND TRANSITION

The National Curriculum spans Key Stages 1–4 with each key stage building on the previous in a spiral curriculum. As a secondary teacher you will need to review the Key Stage 2 National Curriculum to gain awareness of the likely prior knowledge of pupils entering Year 7. This will help you plan their progression through Key Stage 3. A familiarity with your feeder primary school's approach to teaching ICT and curriculum plans is especially helpful.

It is worthwhile spending time in the primary sector to investigate the way ICT is taught. You will find that the ICT capability of Year 7 pupils entering secondary school will depend on a number of factors, which are explored in Chapter 8.

The geographical location of the secondary school will dictate its number of feeder primary schools. This can complicate matters for secondary teachers as a large number of primary feeder schools will result in disparity of pupil knowledge, skills and the areas of ICT they will have covered. At the start of Year 7 there will be a period where pupils are brought to a similar skill level. It is important, therefore, that you assess pupils' capability early on and differentiate lessons accordingly (see Chapters 4 and 7). This will enable all pupils to start their ICT lessons in secondary school in a positive way and progress throughout Key Stage 3.

Schools will take different approaches to finding out the current level of pupils' ICT knowledge – referred to as baseline testing (see Chapter 8). Ideally Secondary teachers would have pupil attainment data (see Chapter 6), examples of pupil work and the time to process this information. This practice is advocated by the Secondary National Strategy. In reality practice differs widely from school to school and this may not happen in a formal way. Some secondary schools have robust transition strategies which enable information gathering regarding pupil performance, curriculum coverage and so on. Chapter 8 explores transition projects and implications for Year 7 teaching and learning.

Reflection Point 3.1

- Investigate how ICT is delivered in feeder primary schools. How might this affect your planning in Year 7?

Reflection Point

TEACHING ICT AT SECONDARY LEVEL

In most schools ICT is now taught as a discrete subject at Key Stage 3 through one lesson per week. The timetable structure within each school will dictate the lesson duration. For instance, some schools will have 50- or 55-minute lessons rather than 60 minutes.

At Key Stage 3 you are also more likely to find that ICT is taught by teachers who are not ICT specialists. This will depend on the number of ICT specialists within each school. If there are insufficient ICT teachers to cover all year groups and classes, then the ICT specialists will be prioritized to examination classes in Key Stage 4 and post-16.

The curriculum content at Key Stage 3 can also be affected by the ratio of ICT specialists to other teachers teaching ICT. *The Framework for Teaching ICT Capability* (DfES, 2002) and associated documents were designed to support teachers (or learning support assistants) who did not specialize in ICT. Many schools have now adapted these materials to their own requirements, rather than adopting them as they were originally presented. Other ICT departments have designed their own schemes of work which fulfil the statutory requirements of the National Curriculum. The content of the scheme of work and the resources used can be influenced by the capacity within the ICT department.

All schools should have ICT mapped across the curriculum, identifying opportunities for developing and consolidating ICT skills through other subject areas. Ideally this mapping should help inform the structure of curriculum delivery within ICT and the other subjects to exploit opportunities to consolidate ICT skills and for pupils to apply their knowledge and skills in different contexts. For example, if mathematics will be using spreadsheets it makes sense to try to sequence spreadsheets in ICT before it is covered in mathematics. This enables capability to be built and developed in ICT and then be reviewed and consolidated in mathematics. From an ICT perspective we benefit from additional consolidation and extension activities for which we lack the curriculum time. The mathematics department benefits from pupils having the ICT skills already in place, enabling them to focus on the application of spreadsheets in mathematics. Unfortunately, this use of mapping does not always occur and it is not always feasible to arrange all curriculum delivery to achieve this aim.

ICT is generally offered as an option in Year 9, but all pupils have an entitlement to access the Key Stage 4 National Curriculum. Schools will meet this entitlement in different ways, often through either offering a range of ICT qualification options or through ICT cross-curricular mapping. The amount of time spent studying ICT at Key Stage 4 will therefore depend on the way in which it is being delivered. Some schools are piloting delivering Key Stage 4 qualifications in Year 9. This appears to meet with variable success: some pupils are well equipped for embarking on Key Stage 4 level study at this stage while others are not. This can result in schools needing to repeat teaching and learning content from Year 9 again in Year 10.

The National Curriculum and the Secondary National Strategy

The National Curriculum sets out what must be taught during Key Stages 3 and 4. Throughout the three iterations of the curriculum, the focus for learning has shifted towards developing ICT capability.

The review of the National Curriculum was completed in 2007 and the new curriculum will be phased into schools from September 2008. Until 2010, trainee teachers will need to have an understanding of the National Curriculum (DfEE, 1999) and the National Curriculum (QCA, 2007).

Reflection Point 3.2

Review the National Curriculum and the *Framework for Secondary ICT*: yearly teaching objectives (see companion website, www.sagepub.co.uk/secondary).

- Are they statutory (mandatory) or guidance documents?
- How do they differ?
- How might they be used by teachers?

The Secondary National Strategy is a whole set of documents, resources and training which has been updated and extended continuously. During 2008, the *Framework for Secondary ICT* (DCSF, 2008b) was revised (see weblinks). The Office for Standards in Education (Ofsted) reports regularly on the outcomes of the Key Stage 3 (now Secondary) Strategy.

Reflection Point 3.3

Review the Ofsted Pilot Key Stage 3 Evaluation and latest Ofsted evaluations of the Secondary National Strategy (see companion website, www.sagepub.co.uk/second ary, for links).

- How have the priorities of national strategies changed over time?
- How successful has the strategy been in meeting its aims?
- How does this compare with your experience in schools?

The Framework introduced the notion of ICT capability. ICT capability incorporates skills, knowledge and understanding. ICT capability comprises:

- skills – these are the techniques which we use when using hardware or software, but also include how we develop search strategies or how we work well with others
- knowledge – comprehension of the underpinning concepts for ICT and an ability to make use of ICT-specific terminology
- understanding – the ability to apply our knowledge and skills to different situations and to be able to reflect on and evaluate our use of ICT.

This is slightly different to the way in which the Framework describes it. They place 'concepts' within 'understanding', but we believe that you should have knowledge of concepts while understanding is usually achieved through practice and reflection on how you have applied your skills and knowledge.

Therefore, we have a National Curriculum which sets out *what must be taught* within ICT and the Framework and associated documents which present *recommendations* and suggestions for how this may be achieved on a practical level. It is important that teachers of ICT understand the difference in status between the National Curriculum and the National Strategy.

While we work within the framework provided by the National Curriculum it is important to consider other opportunities for teaching pupils about and helping them to engage with ICT. This may include technologies or applications which are not explicitly identified in the National Curriculum. It could also be using innovative teaching and learning approaches involving cross-curricular projects which help pupils

Reflection Point

to explore new and exciting applications for ICT outside of the normal classroom environment.

The majority of pupils attain level 5/6 by the end of Key Stage 3. We can assume that they:

- have become fairly independent and discriminating users of ICT
- can match appropriate ICT usage to different purposes and audiences
- can develop and refine their work
- are able to reflect critically and evaluate their work
- are aware of the different ways in which ICT impacts on themselves and society.

In our plans we should aim to move from teacher-led activities in Year 7 to autonomous, independent use of ICT in Year 9. If we look ahead to Key Stage 4, pupils undertaking ICT qualifications need to be independent in the completion of their coursework. In practice pupils still need to be guided through coursework at Key Stage 4.

PLANNING A SCHEME OF WORK

There are generally three levels of planning with which a classroom teacher needs to concern themselves:

- *long-term plans* which set out curriculum time and broad project headings for a year group or key stage
- *medium-term plans* or schemes of work which describe the content of a particular unit of work or topic over a number of weeks
- *short-term plans* or lesson plans which provide the detail of what will happen with a particular class during one particular lesson.

Long-term plans will usually be decided by the head of department or a nominated person in the department. It may well be that the department will share medium-term plans too. It is necessary to meet the Standards that all trainee teachers are able to plan sequences of lessons, which is usually achieved through the development and implementation of a scheme of work. All teachers in the department, including newly qualified teachers, will be expected to contribute to, and often write, schemes of work (including associated resources), which may well be used by others in the department. The schemes of work are then used to develop individual lesson plans. These provide the overview for a particular unit and enable the teacher to see progression and development of the topic.

When planning a scheme of work it is necessary to consider a wide range of factors. Figure 3.1 identifies some of the areas which will need to be drawn together.

We are going to demonstrate one way to build a scheme of work using scenarios to aid our explanations. We will follow Maggie (a trainee teacher) throughout the chapter as she develops a scheme of work. The final result is shown in Figure 3.5 and we would advise you to look at this now. Other practitioners may well suggest

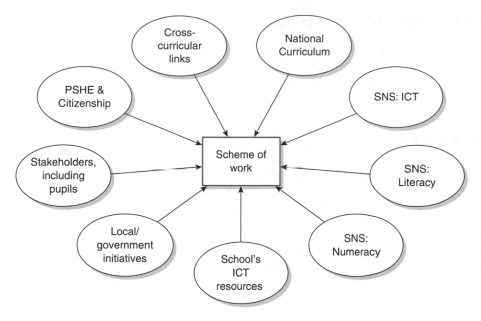

Figure 3.1   Planning a scheme of work

alternative methods. It is up to you to experiment and find a method which suits you. You will gather from this that there is no 'right' way of developing schemes of work, provided that all of the elements are brought together in a way which operates successfully.

Scenario

Maggie is a trainee teacher who needs to develop a scheme of work for a Year 7 class. She has been asked to devise a scheme of work using the following broad learning aim and then discuss this with her mentor:

(Learning aim) Databases: pupils will be able to describe the main components of a database; design a database structure; and construct queries to extract specific information.

It is tempting to begin to think of possible activities at this point. However, it is important to take a step back, thoroughly research the subject and decide what we want pupils to learn. If we commit ourselves to specific activities too early in the process, they may not provide opportunities for pupils to achieve their learning potential. This idea is developed further in Chapter 4.

Planning preparation and research

The starting point for preparing a scheme of work should be the National Curriculum programme of study for ICT (QCA, 2007). In the scenario below, we identify the specific areas of the programme of study – in brackets.

Scenario continued

Maggie looks at the National Curriculum for ICT (2007) and believes that a number of the key concepts can be covered including capability (1.1), aspects of exploring ideas and manipulating information (1.3c), impact of technology (1.4) and critical evaluation (1.5). The key processes which are particularly pertinent will be those under finding information (2.1), some aspects of developing ideas (2.2a, b and d), pupils should be able to use technical terms appropriately and correctly (2.3c) and should evaluate and refine their work (2.4). She will also need to consider range and content (3) and curriculum opportunities (4) which both deal with the breadth of study and relating ICT to wider contexts than just within the ICT classroom.

The *Framework for Secondary ICT* (QCA, 2008) can help ensure specific objectives are being addressed. The learning objectives (see weblinks) show progression year by year, although pupils may move through these more quickly or slowly than indicated.

Scenario continued

Maggie then looks at the Year 7 learning objectives and determines that some of the objectives under 'Finding things out: organizing and investigating' are most appropriate to the topic. Ideally, she would like to provide opportunities to meet all of the relevant objectives in her scheme of work.

Pupils following the National Curriculum are assessed against the Attainment Targets (otherwise known as levels or level descriptors). These are essential when planning progression, designing suitable teaching and learning activities and devising assessment resources.

Scenario continued

Maggie looks at the Attainment Targets and extracts the ones which are relevant to databases. Even though most pupils will be working around level 3/4, she must try to provide opportunities for pupils to meet the higher levels.

In Figure 3.2 we have extracted those Attainment Targets relevant to databases to help us demonstrate progression opportunities. We can identify that at level 3 pupils will be able to use ICT sources which are presented to them, but may not be able to design or create their own. Pupils who are currently working at level 3 should have a target of level 4 or higher.

Level 3	Level 4	Level 5	Level 6
Pupils use ICT to save information			
Pupils find and use appropriate stored information	They use ICT to organize, store and retrieve information	They use ICT to organize, store and retrieve information using logical and appropriate structures	They plan and review their work, creating a logically structured portfolio of digital evidence of their learning
Pupils follow straightforward lines of enquiry	Pupils understand the need for care in framing questions	They select the information they need for different purposes	Pupils use complex lines of enquiry to test hypotheses
	They interpret their findings		
	They question plausibility and recognize that poor-quality information leads to unreliable results	Pupils check the accuracy of information	
		Pupils organize information in a form suitable for processing	
			Pupils develop and refine their work to enhance its quality, using a greater range and complexity of information
		They use ICT to structure, refine and present information in different forms and styles for specific purposes and audiences	

Figure 3.2 Progression through levels

The progression for pupil enquiry is clear across level 3 to level 6 with the expectations for pupils moving from straightforward enquiries to complex enquiries which test hypotheses. This suggests activities whereby pupils at level 3 may interrogate a database to find answers to questions using a structured, teacher-created worksheet, whereas pupils working at level 6 will design their own questions to address a particular problem or issue and then use a variety of sources to find and check the answer.

Scenario continued

As an ICT specialist, Maggie is able to identify from her own knowledge and experience which areas of databases will need to be covered, based on her research into the National Curriculum and the *Framework for Secondary ICT*. She starts by drafting a spider diagram for databases (Figure 3.3).

Figure 3.3 is not complete, but demonstrates how a teacher can start to identify subsections of knowledge around a particular topic. Ideally, this should be broken down as far as possible and may include topics which are later discarded as inappropriate for pupils at this stage.

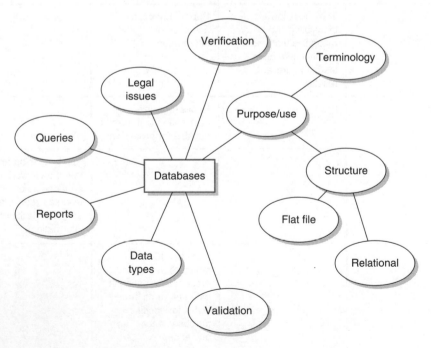

Figure 3.3 Spider diagram: databases

Once the different subsections of knowledge have been identified, it should be possible to start to put them into a hierarchy for teaching purposes. For instance, in our scenario, a pupil will need to know what a database is used for before they start to run queries and reports (see companion website, www.sagepub.co.uk/secondary, video clip, *Starter*, to hear a teacher discussing sequencing learning). The following is the start of a hierarchy for teaching databases at Year 7:

What is a database? What is it used for?
When do pupils use databases?
Terminology
Legal issues
Searching effectively and using a database
Structure of a flat file database
Data types
Collecting data
Creating a flat file database
Validation
Entering data
Creating queries
...

Areas such as relational databases, VBA and so on would be omitted from this list as not relevant at this stage to Year 7 pupils. These aspects may be introduced in future years or key stages as pupils progress through the spiral curriculum (see 'What the research says' section).

Taking the principles of the spiral curriculum, it is possible to start to allocate year groups to each of the subsections within the chosen topic. Our list may now look like that in Figure 3.4.

The majority of these issues will be at least touched upon in Year 7 and then some will be developed in Year 8 and Year 9. Notice how in Year 8 we assume that pupils know what a database is, the related terminology and so on, and the teacher will only need to briefly recap these through starter activities and effective questioning. Some concepts are revisited every year. For example, with 'Legal issues', pupils in Year 7 may have an understanding from a fairly moral standpoint, for instance 'I wouldn't like people to see my medical records' and they may understand that there are laws to enforce this. However, it may not be until Year 8 that pupils are able to identify the laws which protect them and the sanctions in place to help enforce these laws. This is an example of the spiral curriculum.

Encouraging innovation

Britain currently has an assessment-driven culture. Pupils are conditioned for high-stakes assessment, for instance end of key stage tests (commonly called SATs) and CATs which provide baseline data for setting pupils and establishing likely future potential, GCSEs, AS and A2 levels or equivalents. In this culture, risk-taking, innovation and

	Year 7	Year 8	Year 9
What is a database? What is it used for?	✓		
When do pupils use databases?	✓		
Terminology	✓		
Legal issues	✓	✓	✓
Searching effectively and using a database	✓	✓	✓
Structure of a flat file database	✓		
Data types	✓	✓	
Collecting data	✓	✓	✓
Creating a flat file database	✓	✓	
Validation	✓	✓	✓
Entering data	✓		
Creating queries	✓	✓	✓
...			

Figure 3.4 Coverage of databases by year

generally 'trying new things' can result in failure within the education system. Why would you risk innovating or attempting something new if it may mean high-stakes failure? Within your classroom you need to provide the opportunities for pupils to try out new things without risking failure in a high-stake assessment. You will need to examine your long-term plans and schemes of work to identify potential times and units where this would be possible. Pupils also need to know that experimenting at those times is safe, encouraged and that they will not be penalized (either through assessments or socially) if they fail. Ultimately, this seeks to build confidence and creativity.

CROSS-CURRICULAR THEMES

Joined-up concepts make more sense to pupils and lead to deeper learning. The National Curriculum (2007) places more emphasis on cross-curricular teaching and learning. Subjects comprise a mixture of knowledge and skills; traditionally pupils were dependent on teachers who were the holders and disseminators of both. Recent near ubiquitous Internet access has brought into sharp focus the differences between information access and the information skills needed to search for, select and use that information appropriately. The premium placed (for example by employers) on subject knowledge – the facts you can remember – is diminishing. Many of the children we teach today will be employed in jobs that are not yet invented or even envisaged. We need to teach them to adapt to new situations, to find and use information in a meaningful context, and to learn and apply new skills.

Cross-curricular projects are an excellent way of breaking down the barriers pupils perceive between subject areas, for instance planning for a newspaper day where pupils produce a newspaper from scratch in one day (see the companion website, www.sagepub. co.uk/secondary, for links).

In ICT it is often productive for pupils to prepare the contents of a piece of work in other subjects and then to use ICT as a way of integrating the work. For instance, pupils complete a piece of persuasive writing in English, perhaps about a topic they are covering in science such as genetic engineering and then use ICT to produce an informative web page or podcast.

In addition to cross-curricular links with other subjects, you need also to consider and explicitly identify opportunities to build in literacy, numeracy, citizenship and personal, social, health and economic education (PSHEE) learning objectives (see weblinks on the companion website, for further details). These will appear in your lesson plans and scheme of work.

The following scenario demonstrates some opportunities for integration of cross-curricular themes using our database scenario.

Scenario continued

Maggie considers the topic of databases and identifies areas where there may be opportunities for cross-curricular links:

Literacy: pupils will need to understand, use and spell correctly technical vocabulary related to databases.
   I could:

- create some display boards on databases containing new words
- have pupil dictionaries using either exercise books or worksheets
- write new words on the interactive whiteboard then display and recap at the start of lessons
- use homework exercises to define or use key words
- encourage pupils to participate in discussions: whole class, small group and pairs.

Numeracy: pupils could analyse data sets, use numbers and mathematical operators in queries.
   I could:

- encourage pupils to analyse larger data-sets
- ask pupils to write down the queries they will use before applying it to the database.

Citizenship: pupils will be taught about the Data Protection Act.
   I could:

- ask pupils to consider issues from a moral standpoint and discuss before teaching them about the law
- use small groups for discussions to encourage all pupils to participate
- give pupils thinking time to encourage more reflection and considered responses.

The above scenario shows how this may look in practice, identifying cross-curricular issues such as:

- citizenship, through the legal and moral issues raised by database use, and
- literacy, through the use of correct database terminology.

At this stage we advise that you record possible links. You can then research and refine these at the lesson planning stage supported by the use of appropriate resources in class. This may include displays of new terminology, a dictionary section in pupils' exercise book or a learning diary for the unit with a 'New words' section.

Determining the subject matter which needs to be covered and the order in which it should be taught is often the most difficult aspect of planning. We will now start to explore how to plan learning objectives, activities and outcomes. This is further developed in Chapter 4.

DEVISING THE SCHEME OF WORK

Many schools will devise their own scheme of work template which meets their own requirements. The QCA scheme of work template (QCA, 2000) provides a suitable structure containing prompts for most of the aspects of planning we require at this stage. These sections require consideration of the broader picture of planning at this level:

> *About the unit* should be a brief description to enable you and other teachers to get a general picture of the unit.
>
> *Where the unit fits in* should identify what the unit is building on (including progression from Key Stage 2) and where pupils will be going next.
>
> *Expectations* are broad objectives for pupils' capability at the end of the unit. It is unrealistic to expect all pupils to have achieved equally, so we use all pupils, most pupils and some pupils to differentiate expectations.
>
> *Prior learning* gives basic details of what the teacher can expect the pupils to know before starting the unit.
>
> *Language for learning* links to literacy and the technical vocabulary which pupils will be expected to use. This is split into understand, use and spell, and speaking and listening activities. This clearly differentiates the language we use and understand and the way in which we use it to communicate.
>
> *Resources* will include the ICT equipment and software, textbooks and worksheets for the entire unit.

 While it is possible to add further detail, these sections provide the core information which is necessary as an overview. (See companion website, www.sagepub.co.uk/secondary, for link to QCA template.)

At Key Stage 3 a scheme of work would normally cover a half-term period, around six to eight weeks. Sometimes you may subdivide this time into two distinct short projects. Schemes which use the same context over a longer period, say a term, tend to lose pupils' interest.

To avoid ICT becoming skills-based, a carefully crafted scenario needs to be developed. This enables pupils to explore the different facets of ICT capability within a meaningful context and provides opportunities for effective differentiation (see companion website, www.sagepub.co.uk/secondary, video clip, *Lesson Planning*). These ideas are developed further in Chapter 4 – you may wish to explore these before reading further.

Typically schemes will concentrate on skills-building in the first few sessions and then move pupils into a consolidation and development phase where they work more independently to achieve a set of objectives. It is important to build opportunities for pupils to evaluate and refine their work during the unit. Often this is the final activity giving limited opportunities for pupils to refine their work and learn from their mistakes. It is therefore better to either build evaluation opportunities throughout or make this the penultimate activity.

Typically in Year 7 schemes will focus on developing capability within a single software application. As pupils progress they will tackle more ambitious projects which make use of a range of hardware and software to solve a complex problem. These projects enable pupils to integrate and consolidate their ICT capability. For example, project managing the school play would use spreadsheets for budgets, a database and word-processing software for mail shots, and desktop publishing and website development for publicity. This type of project can be used over an extended period, helping pupils develop the skills for independent work and learning necessary at Key Stage 4.

Scenario continued

Maggie needs to devise a suitable scenario or range of scenarios to:

- cover the subsections of databases which she has identified
- fulfil the requirements for progression identified through the National Curriculum and the *Framework for Secondary ICT*
- enhance cross-curricular opportunities.

There are many ways to stimulate ideas for scenario creation. It is often possible to adapt scenarios used by other teachers for your own classes. Ideas can be gleaned from various people and places, including textbooks, Internet sites, official sources, commercial resources, colleagues, school resources, the primary sector or resources to support other curriculum areas (see companion website, video clips, *Cross-Curricular Planning* to hear about this in practice). The following section provides some examples to stimulate your thinking across a range of topic areas. It aims to inform you of the range of resources available rather than providing a comprehensive list. Keep in mind that none are perfectly suited to every class (or teacher). Read them with a critical eye and take the best elements from each.

Secondary National Strategy examples

The Secondary National Strategy resources were introduced from 2002 onwards and are being renewed during 2008. There are a number of elements which are good practice, such as encouraging fitness for purpose, explicitly relating ICT use to audience, developing pupils' knowledge of software beyond average competence, using project-based scenarios which require competency across a range of ICT skills and knowledge.

However, there are aspects of the Secondary National Strategy materials which require careful thought from ICT specialists. Following trialling and reflection, most schools that use the materials have chosen to significantly adapt the material and structure. Our advice would be to evaluate the resources recommended by government as carefully as you would those from other sources.

Examples from the Internet

Teach-ICT.com has a range of resources for all key stages, including worksheets, suggested lesson plans, online educational games and so on. As there is a wide range of resources available from the site, teachers do need to use their professional judgement and will probably need to adapt the resources for their own classes.

Primary teachers of ICT have some really excellent ideas and resources which could be adapted for use in the secondary classroom. Some could be used with Year 7 or Year 8 in order to prompt recollections of prior software used and stimulate discussions. If the pupils have used them in Key Stage 2, reusing it will help them to tap into their prior knowledge and understanding. For instance, Micros and Primary Education (MAPE) (now merged with the National Association of Advisers for Computers in Education – NAACE) have produced a resource called 'Whodunnit?' which features a database of 50 suspects and 15 cases to be solved. Pupils tend to enjoy playing detective and this could be a really nice extended starter activity which would get them using a database and could be used to prompt a discussion on terminology, structures, validation and so on.

Free resources

A range of organizations produce materials to support education at various key stages. Some of the material may not be directly relevant to secondary ICT, but may help to support your teaching or idea generation. Examples include:

- Information Commissioner's Office who provide materials such as 'The Plumstones' which can help pupils learn about the Data Protection Act
- businesses, such as supermarkets, provide case study material on how ICT is used in their business or organizations which provide out-of-school learning contexts. Some organizations provide schemes of work, suggested lesson plans and resources to enhance trips and the resultant learning. Examples include Cadbury World, National Film Museum or Disneyland Paris
- organizations such as English Heritage make resources available online, including photographs and searchable databases.

It is worthwhile reading professional journals and newspapers as these often have sections where teachers share their favourite resources or have news of new resources which are available.

Commercial examples

The website 'Teach with ICT' provides a mixture of free and commercial resources which have been created by ICT teachers and are project based. Scenarios include being on the production team for a film, solving mysteries and project management. Teach with ICT give permission for teachers to adapt the resources to their own classes.

Other commercial solutions are available from a number of educational publishers and usually include electronic resources and textbooks or worksheets for pupils. For instance:

- Sam Learning is an online resource aimed at raising attainment in schools. It covers Key Stages 1–5.
- KeyBytes is produced by RM and covers Key Stages 2–4. It provides an online resource supported by printable worksheets and regular assessment points.
- Nelson Thornes produce a range of resources for Key Stage 3 and 4.

Commercial resources vary in the flexibility granted to teachers to adapt, reproduce and distribute the work. It is always important to check the licensing agreement, particularly when redistributing material, for example on a website or virtual learning environment. Off-the-shelf solutions which cannot be customized to local circumstances need to be extensively trialled and benchmarked against National Curriculum criteria.

Reflection Point 3.4

Choose three resources from different providers and compare their approach.

- Which resources are the most complete for adoption in the classroom?
- Which resources/providers are particularly innovative or creative?
- What are the strengths of each resource and how do they aid pupils' achievement?

Reflection Point

PROGRESSION

A spiral curriculum enables pupils to progress year-on-year as their knowledge of ICT develops, building on their previous understanding. Scaffolding helps pupils to attain a higher level of understanding than they would have been able to achieve on their own. Scaffolding includes how knowledge is presented to pupils, the resources used and teacher intervention in learning (see 'What the research says' section). Essentially, a pupil will not understand relational databases if they do not understand basic terminology, the purposes of a database or a flat file structure. It is important, therefore, to carefully organize the way in which a topic is taught across the whole curriculum, within a unit of work and in individual lessons.

Scenario continued

Maggie decides that the pupils will need to be able to use the correct terminology and have a common understanding of what a database is, how it can be used and any implications of using an electronic database. She then wants the pupils to begin to plan their own flat-file database, collect the data, enter some data and interrogate a data file. Depending on the ability of the pupils, she may want them to consider validation and verification methods, more advanced queries and designing reports.

An extract of Maggie's scheme of work is in Figure 3.5.

The extract (Figure 3.5) shows how pupils' ICT capability is being developed. It does not focus just on ICT skills, but encourages exploratory learning, collaboration, discussion, peer evaluation and refinement of work. This approach will enable pupils to understand the uses of databases and wider issues, to develop the necessary skills and knowledge and to apply these.

Levels

If your scheme of work contains sufficient detail, you should be able to identify what pupils will do and what evidence they will produce in order to achieve a particular level, for example through verbal responses, worksheets, printouts or annotation of their work. The new National Curriculum level 6 states that pupils will create 'a logically structured portfolio of digital evidence of their learning'. This must show how pupils have planned, developed and refined their work, which can be demonstrated by retaining different versions of work and detailed annotation. Reviewing your scheme of work with the levels in view helps ensure suitable activities and opportunities for progression to the higher levels are included.

Reflection Point 3.5

Examine the Attainment Targets and identify how pupils could provide, through a portfolio, suitable evidence for each level. Examine ways in which this could be organized in a portfolio.

Learning objectives Pupils should:	Possible teaching activities	Learning outcomes Pupils will:	Points to note
Activity 1			[Average time to complete: 2–3 hours]
Be able to describe the purpose of a database using everyday examples.	Pupils use a 'Whodunnit?' database to answer queries.	Use a simple database to complete the 5 case studies.	Identify links to literacy in lesson plan.
Use database terminology accurately.	Q&A on databases. Ask pupils for their experience of databases and uses. Pupils to record class findings on worksheets.	Be able to answer worksheet questions posed, use database terminology correctly, describe the purpose of a database and common uses.	
Interpret assessment criteria and use this to set a personal target.	Target-setting for unit.	Set and agree an appropriate target level.	
Evaluate how ICT use can impact on society and some of the legal issues of database use.	Role play on 'legal issues' adapted from Data Protection resource. Pupils work in pairs to answer questions. Plenary feedback.	Be able to answer the set plenary questions and identify legal and moral issues associated with database use.	Link to citizenship.
Activity 2			[Average time to complete: 3 hours]
Identify advantages and disadvantages of using an electronic database.	Manual database paired activity. Pupils to identify difficulties of sorting and searching with a manual database.	Describe in class discussion the advantages and disadvantages of using a manual database.	For some classes, it may be possible to present a choice of topics for different pupils, such as, holidays, pupils, films, music.
Distinguish between and select appropriate data types.	Discussion with pupils on data types using examples from manual database.	Produce a data capture form which meets the assessment criteria including appropriate selection of data types.	Possible homework activity to collect data using data capture sheet.
Design and use a data capture form.	Presentation of the scenario to pupils and discussion of methods of capturing data.	Annotate a partner's work and use feedback to refine and annotate their own.	
Evaluate and refine their work.	Pupils design a data capture sheet and share with another pupil to evaluate and refine.		

Figure 3.5 Computer control scheme of work

Monitoring and target-setting

Many schemes of work focus exclusively upon ICT activities and outcomes. There is, however, good evidence to suggest that building in opportunities to teach pupils to become independent learners, yields substantial learning gains. Understanding assessment criteria, target-setting, responding to teacher feedback, peer and self evaluation are all activities that can be built into the scheme of work. This is explored further in Chapter 6.

SCHEMES OF WORK IN PRACTICE

Once you have completed the first draft of your scheme of work you should revisit it to ensure it contains all of the necessary elements, including:

- sufficient progression opportunities for attaining higher National Curriculum levels
- *Framework for Secondary ICT* yearly teaching objectives
- links to cross-curricular themes, particularly literacy, numeracy, citizenship and PSHEE.

To exemplify progression opportunities let us consider an example from computer control. The relevant aspects of the level descriptors extracted from the National Curriculum (2007) are:

Level 4: They plan and test sequences of instructions

Level 5: They create sequences of instructions and understand the need to be precise when framing and sequencing instructions

Level 6: They develop, try out and refine sequences of instructions and show efficiency in framing these instructions, using sub-routines where appropriate.

The way in which the scheme of work in Figure 3.6 has been written allows the classroom teacher to make decisions about the approach to teaching and learning which is most appropriate. The lesson plans will obviously be tailored to each class (see 'Differentiation', in Chapter 7). Notice how the scheme also provides the framework for enabling pupils to achieve higher levels. If the scheme of work did not include opportunities for pupils to use sub-routines, explore efficiency considerations, test, refine, annotate and explain their choices, then pupils would be unable to present the evidence for the higher levels, even if they had completed the work. It is vital that you consider the evidence which pupils need to demonstrate their attainment.

The scheme of work is not a one-size-fits-all solution. Teachers may use the same scheme of work in different ways for different classes. The following two case studies demonstrate this using the scheme of work in Figure 3.6.

Two classes of differing ability are being taught by the same teacher (Richard) using the same scheme of work. The unit is computer control and the teacher is using Flowol.

Learning objectives Pupils should:	Possible teaching activities	Learning outcomes Pupils will:	Points to note
Activity 4			**[Average time to complete: 3 hours]**
Plan a logical sequence of instructions including decisions in the flowchart. Explain and create sub-routines to increase efficiency. Test and refine their program justifying their choices.	Present scenario of greenhouse to pupils. Ask pupils to plan how the greenhouse should be controlled. A worksheet can be used to help pupils develop the plan. Pupils' plans can be checked through peer assessment or class discussion. Pupils to create the flowcharts to operate the greenhouse. Pupils should print and annotate their work and identify errors and improvements. Discuss sub-routines with pupils. This may be best achieved through a demonstration, as some pupils will need significant guidance with this aspect of control. Pupils to refine their greenhouse flowcharts to include sub-routines. Print and annotate their work explaining their use of sub-routines.	Produce several drafts of annotated flowcharts demonstrating testing and refinement. Answer plenary questions to explain the use of sub-routines to improve efficiency of programs. Explain their use of sub-routines by annotating the final flow chart.	Some pupils will need significant support for this activity. Worksheets should be available which will scaffold planning and testing of their work. Help sheets for sub-routines would be useful.

Figure 3.6   Scheme of work

Class A: 15 pupils of lower ability in Year 8. Some special educational needs (SEN) issues in the group, including challenges around literacy and/or numeracy

Pupils are logged onto the computers and have the greenhouse mimic open on their screens. The teacher has the same mimic open on the interactive whiteboard (IWB). The class have discussed the benefits of sub-routines and have been told they will develop them to control various elements of the greenhouse.

'Right, who can tell me how we start a flow chart?' Yvonne raises her hand, 'We use that oval shape, sir, and put "Start" in it.'

'That's right, Yvonne. Well done.' Richard drags the symbol into position, 'but this time instead of "Start" we are going to put "sub" and type in a name. This is how we start our sub-routine.' Richard demonstrates this on the interactive whiteboard.

'Okay, we want to open the window when it gets hot. Can anyone show me how we will decide that it's hot using the flow chart?' Richard asks Stuart to demonstrate using the interactive whiteboard. Stuart comes to the front and completes the next step in the flow chart. Richard briefly describes what has been done and why.

'Next we need to give the instruction to open the window if the temperature goes above 60. How will we get the window to open?' He asks Reshma to come to the front and demonstrate, again giving a brief commentary as she does so.

'Right, who can tell me what else we need to do to complete the flow chart … yes, Stuart?'

Stuart responds, 'We need to tell the window to close if it goes cold.'

'Excellent. Where will those instructions go, Abid?'

'From the decision, sir?'

'Yes, that's right. Yvonne, how will we get it to keep checking the temperature?'

'Using a loop, sir.'

'Great, but I'm not going to do the rest of the decision and the loops with you now. What I want you to do is copy this flow chart and complete the decision and the loops as we've discussed. Any questions?'

Once pupils have completed the first sub-routine, Richard asks them to have a go at the next one, bringing them back after five minutes to review their progress.

Some pupils in Class A may make significant progress with sub-routines given the highly scaffolded introduction to the topic. Richard would need to give those pupils the opportunity to independently demonstrate their ability if they were to achieve the higher levels. Deciding on how support affects level outcomes is a professional judgement based on experience. To achieve the higher levels, the pupils would need to demonstrate a degree of independence.

Class B: 30 pupils in a higher ability set. No SEN issues

'Right, we've created some flow charts to control the greenhouse, but some of you have identified that it is very difficult to get the different environmental controls to operate as we want. What I want us to do is have a look at some sub-routines.' Richard opens the auto-home mimic using Flowol on the IWB. He has pre-prepared sub-routines to control elements of the house.

'Right, I'm going to run this and I want you to tell me what is happening ...'

The pupils watch the demonstration and describe how the sub-routines are called from the main program. They identify that the program is simpler and more efficient.

'Okay, in a minute I want you to create a sub-routine for opening the greenhouse window, lets see who will be the first to figure out how to start one off and how to call it from the main program. Here's a hint, you need to have the sub-routine in place *before* the main program. Put your hand up when you've got there. You've got two minutes, off you go ...'

Richard writes the two targets on the board to remind the pupils. After two minutes, he calls for attention and asks pupils to report on their progress. Two pupils have managed to complete most of the program, so he asks them to demonstrate using the IWB and they talk through the steps to set up the sub-routine.

'Right, what do you think we should be controlling using sub-routines?' Through questions and answers, Richard describes the objectives for the rest of the lesson.

Richard is encouraging pupils in Class B to be very independent and to work collaboratively to find solutions (see companion website, www.sagepub. co.uk/secondary, video clips, *Independence*, for a discussion of this in practice). He is guiding them to the answers rather than providing them. Given the scheme of work and the approach Richard is taking with this class, they should be able to achieve level 6 and perhaps higher depending upon the evidence that they present for assessment.

TEACHING AT KEY STAGE 4

Many of the principles which we discussed for designing a scheme of work at Key Stage 3 also apply at Key Stage 4 (and beyond). ICT is a mandatory entitlement at Key Stage 4 – all pupils must have an opportunity to access the Key Stage 4 National Curriculum for ICT even where they do not opt for ICT as an award-bearing subject. Schools typically choose to meet this entitlement through:

- cross-curricular delivery of ICT
- level 1 or 2 awards made by award boards such as General Certificate of Secondary Education (GCSE), Diploma in Digital Application (DiDA), Oxford, Cambridge and RSA (OCR) Nationals. The specifications for these qualifications are mapped to the National Curriculum (2007) programme of study
- building a curriculum based on other qualifications which may not meet all of the requirements of the National Curriculum, for example vendor-accredited qualifications or the European Computer Driving Licence.

Where schools opt for cross-curricular delivery, they will map ICT opportunities against the National Curriculum (2007) programme of study. For example, they cover spreadsheets, Internet searching and GIS in geography, in mathematics they use control software and in English, word processing, desktop publishing and presentation skills.

Reflection Point 3.6

What may be the implications for pupils and teachers of using a cross-curricular delivery model for ICT at Key Stage 4?
   How might this affect the development of 'ICT capability'?

Some schools are creative in the way in which they meet the statutory requirements for the National Curriculum. For instance, ICT may be part of a carousel of subjects in Key Stage 4 or cross-curricular delivery may be supplemented through special projects such as an Enterprise Week where skills are developed and enhanced in a work-related situation.

FUNCTIONAL SKILLS

The government's white paper, *14–19 Education and Skills* identifies that 'GCSEs do not fully secure achievement in the functional core of maths and English' (DfES, 2005a: 21). It goes on to state that ICT is an essential skill in the modern world and that it is necessary to identify and offer a functional skills unit for ICT building on current provision. At the time of writing this book, the award boards are piloting the functional skills qualifications.

   The pilot functional skills qualifications are currently stand-alone but there are plans to eventually integrate them into relevant Level 1 and 2 qualifications and diplomas at level 3. The mathematics, English and ICT GCSEs will integrate functional skills into their course specification. The pilot functional skills assessment methods are based on practical situations and realistic contexts.

TEACHING COURSE SPECIFICATIONS AT KEY STAGE 4

Award-bearing qualifications at levels 1 and 2 are mapped to the National Curriculum. There is no need to assess National Curriculum levels at Key Stage 4.

   When you start to teach a course specification, it is vital that you check the original specification. The specification will provide all the details of curriculum coverage, coursework requirements, examinations, assessments, suggested reading materials and so on. The classroom teacher must have a thorough understanding of the specification requirements. It is also useful to look at reports from previous examination years to identify areas which the examiners felt were weaker or needed to be addressed differently. These are usually available through the award boards' websites. Also from these websites you can access teachers' guides, previous examination questions and so on. Many award boards provide essential training and moderation events, and you should try to attend these wherever possible.

Although qualifications change, essentially there are two types of ICT qualification: vocational, such as DiDA and OCR Nationals, and the academic GCSEs. It can be argued that there is increasingly a blurring between the two types of qualification. Usually the qualifications will consist of coursework and external assessment under controlled conditions via examination. Our purpose here is not to examine each qualification in detail but to take a more holistic approach regarding planning for delivery.

The weighting for examination and coursework currently favours coursework, meaning that teachers tend to place most emphasis and curriculum time on the coursework element of the qualifications. Where theoretical knowledge will be tested, though, there needs to be a balance between the theoretical and practical aspects of the course. There are different approaches to the delivery of the underpinning theoretical knowledge:

> *In parallel to coursework*: the pupils are taught the theoretical aspects required when they reach appropriate points in the development of their coursework.
> *Front loaded*: the pupils are taught all of the theoretical content at the start of the course and are then expected to utilize this for the development of their coursework and as a revision aid.
> *Just in time*: once the coursework is completed, pupils have a crash course on the theory before the examination, usually using the context of their coursework experience.

Reflection Point 3.7

Consider the advantages and disadvantages of each method. Discuss with your mentor in school the approach used and their reasons for selecting this method.

Even qualifications which focus on the practical application of ICT need an understanding of the underpinning theory. It is important for pupils to be able to apply ICT principles and concepts across other software, hardware and situations. For example, pupils should understand that all spreadsheet packages perform certain functions, not just the software package the school uses.

At Key Stage 4, pupils want guidance on passing their qualification with the best possible grade. The lessons from developing a scheme of work at Key Stage 3 apply equally at Key Stage 4 and in some ways it is simpler as the course specification requirements are far more explicit. It is necessary for the teacher and pupils to be very clear about the requirements and how best to succeed. You will achieve this through your teaching, pupil guidance, ongoing assessment and the support materials which you devise and use in your classroom.

Pupils need to have a clear understanding of how they will be assessed (see Chapter 6). This will mean sharing the assessment criteria with the pupils, discussing it and using it on a regular basis. This is obviously directly relevant to coursework, but can also be applied to preparation for examinations, through the use of mock questions and discussion of the marking criteria.

SUPPORT MECHANISMS FOR COURSEWORK

When pupils are working on coursework, you will still need to have a scheme of work in place. This will contain broader headings than at Key Stage 3, providing more scope for pupils' independent working. The scheme of work will be based around the external deadlines which are set by the award board to enable moderation and final submission of coursework in adequate time. You will also want to include interim dates in your scheme of work, enabling monitoring of coursework completion and grades. It is important to plan review and revision sessions at Key Stage 4 and to note significant deadlines.

During Key Stage 4 and post-16, your medium-term planning will need to be more flexible to allow you to react appropriately to learner needs. You are more likely to be involved with a more diagnostic approach to teaching where you assess pupils' knowledge and understanding as coursework progresses. You will then respond to your diagnosis of their current understanding using immediate feedback and support to either a whole class or a sub-group within the class. This is not to suggest that you do not still have a predetermined scheme of work, just that the way it is written will be less prescriptive.

During examination years, you will be regularly monitoring, assessing and providing formative feedback to individual pupils. Pupils are eager to receive regular feedback on their coursework and need reassurance that they are making good progress towards their target grade. It is worthwhile investing time in self and peer assessment activities to help pupils to develop a good understanding of the assessment criteria for themselves.

Assessment criteria in course specifications at Key Stage 4 influence your scheme of work in much the same way as National Curriculum attainment targets at Key Stage 3. See Chapter 6 for examples.

CONCLUSION

You should now be aware that there are a host of factors (many of which are explored further in the following chapters) to consider when planning in ICT. This chapter has given you some practical strategies to help you to start developing your own schemes of work. You will need to spend time developing your knowledge of the National

Curriculum, the Attainment Targets (levels), the *Framework for Secondary ICT*, course specifications and cross-curricular themes. While this will at first be difficult and time-consuming, it will become easier with practice.

Always try to ensure that your plans include sufficient opportunities for pupils to progress and to learn in different ways. This will help to keep pupils engaged in your lessons.

Good medium-term planning makes your life easier when you start planning individual lessons. The more time and effort you spend on your schemes of work, the less time you will need to use for thinking and development once you are involved in daily lesson planning.

What the research says: curriculum design

First, it is important to understand that children's cognitive development progresses through various stages. Piaget suggested four developmental stages through which all children progress sequentially. Subsequent researchers have largely confirmed the sequence but some have disputed the age ranges Piaget gave for particular stages (Shayer, 1978, cited in Parsons et al., 2001: 48). The four stages proposed by Piaget are:

1. Sensorimotor (birth–2 years)
2. Preoperational (2–7 years)
3. Concrete operational (7–11 years)
4. Formal operational (11 years and over).

The two stages which concern the secondary sector are 3 and 4 above. Children at the concrete operational stage are able to organize their thoughts and think logically, and can apply themselves to concrete problems. They are not able to think in more abstract terms. Children in the formal operational stage are able to formulate various hypotheses and consider problems which are beyond their own experience. They are able to deduce solutions or conclusions using the rules and principles they already know.

For teachers this means that we may sometimes be asking pupils to complete a task which is beyond their current cognitive stage. Researchers have found that clear, easy to understand instructions and the way the learning activities are structured can result in children reaching a higher cognitive stage than their age would indicate (Parsons et al., 2001; Slavin, 2003), although this progress may be limited to that topic or subject area.

Cognitive development influences how a child perceives its environment and engages with learning. Vygotsky theorized that children learn best in their zone of proximal development (ZPD). There are essentially three zones in which learning activities can be placed:

1. Learning which has already been mastered or is too easy and presents no challenge or opportunity to develop
2. Learning which can be achieved with support of an adult or peer, but cannot yet be achieved independently (ZPD)
3. Learning which is too difficult and will demotivate the learner.

(Continued)

(Continued)

Teachers should strive to present learning activities and opportunities within the ZPD of the pupils. 'Scaffolding' involves providing support which is needed to enable a pupil to progress. Scaffolding should not be more or less than they require and the level of scaffold provided should be reduced as the pupils' understanding develops. Daniels (2001: 107) explains that 'scaffolding involves simplifying the learner's role rather than the task'. He goes on to explore different levels of scaffold ranging from asking a prompt question through to demonstrating techniques. The scaffolding required will vary between pupils and the scaffolding can be provided by peers as well as by adults in the classroom.

Pupils progress through different cognitive stages and need support to maximize their learning from appropriate activities. The way in which we structure learning is therefore important. Jerome Bruner first advocated the use of a spiral design to teach the curriculum. This refers to the way in which a person increases their depth of knowledge and understanding about a topic by building on their prior learning.

It is easiest to explain a spiral curriculum through the use of an example. A pupil in Year 7 learns that spreadsheets use formulae to calculate totals, that the variables can be altered and that results can be presented in a graph. In Year 8, these principles are briefly revisited and the teacher then introduces functions for efficiency, relative and absolute referencing and tools such as conditional formatting and comments to improve understanding of the spreadsheet functionality. The pupil is still learning about spreadsheets, a topic covered the previous year, but their understanding is deepening and broadening while reinforcing the basic concepts first introduced to them. Figure 3.7 presents a pictorial representation of this.

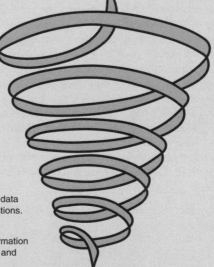

Key Stage 4: pupils analyse a problem, design a solution, implement and test it using appropriate database software. They evaluate their solution against end-user requiremens.

Key Stage 3: pupils design and create databases and data collection methods. They search for data using multiple criteria and check it is reliable.

Key Stage 2: pupils enter data into existing, simple databases, classify data and use a database to answer questions.

Key Stage 1: pupils search for information using simple databases, CD-ROMs and the Internet.

Figure 3.7 Spiral curriculum

Bruner (1977: 13) suggests that early teaching of subjects should have an 'emphasis upon the intuitive grasp of ideas and upon the use of these basic ideas. A curriculum as it develops should revisit these basic ideas repeatedly, building upon them'. He hypothesizes that any knowledge can be taught and learnt, if the teacher is able (and willing) to 'translate' the material to make it accessible for children at a particular cognitive stage. He suggests that early teaching of concepts, ensuring pupils have an intuitive grasp of the subject, aids the learning of more complex material later on.

The National Curriculum has been designed based on Bruner's theory of the spiral curriculum. Pupils are introduced to basic ICT concepts during Key Stage 1 which are then developed and built upon during the other key stages. By Key Stage 4, the expectation is that pupils are independent and discriminating users of ICT.

Further reading

Black, P., Harrison, C., Lee, C., Marshall, B. and Wiliam, D. (2003) *Assessment for Learning: Putting it into Practice*. Maidenhead: Open University Press.

James, M., McCormick, R., Black, P., Carmichael, P., Drummond, M., Fox, A., MacBeath, J., Marshall, B., Pedder, D., Procter, R., Swaffield, S., Swann, J. and Wiliam, D. (2007) *Improving Learning How to Learn: Classrooms, Schools and Networks*. London: Routledge.

Parsons, R., Hinson, S. and Sardo-Brown, D. (2001) *Educational Psychology: A Practitioner-researcher Model of Teaching*. London: Thomson Learning.

Weblinks

Live links to each of these websites can be found on the companion website, www.sagepub.co.uk/secondary.

Framework for Secondary ICT – www.standards.dcsf.gov.uk/secondary/framework/
The National Curriculum (2007) – http://curriculum.qca.org.uk/
The QCA provide information on qualifications, National Curriculum reforms, Assessment for Learning and other education initiatives – www.qca.org.uk/

4 PLANNING TO TEACH AN ICT LESSON

This chapter covers:

- how to think through, prepare and use a lesson plan
- finding an appropriate level of challenge for your pupils
- strategies for generating ideas for activities
- developing resources
- structuring and pacing lessons
- developing your teaching technique – making lessons memorable
- planning and managing project work.

When we plan a lesson we quite understandably become very focused on classroom activities. We commonly ask ourselves two questions:

- What will the pupils (and teacher) do?
- How will I fill the hour with productive activities?

Before we rush into answering these questions it is important to take a step back and consciously refocus, to ask:

- What do we want to achieve? (Aims)
- What will they learn? (Learning objectives)
- How will I know what they have learned? (Learning outcomes)

This chapter looks at the planning you need to undertake before you take your first step into a classroom as a teacher. It focuses on the thinking you need to do and the things you need to prepare and take with you so that you feel as prepared as possible. As well as ensuring good learning takes place we hope that being prepared will give you a large confidence boost and set you on the path to becoming an excellent teacher.

LESSON PLANS

The most obvious piece of paper to have in the classroom is a lesson plan, but there are other items to take with you. These include:

- a seating plan
- pupil register and records (mark-book)
- any relevant textbooks or other source material
- handouts/worksheets
- a backup-task/lesson in case the technology fails
- spare pens and pencils!

At the end of this chapter is a complete lesson plan which draws together all of the elements discussed. Although the output of this chapter is a lesson plan, it is important to realize that the thinking process leading up to the plan is as important as the finished document.

You should go through the lesson planning process for every lesson. Where you are repeating the same lesson you may only need to refine the plan based on your reflection of the previous lesson and amend any details specific to the progress of each class. Base each lesson plan on your medium-term plan (scheme of work) which should be in place at the beginning of each term or placement. Do not plan lessons in detail more than a week or two in advance as it is likely that you will need to make significant changes as you monitor pupils' learning and progress. However, you can have a number of future lesson plans sketched out and add detail as you go along. Never go into a lesson without a plan, remember that being prepared translates into a healthy dose of confidence – even if you have to be flexible, adapting the lesson as you see how pupils respond. Also remember that for any given lesson it is always better to have too much to do than too little – in fact, beginning teachers tend to be quite ambitious anyway, so this is rarely a problem.

Your institution will have its own lesson plan format, it is likely that this has similar headings to those you will find in the example at the end of the chapter (Figure 4.12). Take a look at this now for an overview and then move on to the next section to examine the fine detail.

Using a lesson plan

A lesson plan is a *planning* tool, containing all the information and decisions you need to consider before setting foot in a classroom. However, when you are teaching a class it can be difficult to refer to the lesson plan document quickly, precisely because it is so dense with information.

Consider a live stage show – the director will plan the show using a script which will include dialogue, stage set-up, scene transitions, lighting cues, props, music, sound effects and so on. When the actor is on stage the information they need is (at most) prompt cards to remind them of key lines of dialogue. If they were given the director's script they would suffer serious information overload. As a teacher you are both director and actor, so you need all of the relevant information (or at least the bits you are likely to forget) available in a manageable form.

Occasionally beginning teachers are over-reliant on the full plan during the lesson – their 'performance' becomes stilted, with no flow or spontaneity as they check off each point on their plan. At the other end of the spectrum some teachers abandon the plan then later regret missing the key points they had spent so long preparing. Some teachers can retain nearly everything in their memory with little need of prompts. Most of us are not so lucky and need something between a full lesson plan and keyword prompt cards. Strategies which can help here include:

- highlighting on the lesson plan only those key points likely to be forgotten, such as the sequence of activities and question phrasing
- transposing the key points onto a single piece of paper for easy reference during the lesson
- building prompts into the resources you are using – for example, a slideshow which includes the key questions you want to ask the class.

There is no single best approach and you may use a combination of these and other strategies. The important thing is that you find a system which works effectively for you (see companion website, www.sagepub.co.uk/secondary video clip, *Dealing with Complexity*, for a discussion of this in practice).

LEARNING AIMS AND OBJECTIVES

Academics argue (and will continue to do so) about the fine differences between aims, objectives and outcomes, and you may wish to contribute to the debate as part of your ongoing studies. For now, as beginning teachers what is important is that you have a framework which helps you plan effective lessons. Fortunately, while the fine detail of the definitions is debated, there is broad agreement about the spirit of these terms.

Learning aims

Learning aims state in quite broad terms what you want your pupils to achieve. They reflect your high, but realistic, aspirations for the class. The purpose of a learning aim is to provide direction, justification and context for the learning. Later on, when we are planning specific activities, it is useful to return to the learning aim to check that everything that we have planned truly matches up with and contributes to our original vision.

Beginning teachers will probably find that broad learning aims have been defined in advance by a combination of more experienced teachers, existing schemes of work and examination syllabuses. Nevertheless, you should be able to interpret, evaluate and refine existing aims.

Example learning aims

To be safe and considerate online users, having a broad understanding of e-safety issues, precautions and practices.

To identify, use and evaluate a set of graphic design principles, practices and techniques for an identified audience.

To be able to create a computer-based model of a real-world scenario and to be able to evaluate the strengths and weaknesses of such a model.

The same learning aim is likely to be used across a unit of work and will persist from lesson to lesson.

Learning aims tend to be too broad and generalized to provide clear assessment outcomes. The gap between a broad learning aim and individual learning activities is too great to cross in a single leap – to get there, we need to use the stepping stones of learning objectives.

Learning objectives

Taking the time to establish our learning objectives provides a powerful way of focusing our attention on *learning* rather than *activities*. Time spent on these at the beginning of the process helps us in a whole variety of ways later on, not least in differentiating the learning (see Chapter 7).

The same learning objectives we define in our scheme of work will then be used in individual lesson plans and are shared with pupils so that they understand the purpose of an activity. These objectives will ultimately be used to inform our learning outcomes and assessment criteria. It is therefore worth spending a little time to craft good objectives from the beginning.

Writing learning objectives is often made easier at first by going through a set of step-by-step refinements rather than aiming for a perfect final document on the first attempt – remember this is a thinking process. Start by getting your main ideas down and then use a framework to go back and improve the objectives.

Imagine you have been asked to prepare two or three lessons based upon the topic of email. A broad learning aim for this seven-lesson unit has been developed using the concept of ICT capability and the National Curriculum (key processes 2.3b and 2.3c):

Learning aim: Pupils can select the most appropriate method to confidently communicate information using digital and non-digital means effectively, safely and responsibly. They use technical terms appropriately and correctly.

Reflection Point 4.1

Before continuing, write down three learning objectives that you think pupils could achieve on the topic of email.

Reflection Point

The following statements are fairly typical of first attempts at this exercise:

1. Pupils can create an email account and send an email.
2. Pupils can open an email message and respond, adding an attachment.
3. Pupils can complete an email wordsearch.
4. Pupils write the definitions of email, reply, reply-to-all, forward, attachment, send and filter.

All of the above are in fact *activities*, not learning objectives. Does this really matter as long as teachers and pupils know what they are doing? We would strongly argue that it does. Settling on activities *before* we know what we want pupils to learn leads to lessons which tend to be skill-based, unfocused (in terms of pupils and teachers knowing why they are doing what they are doing) and, worst of all, inflexible (how would you differentiate the above?).

Let us take a step back and think about what we might want pupils to learn:

1. Pupils know the key vocabulary.
2. Pupils know the relative advantages and disadvantages of email, 'snail mail', telephone and face-to-face communication.
3. Pupils know how to send, receive and attach.
4. Pupils know the potential dangers of email – contact with strangers, malware, phishing.

This is a better approach because we are now not strait-jacketed by specific activities. We could devise several different activities for pupils to meet the same learning objective. For example, to meet the third objective, pupils could do any of the following (or a combination of them):

- produce a help-sheet for first-time users
- do a demonstration to the class
- send messages to each other or the teacher
- take part in a penfriend project.

While these objectives are an improvement, there is scope for (at least) one substantial improvement. We could improve upon the verb 'know' which is a rather vague concept; it would be better to use a specific verb which could also indicate the level of challenge involved in the learning. Fortunately for us, more than half a century ago, an academic educational psychologist produced a framework for doing this which teachers and schools continue to use to this day. His name was Benjamin Bloom.

Taxonomy of Educational Objectives – Bloom's Taxonomy

Benjamin Bloom believed that the majority of learners could be successful provided that they were given sufficient time and support. Central to his argument was the idea that all learners should be judged against clear objective criteria rather than a competitive system where only the top *n* per cent of a cohort are judged successful. He recognized that the

	Original taxonomy (1956)	Updated taxonomy (2001)
	Evaluation	Creating
	Synthesis	Evaluating
	Analysis	Analysing
	Application	Applying
	Comprehension	Understanding
	Knowledge	Remembering

Level of cognitive challenge (vertical axis label, arrow pointing up)

Figure 4.1   Bloom's taxonomy updated

education system often overemphasized the memorization of factual knowledge and he believed that the skills associated with higher-level mental processes were more important.

Bloom headed a research group at the University of Chicago to develop a taxonomy of educational objectives (do not be put off by this term, it simply means a way of classifying and ordering a set of items, from Greek *taxis*, 'arrangement' and *nomia*, 'method'). The group worked to develop taxonomies in three domains – cognitive, affective and psychomotor. Their work in the cognitive domain resulted in the *Taxonomy of Educational Objectives, The Classification of Educational Goals – Handbook 1: The Cognitive Domain* (Bloom, 1956). This has become one of the most influential education theory texts of the twentieth century and its ideas have been adopted and developed by education institutions across the globe.

Bloom's original work was most significantly updated in 2001 by Anderson and Krathwohl (see the weblinks on the companion website, www.sagepub.co.uk/secondary for further discussion behind the changes). The updated taxonomy was an attempt to respond to the growing use of the taxonomy in fields beyond its original intended audience (a simplified summary of the changes can be seen in Figure 4.1). In our opinion the updated version is more useful to teachers as a planning tool and we use these categories throughout the rest of this chapter (see Figure 4.2 for an overview). The important thing you need to take away from either model is that it is easy for our classroom practice to focus on the bottom two aspects (remembering and understanding). However, our lessons can become more challenging, worthwhile, interesting and even fun by focusing more of our practice upon learning to apply, analyse, evaluate and create. This is not to say that the first two levels are not important, there will be substantial elements of both in all of our teaching – but this should not be all that we do.

Figure 4.3 illustrates how we could use the taxonomy to be very specific in our learning objectives and increase the level of challenge and interest. We will use our email learning objective two: pupils know relative advantages and disadvantages of email, 'snail mail', telephone and face-to-face communication.

This example shows how we might use the taxonomy to set an appropriate level of challenge for a given learning objective. We would not expect every pupil or class to achieve every level in every lesson, we select the level which is appropriate to our

Remembering: Retrieving, recognizing and recalling relevant knowledge from long-term memory.

Understanding: Constructing meaning from instructional messages. These could be oral, written or graphical in nature. Subcategories include interpreting, exemplifying, classifying, summarizing, inferring, comparing and explaining.

Applying: Carrying out or using a procedure in a defined situation.

Analysing: Breaking material into constituent parts, determining how the parts relate to one another and to an overall structure or purpose.

Evaluating: Making judgements based on criteria and standards.

Creating: Putting elements together to form a coherent or functional whole; reorganizing elements into a new pattern or structure. Subcategories would include planning, generating and producing.

Figure 4.2 Hierarchy of cognitive skills from least to most challenging (adapted from Anderson & Krathwohl, 2001)

Category	Typical learning objective	Possible activities
Creating	Pupils can examine how functions have been added to early email systems over time and hypothesize how email may evolve in the near future.	Research the rise of email, social networking, instant messaging and mobile technologies. Create a detailed description for a device that might see these technologies converge in the near future.
Evaluating	Pupils can justify the use of each method from a social, economic and technological perspective. Construct a business case for using email, snail mail, telephone, face-to-face or a combination, or some other appropriate technology.	'Our school should use email for all communications in order to protect the environment.' Use a spreadsheet model to assess the costs and benefits of both mail systems – present findings to the headteacher.
Analysing	Pupils can break down the steps necessary for the mail function (composing, addressing, sending, tracking) and draw out relative advantages and disadvantages of alternate methods at each stage.	They can draw analogies between email and snail mail. Troubleshooting business case studies – 'Why did this email marketing strategy succeed/fail.'
Applying	Pupils can choose the most appropriate communication method. They can send a message using any method.	Given a list of possible scenarios, select the most appropriate method.
Understanding	Pupils can compare email, snail mail, telephone and face-to-face communication listing the advantages and disadvantages of each.	Complete a table of advantages and disadvantages.
Remembering	Pupils can define email and snail mail.	Select the correct definitions in a quiz. Write the definition on the whiteboard.

Figure 4.3 An example of the taxonomy in use

local circumstances. The point we are trying to make is that if *all* of your learning objectives start 'Pupils can describe' or 'List' or 'Remember', then they are never being stretched to do something challenging or interesting, and this may ultimately lead to classroom dissatisfaction (theirs and yours). In this case, think about whether you can set a more challenging (but realistic) learning objective using Bloom's taxonomy.

Notice how the verbs in each objective reflect the relative complexity of the task, 'define' > 'compare' > 'choose' > 'break down' > 'justify' > 'examine and hypothesize'. In turn each verb lends itself to a subset of possible activities. There are many useful web resources and diagrams which can help you choose the appropriate verb in your learning objective alongside related learning activities; these will help you broaden your teaching repertoire. You can find an example in the next section and a selection on the companion website, www.sagepub.co.uk/secondary.

In everyday classroom practice, for any given activity there will probably be an overlap between levels of learning both in terms of the task itself and what the children learn and produce. So, in a website design lesson the activity may require pupils to *remember* and *apply* various techniques, *evaluate* the impact of their web page on an audience and *demonstrate* understanding by creating a user guide so that someone else could update the website. While all children in the class may be able to remember and apply the techniques, the attempts to understand and evaluate may be superficial for some at their stage of learning and they will need further opportunities to acquire these skills in subsequent activities.

It is possible to debate the precise meaning of each term in the taxonomy and how it applies – for example, is our 'Applying' example really 'Application' as Bloom intended? Should we instead focus on *using* email and snail mail by sending an email and a physical letter? Before you get too tied up in this kind of debate, do not forget that it is the spirit of the taxonomy that matters, alongside your professional judgement. If you think a particular objective moves your pupils up the cognitive ladder, then it probably will.

Reflection Point 4.2

Rewrite your original learning objectives using Bloom's taxonomy.

Learning objectives using Bloom's taxonomy (level is in brackets):

1. *Pupils can **recall** the key vocabulary and use it in their work.*
   (Remembering/Understanding)
2. *Pupils can **explain** the main functions of email and 'snail mail'. They can **compare** email, 'snail mail', telephone and face-to-face communication, **choosing** the most appropriate method for a given scenario.*
   (Remembering/Understanding/Applying)

3. *Pupils **demonstrate** the practical skills of sending, receiving and attaching.*
   (Applying)
4. *Pupils can **identify** the potential dangers of email – contact with strangers, malware, phishing.*
   *They can **judge** when their actions constitute an unacceptable risk.*
   (Analysing/Evaluating)

THE JIGSAW OF LESSON PLANNING

Once we know what we are trying to achieve (aims) and what we want pupils to learn (learning objectives) we need to think through and combine a number of elements to create a meaningful learning experience. The actual process of planning the lesson is rarely a linear (step-by-step) experience; it is more like doing a jigsaw. You will develop ideas and elements, see how they fit and then go back and modify the lesson until you have a workable plan. The elements we need to create and combine are:

- an overall *context* for our lesson
- *activities* that we want pupils to undertake
- *resources* to interest pupils and promote independent learning
- *outputs* that pupils will produce
- *assessment criteria* for those outputs
- *timing and structure* of the lesson.

How then do we move from a set of learning objectives to an interesting context with a set of good classroom activities and resources which result in a set of clear outcomes that can be assessed?

Sometimes a context will present itself first, for instance the school may have an environmental project which you can use or there may be a news story that you know will spark pupils' interest. At Key Stage 4, many examination boards provide a specific context which must be used. At other times, you may identify a resource or activity that you know pupils will like (which meets the learning objectives) and so you build a context around the activity. Sometimes you will have to invent a context and resources from scratch in order to meet your learning objectives. Equally important at this stage is deciding how the work will be judged or assessed. A common experience of beginning teachers is to embark upon a substantial ICT project over several weeks without being really clear about what you are looking for in the work. Once the work is handed in you may make a set of value judgements about the relative presentation, effort and quality of the work, and probably end up ranking the work against the others in the class or year group. Remember, this is the situation we are trying to move away from. If the criteria are agreed and clear right from the outset, our teaching is more directed at achieving the outcomes and pupils feel happier that they understand what is expected. It also makes peer and self assessment possible (see Chapter 6). We will then need to put all of these elements into some kind of coherent structure.

Your goal in all of this is to create *memorable* experiences – those that pupils talk about in the school playground or at home with parents. Memorable lessons take pupils' own understanding, experiences and interests and use these to explore new ideas and concepts. I can still distinctly remember a chemistry lesson from 20 years ago when our teacher took what we knew from our laboratory work and showed how it applied to the real world. We understood theoretically that when fossil fuel burns it releases carbon dioxide, her explanation of how this gas could create a greenhouse effect (long before the term was familiar in the media) and its possible effects upon sea levels brought the chemistry to life. The sequence of events was set out so simply and powerfully that many of us have probably retold the tale many times since – such is the power of a good teacher.

Reflection Point 4.3

Think of two activities or lessons you have experienced as a learner (preferably with the same teacher), one that you enjoyed and one which you did not enjoy. Thinking purely about the nature of the activities make a list of the key elements that made one successful and the other not.

It is likely that the lesson you enjoyed:

- was directly relevant to your interests or aspirations
- built on what you already knew – so that you did not cover old ground
- was the kind of activity you liked, for example a practical activity
- was difficult (just at the edge of your ability), but fun
- had a very specific output, for example, an answer to a hard question, a physical piece of work, a performance or presentation
- gave you the chance to feel clever and be creative
- provided opportunities for dialogue (both teacher–pupil and pupil–pupil) and group work
- was well paced and limited to a specific time period.

Much of the above depends on the teacher's knowledge of their pupils. This is challenging for beginning teachers. You may have some data or general information about the pupils, but you most likely will need to supplement this with some baseline questioning or assessment.

Baseline questioning

If you have been in a situation where a tutor either covers a topic you already fully understand or assumes knowledge you do not have, you will empathize with those pupils who are bored and perhaps act inappropriately because a teacher has not taken into account their various starting points (prior learning). To be effective you must find out what children know and can do, and build your activities from there. Timing is important, it is not good to find out at the beginning of a lesson that the class are competent and confident in everything you had planned – 'Miss, why are we doing this all over again?' It is better, if possible, to build this assessment into an earlier lesson, perhaps your plenary of the previous lesson so that you have time to amend your plans. Often the simplest way to ascertain prior knowledge is through questioning, but be aware that while children may have completed some learning in the past, they may not remember the terminology that you use. For example, a common response to 'Who has used LOGO?' from 11-year-olds is a room of blank expressions. However ask, 'Who has used a robot called a turtle which sits on a sheet of paper and responds to instructions like Forward 100?' and you will usually be rewarded with some enthusiastic head-nodding. You will then need some further questioning to understand the extent of their knowledge.

Do not assume that just because 'We did this in Year 8', that they have met all of the learning objectives – staff may have been absent, other pressures may have resulted in some rushed teaching or the children may simply have forgotten. Often it is good to use a mechanism like thumbs up or traffic lights to gauge prior learning using a question like 'Who is confident that they can come to the front and demonstrate how to use a Master slide? Red = No idea, Amber = I think so, Green = Definitely'. This gets around the automatic response of pupils to nod at you if you ask 'Do you all know how to do Master slides?' Traffic lights also help you subgroup a class into flexible ability groups (see Chapter 7).

Once you have an idea of pupils' prior learning you can plan your activities in more detail. Most of the time you will plan a central activity which is achievable for most learners and then differentiate the task, outputs, resources, support or a combination of these to suit learners with a larger or smaller learning gap to traverse. Remember that task difficulty can be graduated so that everyone can achieve something worthwhile. Also think about having the right level of 'scaffolding' for the learner – you want to provide the minimum support which enables them to learn for themselves, but not so little that they become frustrated. Chapter 7 deals with these ideas in greater depth.

Generating ideas and subject research

How do teachers begin to generate ideas which lead to really good teaching activities and outcomes? Ideas for activities come from many different sources. A good starting point is personal experience. First, as learners ourselves we may have been exposed to a particularly brilliant or engaging activity that we can replicate with our own pupils. (It is surprising what you can re-learn by going through your old projects, files or workbooks). Secondly, by observing other teachers or looking at their resources we can learn what works, and equally important what could be improved. This could include teachers from other disciplines and age phases. Thirdly, self-reflection of lessons we have taught helps us refine or redesign activities to meet our learning objectives. Be aware when selecting activities that you may need to consider approaches that would not be your own preferred approach as a learner. Many learners will respond best to activities which may be outside your own comfort zone. Perhaps you learn best by reading and reflecting, but this will not suit more active learners who may prefer to role-play a situation.

ICT textbooks and online resources offer a range of ideas which can be adapted into useful classroom activities. It is rare that these resources will meet all your needs in terms of learning objectives and pacing, so they will need some degree of adaptation. Remember to demonstrate good practice by providing an acknowledgement of the source material.

Talking with pupils about their interests and influences often sparks ideas; in fact, finding out about each others' interests can be a good project in its own right in the context of presentations or databases. You can then integrate some of these ideas into activities in subsequent lessons. Do be careful about generalizing too widely – not all pupils want to construct a fantasy football league or a poster about their favourite celebrity. The idea of an appropriate context is explored later in this chapter.

Some online games (particularly multiple-choice recall-type questions) can be engaging for a class, but take up far too much time compared with, for example, some quality classroom dialogue, which could accomplish the same learning in much less time.

Resources from other subjects can also be a source of inspiration. Why not use a mathematics model within a spreadsheet activity, use a history context for comparing online versus traditional research methods or an English activity as the basis for a presentation to an audience?

Current news stories are often a great source of ideas, it is well worth checking science and technology headlines on a daily basis. You can use these to provide a real-world context for your teaching and sometimes base an entire project around a news story. For example, as we are writing this news is breaking of the loss of several disks containing the personal details of 25 million people in the UK by one government department. This would provide a really interesting context for discussions about the Data Protection Act and possible identity theft. See the suggested weblinks at the end of the chapter and the companion website, www.sagepub.co.uk/secondary for links. News stories have the added advantage of dramatic pictures and video which seize pupils' attention at the beginning of a project.

As discussed in the previous section, Bloom's taxonomy can help us select a range of activities which match a particular type of learning objective. Figure 4.4 shows how the verbs we have chosen for our objectives can indicate the types of activities we might choose.

Many of the activities we enjoy teaching have a 'wow factor' which typically demonstrate the power of ICT (if the children whisper 'cool' you have hit upon the wow factor). This does not necessarily mean all-singing-and-dancing multimedia; often simple demonstrations in the hands of pupils can have great impact. Examples might include:

- presenting information in a way previously impossible such as the online NPAC Visible Human Viewer, Google Earth or the Hermitage Museum's Digital Collection image search
- examples of artificial intelligence and neural networks such as A.L.I.C.E. (Artificial Linguistic Internet Computer Entity) or 20Q online (also the hand-held game version)
- using simple commands to build beautiful, complex repeating patterns in LOGO
- demonstrating simple decision-making techniques (for example conditional formatting or 'IF' statements in spreadsheets) often promotes an interesting 'But how does it know?' discussion
- using spreadsheets to perform many simultaneous calculations to illustrate speed of processing – a simple example is a life calculator which when given your date of birth calculates how old you are in years, days, minutes and seconds. By assuming you live to be 85, it could also tell you how many hours you will spend in various activities – talking, sleeping, reading, watching television, playing computer games and so on

	Remembering	Understanding	Applying	Analysing	Evaluating	Creating
Verbs	Define	Compare	Carry out	Break down	Appraise	Assemble
	Describe	Comprehend	Change	Categorize	Compare	Bring together
	Identify	Explain	Demonstrate	Classify	Conclude	Build
	Know	Extend	Employ	Compare	Consider	Combine
	Label	Give examples	Execute	Contrast	Contrast	Compile
	List	Interpret	Manipulate	Deconstruct	Criticize	Compose
	Locate	Make links	Modify	Distinguish	Critique	Construct
	Memorize	Match	Operate	Define	Decide	Develop
	Name	Paraphrase	Perform	Discover	Defend	Devise
	Note	Paraphrase	Prepare	Examine	Determine	Formulate
	Recall	Re-state	Show	Explore	Discriminate	Generate
	Recap	Rewrite	Solve	Identify	Form an opinion	Hypothesize
	Recite	Select	Use	Illustrate	Interpret	Innovate
	Recognize	Summarize		Infer	Judge	Invent
	Repeat	Translate		Investigate	Justify	Make
	Reproduce			Outline	Recommend	Organize
	Select			Predict	Relate	Plan
	Spell			Prioritize	Select	Produce
	State			Probe	Weight	Summarize
				Question		
				Solve		
				Sort		
				Subdivide		
				Summarize		
				Work out		

(Continued)

Example activities	Remembering	Understanding	Applying	Analysing	Evaluating	Creating
	Write the definition. Devise a mnemonic. Fill in the gaps. List the words. Complete the crossword. Read and learn. Say the ryhme.	Complete a comprehension. Rewrite for an audience. Provide 3 examples. Explain in your own words. What are the advantages and disadvantages? Interpret a graph.	Use your skills to produce a poster, spreadsheet, presentation. Complete the missing steps. Explain how you ... Write a user guide. Sequence the instructions. Show your partner how to ... Find the information. Conduct a survey.	Draw a diagram to show the relationships. Construct a concept map. Plan the steps you will need to take. Solve the mystery or problem. Predict what would happen if ... Reduce the number of steps. Find out what the audience wants. Refine your search strategy. Define the fields you will need. List the validation rules. Analyse your survey results. Identify the pattern. Predict what would happen if the price increased by 10%. Identify the design features used. Troubleshoot the problem.	Present a balanced view. Annotate your work with suggested improvements. Use the assessment criteria to peer-evaluate your partner's work. Prepare for a debate on the issue. Identify the effectiveness of the design features and suggest improvements. Select the software to use and justify your reasons. Identify and challenge the assumptions that the webpage designer has made. Evaluate the impact of the decision. Select the most effective solution. Identify bias in a website.	Use a number of sources to produce an overall summary. Design, implement and refine a product or system. Experiment to find the optimum solution. Use your survey data to identify audience needs and use persuasive writing and design skills to meet those needs. Use a variety of electronic and 'traditional' sources to investigate a hypothesis. Create a game which tests your classmates' knowledge.

Figure 4.4 From objectives to verbs to activities

- using quiz-generating tools such as Hot Potatoes to make quizzes for fellow pupils or presentation templates which allow you to recreate popular television game shows
- collaborating with other schools, organizations or experts using tools such as Google Docs
- simple animation tools, for example to generate graphics image format (GIF) animations
- using a webcam to generate stop-frame animation
- simple audio recording and/or sequencing
- projects which examine the impact of miniaturization, exponential rise in data storage capacity, increase in computing power (Moore's Law) or rapid rise of World Wide Web usage
- looking back at past uses of technology and associated attitudes (the free British Pathe News clips are an excellent source here).

 Examples and weblinks for the above are available via the companion website, www.sage pub.co.uk/secondary.

Hopefully, you are now beginning to generate your own ideas. As these bubble up and you start to research your subject and invent activities we would offer three pieces of advice:

1. Record everything that you find, either electronically or on paper – otherwise you will not be able to locate that brilliant website you found last week.
2. Research needs to be deep and broad: deep because you need to anticipate the children's questions and find the answers in advance; broad because knowing about related or surrounding topic areas helps you answer unanticipated questions and set interesting extension tasks or questions.
3. Once you have amassed a desktop full of background materials, websites, ideas and possible activities, do some really hard pruning and selection so that you are only presenting a manageable 'chunk' of learning in any one activity.

 (See companion website, www.sagepub.co.uk/secondary, video clips, *Lesson Planning* to hear about this in practice.)

A practical example

In this example we follow a beginning teacher, Jason, as he generates ideas, evaluates them and plans his lesson. Because this is not a linear journey we will see how he moves between stages by imagining what would happen in a classroom. The final lesson plan is at the end of this chapter and related resources are on the companion website.

Jason is to teach a seven-week topic covering control and modelling. The scheme of work identifies these National Curriculum links:

1.1.c Apply ICT learning in a range of contexts and in other areas of learning, work and life.
2.2.d Design information systems and suggest improvements to existing systems.
2.2.e Use ICT to make things happen by planning, testing and modifying a sequence of instructions, recognising where a group of instructions needs repeating, and automating frequently used processes by constructing efficient procedures that are fit for purpose.

2.3c Use technical terms appropriately and correctly.

4d   Apply ICT to real-world situations when solving problems and carrying out a range of tasks and enquiries.

Expected level 4 Attainment Target: *'They plan and test sequences of instructions. They use ICT-based models and simulations to explore patterns and relationships, and make predictions about the consequences of their decisions.'*

In his first lesson he wants to provide an overview of the unit and key concepts. He has settled on the following learning objectives (LOs):

Lesson 1 of 7

1) Pupils can apply the terms *input, process, output* and *feedback* to describe how real-world systems work.
2) Pupils can use the idea of a computer program to invent instructions which control a device or process. They can deduce the effects of imprecision in computer instructions.

Jason begins sketching out his lesson plan starting with the main learning points he thinks he will need to cover, using textbooks and his own notes to help. He finds and records definitions for the key vocabulary.

To meet LO1 he thinks it would be useful to display pictures of various devices (alarm clock, washing machine, microwave oven, aircraft autopilot) on the board and have pupils list the input, process and output. As he thinks about these examples he realizes some potential for confusion between looking at devices as a whole and looking specifically at the computer control element – this is a distinction he will have to make clear. He works it through to ensure his own subject knowledge is sound (Figure 4.5).

He decides a thought experiment would be useful for the pupils to understand the idea and plans some questions/activities:

1. Display a picture of a washing machine. *'On your wipe boards write down the inputs and outputs for this device – you have 30 seconds – go.'*
2. Ask everyone to hold up their boards ask for further explanations where necessary and capture the key answers on the board – if necessary prompt so that there are a mixture of whole system and computer control responses.
3. *'Thanks for those brilliant answers. Remember the things we are interested in are those that the computer inside the washing machine "knows" about – INPUTS, and the things it can directly control – OUTPUTS. Close your eyes. Imagine you are the computer that "lives" in the washing machine – your job is to get the clothes clean. Think about what* **senses or sensors** *you have that tell you what's going on in the washing machine and what* **devices** *you can control in order to wash the clothes.'*
4. Take feedback from the class – ask a volunteer to update the list on the board so that we are only left with computer controlled inputs and outputs.

Device	Whole system	Computer control
Alarm clock	Input – current time, alarm time Process – is current time = alarm time? Output – alarm on	Same as whole system
Washing machine	Input – clothes, washing powder Process – wash clothes Output – clean clothes	Input – select wash programme, detect water temperature, drum speed and water level Process – make decisions about water level, temperature and drum speed Output – fill/empty, heat, spin
Microwave oven	Input – food Process – cook Output – hot meal	Input – power level and time selector, door switch Process – is door closed? Countdown time. Has time reached zero? Output – power on at selected level/turntable activated, power off
Aircraft autopilot	Input – fuel, people Process – fly to destination Output – arrive safely	Input – destination co-ordinates, current position (GPS), set altitude, set speed Process – set direction and air speed Output – engine speed, rudders, flaps, landing gear up/down

Figure 4.5 Thinking through Input-Process-Output

Jason is happy with this – the pupils are working things out for themselves; he could have saved a few minutes by telling them the answers, but he thinks fewer pupils would understand and the experience would be less meaningful and memorable. At the end of the activity he will have a list of keywords that he can then refer back to throughout the lesson. He notes that a homework which extends this work might provide useful practice and cement the learning.

The idea of sensors and devices is a good one – Jason realizes that it will be necessary to expand upon this so that the pupils know a range of specific devices that can be used. They could add the names of the relevant devices to each input and output. Once completed the class need to turn their attention to *process* – how does the computer make decisions about what to do based on the information received through its inputs?

For learning objective 2 (LO2) Jason has observed lessons where the teacher or a volunteer pretends to be a mechanistic robot and the class issue instructions, he thinks this is an engaging approach. He could then progress to look at the differences between natural language (English) instructions and using flow-charts. The next step would be to get pupils to design or label some devices showing inputs and outputs and ask them to write some 'If … happens … then do this …' type statements for the process. Finally, he wants to introduce the idea of a feedback loop.

Thinking through the role play he lists a number of possible scenarios – making a cup of tea or a sandwich, copying a picture, assembling a Lego model, stacking coloured blocks. He decides that making a sandwich will be a good visual demonstration and any group that wins gets a reward – they can eat the finished sandwich (provided he has checked about food allergies of course)!

He decides that what is important in this activity is that the pupils realize that computer devices have to be programmed carefully in advance of the situation where they are expected to perform (human operators do not stand at the washing machine issuing instructions to add water or washing powder) – the programmer has to work everything out in advance, anticipating all eventualities. Group work seems a good option here; he can use mixed-ability groupings and will have time to take feedback from each group in a way that would be impossible with individuals within the timescale. With 20 in the class he decides on four groups of five. The task will be to provide a kitchen robot with all the instructions it needs to make a jam sandwich – all the ingredients and utensils will be laid out on a tray so that they can see the context. The groups will have three minutes to record their instructions on a flip chart – the teacher will then act out the robot role as each group reads out their instructions. He plans to be deliberately obtuse – a comment like 'put the butter on the bread' will result in the tub of butter being placed on the packet of bread unless he has first been instructed to open both items, use the knife and so on. Jason anticipates that the learning that will come out of this activity will be that pupils will understand the difficulty in providing unambiguous, precise instructions which anticipate all eventualities. He plans to end the activity by giving 30 seconds' thinking time for individuals to say why the task was so hard – feedback will be recorded on the board. Again there are faster ways to do this learning, but they are unlikely to be as memorable or meaningful.

In the back of his mind Jason anticipates his class asking: 'But *why* are we doing this Sir?' He needs a context to make pupils understand why these ideas are important. He wants them to understand that engineers and computer programmers go through this process whenever they create a computer-controlled device. Scanning the BBC's technology headlines he finds a news story '*Robot glider harvests ocean heat*' (Fildes, 2008), which describes an autonomous 'sea-going robotic glider that harvests heat energy from the ocean'. The story includes a striking picture and links to additional details. He realizes that this device neatly bridges the two main themes of the seven-week topic – it is a device controlled by a computer program and the data it collects is used back at base to produce a computer model (say, of how currents flow in the ocean). On reading further, he learns that the robot senses its surroundings in order to glide at a specific depth and direction – a perfect example of feedback. He begins to consider the possibility of using autonomous robots as a main context for this lesson. Further searches find a commercial robot manufacturer, iRobot, which supplies home and military robots that perform tasks from home vacuuming to bomb disposal. He thinks iRobot's co-founder, Helen Greiner, will be a great role model for the girls in the class, in what can be perceived as a male-dominated field.

Jason decides to add a third learning objective he was planning to leave until a later lesson:

3) Pupils can explore the relative advantages and disadvantages offered by independent robotic devices.

Initially Jason thinks that he could set a task for the remainder of the lesson and home-work in which pupils design their own robot, for example to tidy their room. On reflection he realizes that this is an awfully complex (and time-consuming) task to meet the learning objective. Furthermore, he has come across many existing examples of robots in his research and realizes that asking pupils to speculate about the inputs, processes, outputs, sensors, devices, advantages and disadvantages of these existing robots would meet the objectives admirably. He could follow up the previous activity by asking them to also think about the situations a programmer would have to anticipate. There is a great deal of scope in terms of what the pupils could produce as an outcome for this activity. Jason's initial ideas include:

- a simple report or table listing the characteristics of the robot
- answers recorded against teacher-set questions
- a news report to the class
- a sales poster for the robot
- labelling a diagram of the robot
- preparing to be in the 'hot seat' where they are the expert answering questions from the rest of the class about their chosen robot.

In selecting an appropriate activity (or set of activities) Jason will need to consider whether the work is to be completed individually or in groups, how the work will be assessed and how much time is available in lessons for sharing findings with the class and teacher feedback.

Jason decides that for this activity sharing their findings with the class is more important than completing an individual assessment (there will be time for this later). He decides to give them a group task with a choice of outputs for next week. They can either produce:

- a live news style report accompanied by a short on-screen presentation, or
- a sales poster for the robot accompanied by a short verbal presentation (the poster may be hand-drawn or produced using a computer).

As the timescale is so short for this task, Jason decides to provide a high degree of scaf-folding with a template pre-prepared for the news script and poster. Pupils can then focus on the topic rather than spending large amounts of time creating a script or designing from scratch.

Jason is well on the way to planning an engaging lesson, he has a potentially inter-esting context has supplemented his own subject knowledge by using textbooks and websites, and has some initial ideas for activities. The next step will be to begin to plan the lesson in detail in terms of activities, outcomes and assessment criteria.

Activities, outcomes and assessment criteria

Activities – what will they do?
Outcomes – what will they produce (or what questions are they able to answer)?
Assessment criteria – what are the quality criteria that let you know what they have learned and the extent of their expertise?

These three elements are closely interrelated and you will need to consider all three in parallel. In the previous example Jason has a clear idea of what pupils will do (activity) and produce (outcome) as in Figure 4.6.

The best activities 'sell' an idea and make learning meaningful. Jason has tried to create activities which:

- are simple to describe
- use prompts to help pupils understand what is required – demonstrations, examples of good and poor work, worksheets with clear signposts of what is important
- hang together within an overall context which makes sense to pupils
- use a combination of stories, analogy, mystery, novelty and everyday experience to sustain interest and help pupils understand difficult concepts
- are creative (even fun) within structured parameters – 'Make a website on any topic of your choosing' is too open a task for most pupils who will spend most of the allocated time deciding upon a topic
- are 'hard fun' – they make you think almost without you realizing that you are working hard.

Activity	Outcomes
Labelling devices (input, output, sensors and devices)	Screenshots from interactive whiteboard as pupils do the class task Homework sheet
Issuing commands to make a sandwich	List of instructions A sandwich (perhaps) List of reasons why programming is a difficult task
Either Produce a sales poster for an existing robot and present to class. Target audience – potential buyers	Script/notes Poster Bibliography and search terms used
Or Prepare a children's science news report about an existing robot. Target audience – 10- to 14-year-olds	Script Presentation with images Bibliography and search terms used

Figure 4.6 Identifying and aligning activities and outcomes

Similarly for learning outcomes, Jason has tried to ensure that what the children do or produce:

- has clearly identified outputs
- is not 'busy work' in which the children are kept busy, but learn very little – for example, copying from a book or repeating many examples of the same task
- allows pupils to reach higher levels of the National Curriculum (through recording their searches, acknowledging sources and writing for a target audience).

Reflection Point 4.4

It is possible to unwittingly design activities which only allow pupils to access the lower-level descriptions of the National Curriculum, yet a simple extension of the task can provide more challenge and opportunity to reach higher levels. In each of the examples below, how could the activity be amended to provide access to the next National Curriculum level?

1. Keep a record of the search terms and web pages you have used and present these in a list.
2. Explain how you used the main functions of the software to produce a leaflet.
3. Produce a poster inviting people to the school show.
4. Explain what you think will happen to profits if the ticket price increases by £1.
5. Use this website … to find out the answer to these questions …
6. Produce and print a flow chart to control the pelican crossing.

Jason has specified what the children will produce, but has not yet considered the criteria that pupils will be assessed against – what do they need to do to demonstrate they have truly met the learning objectives? Jason needs to consider how he might distinguish between the quality of one piece of work which is excellent against another which is weaker overall. In short what does 'good' actually look like? To make this decision and illustrate the differences to the class it is helpful to use similar work from previous classes. Where this is not possible, you can imagine and create examples of work that pupils might produce and use these to help define your criteria. Jason considers the following to be important criteria for the main task:

- completeness/volume of responses – all or most inputs, outputs, sensors and devices have been identified, and pupils suggest at least two advantages and disadvantages of robots over humans to perform the task
- accurate use of terminology in the written and oral work

- a balanced evaluation of, for example, advantages and disadvantages of robots over humans.
- use of language and images appropriate to the target audience – with justification
- creativity, for example, in anticipating the situations the robot may face
- expert knowledge – ability of pupils to anticipate and answer questions from peers and teacher.
- research skills – what search terms were used and are sources acknowledged (perhaps some opportunity to evaluate)?
- overall presentation of the work.

Jason may choose to expand his list of assessment criteria by developing and agreeing them with the class – see the 'Starters' section of this chapter for one example of how to do this.

Teachers (often subconsciously) prioritize the first and last items in this list ('How much have you done and how neat is it?'). It is, after all, human nature to want to reward hard work – and there is no more visible sign of this than the quantity and presentation of a piece of work. Armed with this knowledge we can inoculate ourselves against its effect and concentrate on the more important criteria which identify the *quality* of the actual *learning* that has taken place (see Chapter 6 for further details). This is not to say that presentation is unimportant, but it is a skill which takes time to develop and we should not downgrade a piece of work disproportionately on the grounds of presentation alone. (See companion website www.sagepub.co.uk/secondary video clips, *Independence*, to hear about this in practice).

Jason now has the main elements of a lesson planned, the next challenges are to structure his ideas into a one-hour period and prepare the resources he needs.

Structuring and pacing

Organizing ICT projects within the time available (often an hour a week for Key Stage 3) is challenging. Typically the time spent using the computers is a maximum of 45 minutes and many pupils spend a proportion of this time simply remembering where they were up to from the previous week. Projects which span several weeks can easily telescope out into a much longer time frame than previously anticipated. A major part of an ICT teacher's job therefore is to keep pupils focused and on track.

In our observation of teachers we often distinguish between 'teaching time' – where the teacher is working really hard to explain, motivate and enthuse, and 'learning time' – where the children are working hard to meet their learning goals. Where the balance is towards 'teaching time' children are often entertained and the teacher feels like they are 'teaching their socks off', but actually there is only limited learning taking place. Perhaps this happens because in an observation situation teachers feel more pressured to 'perform'. Ultimately what matters is the learning that takes place, and this is what observers are looking for – even if teacher dialogue takes up only a small part of the overall lesson.

Be realistic in the time you allocate to activities (the work usually takes longer than you think). It helps to build in some 'wiggle room' so that less important elements are towards the end and can be deferred to a later time if it becomes necessary. Whenever you set an activity tell pupils how long they have and regularly remind them how long they have left – an on-screen timer is an excellent way to do this (see companion website, www.sagepub.co.uk/secondary). If tasks are complex, break them up into manageable time chunks and tell them how long they have for each part. Try to ensure that activities are varied from task to task both in terms of the type of activity and pacing, with some short tasks balancing longer project-type work.

Teachers often feel pressured to 'cover the curriculum', moving quickly through activities, sometimes before learning has been fully consolidated. There is a real tension here between curriculum coverage, providing opportunities to consolidate and link together learning, and ensuring that there is sufficient pace to maintain children's interest. This is a difficult balancing act and your approach will vary between classes.

> Although good pace is a key factor in successful teaching, there are occasions when pupils are rushed through new work in particular applications. They follow instructions closely, often using work sheets, and achieve the desired end, but without a clear understanding of the underlying concepts. In the best lessons, teachers set work which is demanding and which requires pupils to apply knowledge and skills developed previously; they encourage experimentation and discussion. (Ofsted, 2002: 3)

As a general principle, in our view it is essential that pupils have an opportunity to fully understand a concept before moving on. It is particularly important that pupils have an opportunity to learn from their mistakes and so you need to build in time where pupils can correct, extend or redo work in response to your feedback or peer/self assessment.

When Jason starts to plan the lesson he realizes that there is perhaps too much teaching time and too many activities to fit in during the hour. As a result, he changes his original idea for a 'Robots' presentation into a web-quest where the pupils can find information for themselves (and by asking them to record their searches he creates an additional opportunity for them to demonstrate ICT capability). He decides to use the sandwich-making task as a plenary and to only start the production of the script or poster during the next lesson. This also allows him to add a homework task in preparation for next week's lesson giving an opportunity for some independent learning.

Starters

The tripartheid lesson structure of a starter, main activity and plenary has become ubiquitous in secondary school ICT lessons, particularly at Key Stage 3. There are good reasons for using this structure, many of which are outlined in the Key Stage 3 (now secondary) National Strategy.

Beginnings of lessons can easily become derailed by administrative tasks such as collecting homework or taking the register, by leaving these tasks until the children are on-task it is possible to improve the pace of the lesson. Starters can be used to engage children in meaningful activity as soon as they enter the room. This makes best use of the time when pupils are most alert, focuses their attention and reduces inappropriate behaviour. Starters are most often used to:

- recap previous learning
- introduce a new topic
- carry out baseline assessment to find out their starting position
- share learning objectives
- set targets
- demonstrate a skill
- or simply to get pupils thinking.

Your starters will vary in timings, usually between about 5 and 15 minutes. While you will often plan a single activity, sometimes it may be better to subdivide your starters. For example, where a class typically arrive with low energy levels you could engage them in a quick mental warm-up activity before beginning the main starter.

Where pupils do not all arrive at the same time it is a good idea to plan starter activities which do not require direct teacher explanation. You can then develop a routine where pupils know that when they arrive there will be a time-limited task to complete at their desk or workstation (a laminated reusable task sheet is a good idea). If pupils have low reading ages you will have to carefully consider the language used on these tasks and complement them with clear diagrams, perhaps even a slideshow or video with narrated instructions. As with all learning activities, the tasks you produce need to be focused, meaningful and challenging – pupils who start every lesson with a standard word-search are simply performing a pattern-matching exercise that the average seven-year-old could accomplish – use Bloom's taxonomy to help.

Many effective teachers use an element of novelty to secure pupils' attention, perhaps a provocative question – 'What if … microchips stopped working?', visual cue – striking image, video or animation on the whiteboard, or perhaps a piece of music, sound effect or audio clip related to the topic.

It is easy for starters to overrun. You need to make a professional judgement here, if the quality of discussion and learning is good then you may need to be flexible in the use of the planned lesson time and readjust accordingly. However, be aware that tasks will most often fill whatever time is made available. Using a visible timer with reminders can speed up the pace at which pupils work and help you stay on track. A healthy element of competition can also be a good tactic for maintaining pace.

Starters do not have to be overly complex. The following idea for a lesson starter is simple, time limited and requires no technology, yet it yields excellent results, gets children focused on assessment criteria and can be displayed as a visual reminder throughout the duration of the project. In our experience most children are far more focused on the feedback because of the visual cue they produce, rather than just listening to each other answer questions.

Lesson starter: agreeing assessment criteria

Split the class into groups of four, provide a piece of flip-chart paper and an instruction giving them five minutes to use only pictures to describe a concept such as 'Things that make a good sales poster' (giving each group member a different coloured pen is a quick way of assessing individual contributions). Each group then presents their results and takes questions from their peers. The teacher can refine all of the feedback into a single set of agreed assessment criteria which can be used throughout the project.

Remember those learning objectives we examined earlier in the chapter? A starter is the perfect time to explain them to the class. We do not need to do this as soon as the pupils enter the rooms; in fact this can sometimes spoil some of the novelty factor you are trying to build. In these cases it is more appropriate to share the learning objectives just before the main activity. Many schools share objectives and outcomes in all lessons using a two-phase approach with the headings WALT (**W**e **A**re **L**earning **T**oday) and WILF (**W**hat **I**'m **L**ooking **F**or).

Reflection Point 4.5

Consider these two examples of WALTs and WILFs. How do they differ in approach? Are they equally helpful to pupils?

Example 1

We Are Learning Today – To query the data in the database
What I'm Looking For – Pupils who can quietly finish all the database queries

Example 2

We Are Learning Today – How these words and symbols ['AND', 'OR', =, <, >, *] help us to ask questions using our database
What I'm Looking For:
Pupils who have written on the worksheet the queries they have tried and the results
Pupils who can answer this question in the plenary – 'Which query is likely to give more results and why?
Height = 1.8m
Height <1.8m
Height >1.2m AND Height <1.8m.'

WALT is used to explain your objectives in pupil-friendly terms. *WILF* describes the concrete learning outcomes that pupils will achieve, these are the things they will produce or the questions they will be able to answer. WALTs and WILFs are sometimes simply displayed and read through; this can result in a mechanistic exercise with few gains for pupils or teachers. It is more constructive to give pupils a moment to fully understand them and have an opportunity to ask or answer questions.

Jason often uses WALT and WILF at the beginning of his lessons to provide pupils with a route map for their learning – notice how he has reworded the original learning objectives into pupil-friendly language:

Scenario

'OK, here's our WALTs ...' (he has them ready on the flip chart):

We are learning today ...

1) How the words *input, process, output* and *feedback* help us make machines that work.
2) How we can write instructions called computer programs which can control machines – even when we are not there.
3) To justify why some jobs might be done better by robots, while others might be done better by humans.

'Emily, what do we need to know in order to do number 1?'
'What those words (input, process, output, feedback) mean.'
'Excellent – Iqbal, anything else for the first point?'
'Some examples of the kinds of machines.'
'Yes, and we'll be doing that in just a moment.'
'In point 2 we'll be looking at programs – has anyone here written a computer program?'
'Sir, we did it in primary school – with that turtle robot.'
'Excellent, Josh, hands up who else has done that ... I see we have quite a few expert pro-grammers today. Kyle, what does 'justify' mean in point 3?'
'Erm, it is like saying why we would use a robot.'
'Exactly – and perhaps why we didn't choose a human – we could say the advantages and disadvantages of each. Here's our WILF ...'

What I'm looking for – pupils who ...

1. Can accurately label the inputs, outputs, sensors and devices of a machine – on the whiteboard and for homework.
2. Can guess what sensors and devices robots might use.
3. Can explain what robots can do better than humans.
4. Can explain what humans can do better than robots.
5. Can answer these questions in the plenary:
   a. 'What does a computer programmer do?'
   b. 'Give a reason why it is so difficult to write good computer programs.'

Jason has his WALT and WILF on a flip chart – this is a good idea, because it will be permanently displayed throughout the lesson, unlike if he used a projected image for example. This is useful because some pupils take more time than others to read and understand information. Also we have all had the experience of 'zoning-out' for a moment and then realizing we need to catch up with what has just been said – a permanent visual reminder helps in these circumstances. Remember to include these details in your lesson plan so that you have, for example, flip-chart paper and pens to hand.

For this lesson Jason's starter will be longer than average because he is introducing new concepts and topics. This does not concern him because he knows that the second lesson will have a short recap starter and then a large chunk of learning time. (See companion website, www.sagepub.co.uk/secondary, video clips: *Starters*, to hear about this in practice.)

Main activity

By the end of the starter phase pupils are usually eager to get on with the main task, particularly when it is computer based. It is tempting to release them immediately, but a few minutes with the whole class confirming their understanding and answering questions now will save you lots of repeated messages later on. Plan to describe the task to them, including how resources will be used. Visual cues such as screenshots can save lots of teacher talking here – a picture really is worth a thousand words. Have the steps they need to undertake written out either on a whiteboard or a worksheet, or both. Finally, check their understanding by asking probing questions – 'Janelle, remind the class what we do for step 2' is much better than 'Do you all understand?'

The main activity phase of a lesson is dominated by children being engaged in learning tasks supported by their teacher and other peripatetic staff. Resist the temptation during this phase to plan many teacher instructions, questions or transitions. Only intervene at a whole-class level when absolutely necessary, for example if you feel the majority of the class have misunderstood the task. In these cases it is essential that you secure the attention of the whole class before beginning your instructions (see Chapter 5 for suggested strategies).

Planning and preparing worksheets or computer-based resources which guide pupils through tasks prevents beginning teachers from becoming overly reliant on lots of verbal teacher instruction. This is not just a technique to save your voice, interpreting and following instructions is an important life skill for children. It also results in a calmer atmosphere and provides an opportunity for differentiated self-paced learning. These resources are time-consuming to prepare, but once in place can be refined and used many times. Some of the resources we have developed during our training have been adapted and used with many classes and hundreds of children. Later in the chapter we examine the kinds of resources you could produce.

As with the starter, setting timed targets and displaying an on-screen timer can be really helpful in maintaining pace and focus, as can an element of competition.

Once children are settled, main activity time can provide a good opportunity to conduct individual and small-group assessments so that you can check pupils' understanding in depth. These may range from simply asking pupils to describe some of the key concepts, through to more formal recording of their progress to date and target-setting. By using a mark-book to record outcomes from these assessments you can ensure that everyone gets your attention over a period of weeks.

Plenaries

A plenary phase of the lesson is most often used to consolidate the children's learning. The emphasis should be on pupil talk/activity rather than on teacher explanation. Plenaries are typically used to:

- recap the key points from the lesson
- assess and record pupils' understanding against selected learning objectives
- identify misconceptions
- introduce the next lesson (possibly including some baseline questioning of pupils' current knowledge).

Teaching an effective plenary which explicitly links back to the learning objectives of the starter is a high-level professional skill. Where plenaries take place at the end of a lesson the children will often want to continue working on the task and may be mentally tired or focused on the next lesson. There is often a considerable amount of administration to conduct – logging off, collecting worksheets, tidying up and so on. Our advice here is to finish the main activity in plenty of time for the plenary, keep the plenary format as simple as possible (do not introduce lots of new ideas or resources) and make use of carefully planned routines to deal with the administration (Chapter 5).

There is no reason to wait until the end of a lesson to have a plenary. In many circumstances it is better to have an interim or mini-plenary whenever you want to consolidate learning. For example, you could stop the class and display examples of pupils' work in progress (perhaps using remote control software); then discuss the relative strengths of each and draw attention to the key parts which everyone needs to focus on.

Try not to be tempted to rush through a plenary; doing this sends a clear message to children that this time is not really important. It is better to hold over activities until the next lesson rather than rush through an activity, which it is not possible to complete meaningfully.

Selecting and developing resources

Resources serve to provide a stimulating context, structure the learning experience and promote independence. They complement direct teacher instruction by providing access to the learning even when the teacher is supporting other pupils, presenting learning in different forms and enabling children to work at different rates.

Many resources are well established in all schools. They are familiar to staff and pupils and there is a great deal of existing advice about how to make the most of them within an educational setting. Resources in this category would include textbooks, newspapers, websites, worksheets, presentations and use of broadcast or pre-recorded video and audio programmes.

Other resources are at various stages of adoption in many schools, who are typically still discovering their potential. These would include quiz generators (sometimes coupled with classroom voting systems), video filming/editing, video conferencing, interactive whiteboards (and their associated curriculum resources), virtual learning environments and video tutorials.

Our final category of resources are more likely to be in the pilot stage of evaluation in a smaller number of schools. These might include for example use of immersive environments/virtual worlds, games creation software in an educational context, social networking and blogging.

ICT teachers have an advantage in terms of IT skills and access to hardware and software when compared with many of their peers. However, pupils have correspondingly higher expectations of what ICT teachers will do with the technology. They understand the potential of technology to interest and engage them through computer games, social networking and interactive resources and may expect teachers to bring these resources or experiences into the classroom. There are undoubtedly opportunities here – both in terms of contextualizing learning and using the actual technologies. There is also a cost in terms of teacher time and, often, software or hardware purchase. You will need to exercise your professional judgement and experience when making choices about the resources to use or develop. It is easy to be overawed by a software demonstration or seduced by a free software application which shows potential. As with everything else you need to think about what you want the children to learn and the best use of your and the children's time (including your time outside the classroom to develop and evaluate the resource).

In each lesson it is likely that you will be combining resources you have created or adapted with existing 'off the shelf' resources. Whenever you create, adapt or select a resource you need to consider the following general points:

- How closely does it meet the learning objectives? Is its purpose clear?
- The clarity of language used – does it match pupils' reading ages and stretch them to understand and use new vocabulary? (See next section.)
- The clarity of the design – do design elements enhance the resource by making it both interesting and clear? Your time will be well spent in examining and practising some basic page and screen design principles. An excellent resource to start this process for teachers and pupils is *The Non-Designer's Design Book* by Robin Williams (2008).
- Has anyone else reviewed or used the resource?
- The inclusion of pictures/screenshots and how these are linked with the text.
- Are questions used to make pupils think and are these clearly written?
- Does the resource provide differentiation opportunities – either graduated tasks, or different versions of the resources?
- Are there copyright restrictions on adapting or copying existing material?
- Has the resource been used successfully with similar groups?
- Does the resource provide variety and challenge?
- Does it provide opportunity for a broad range of pupil outputs – rather than mechanistically following a set of instructions?

Paper-based resources offer portability and convenience, but can be very time-consuming to produce, copy and collate. Electronic resources can incorporate interactivity to varying degrees, colour at no extra cost and offer a great deal of flexibility in even basic functions like expanding text boxes which do not constrain pupils in the same way that spaces on a worksheet might. They can be easily changed and updated without having to reissue paper copies. They can also be linked to associated resources – increasingly VLEs are being used by schools to provide a means of hosting materials and making them available from any Internet-connected computer. Obviously, electronic resources require access to a computer, laptop or PDA and this may prevent access for some pupils outside the classroom.

If the resource is paper based, consider:

- Is the resource to be reused or written on? If the latter, is there sufficient space for pupils' wide variety of handwriting?
- Is colour important, or will black and white be sufficient?
- How will the resource be produced, who will do this and what is the lead time required?

If the resource is electronic, consider:

- How is the resource distributed to pupils, for example do they need to create their own local copy of a class template?
- How easy is the resource to navigate?
- To what degree can the resource be customized to suit your pupils?
- Will the resource require lots of application switching, for example does it require pupils to juggle a video tutorial, text instructions and the application they are using for the work, all at the same time?
- Is access required outside the lesson? If so, how can children without a computer do this?
- When using pre-recorded television programmes or clips, how will you provide a focus so that children watch actively rather than passively?

In the example lesson Jason will need to create a variety of resources as in Figure 4.7.

Examples of the completed resources are available via the companion website, www. sagepub.co.uk/secondary.

Resources and reading ability

Sometimes beginning teachers rely on direct teacher instruction rather than preparing resources such as a worksheet because their typical experience is that 'Pupils don't (or can't) read the worksheets'. Lessons with such classes are often 'follow-me' demonstrations where the teacher does something on the whiteboard and the class copy it on their screens. This becomes unsatisfactory from both a teacher and pupil point of view. The teacher is unable to give individual attention, for when they do the rest of the class is sat waiting for the next instruction. The class proceeds at the pace of the slowest child to follow the instruction (who probably feels under pressure from peers) and very little learning takes place for anyone. Our challenge in such lessons is 'How will these children ever learn a degree of independence and how will they function in the real world where instructions are not spoon-fed in this way?'

What can we do to help children who are unable or reluctant to use resources?

The school's SEN co-ordinator can be an invaluable source of information, strategies and resources to help you (although note that these children are not necessarily

Lesson 1 Resource	Comments
Computer-controlled devices presentation	This actually needs to fulfil two functions – a standard presentation and a whiteboard resource which enables pupils to write and save the labels
Homework sheet – 'Input, process, output' and 'Thinking about robots'	Paper based – pupils can write short answers on the sheet. Electronic version also available for those pupils who prefer to type their responses
Robotics web-quest	Embed hyperlinks to the robot websites
Bibliography template	Available electronically
Incomplete concept map	On whiteboard to complete during the plenary
For subsequent lessons, he will also need to produce:	
Task sheet for the robotics task	Available as a paper-based and electronic resource to provide maximum access
Templates for the news report, script and poster	Electronic versions provided as this will be worked on in class. Poster template may be printed and drafted by hand
A peer evaluation sheet	Paper based – Jason would normally use an electronic sheet to help with collation, but he wants pupils to be able to make notes at the front of the room while watching the presentations and also does not want distracting keyboard noises while these are taking place

Figure 4.7 Identifying the resources required

identified as having a special educational need). They are likely to suggest adapting the resources:

- Can the language be simplified?
- Do additional interim steps need to be added to instructions?
- Can more use be made of labelled pictures and screenshots to reduce the quantity of text and make meaning clearer?
- Can the resource be changed into an alternative format, for example a presentation or video tutorial with a mixture of text and narration? (Also see the 'Independence' video on the companion website.)

Once we judge our resource suitable we need to think about how we introduce the material to the class and get them used to the routine of using resources. You can do this gradually, asking them to use a resource just for a portion of the lesson. Your initial attitude is all-important here – you need to have an unwavering expectation that they can and will use the resource rather than demanding your constant attention, as in the following example:

Scenario

Ryan: 'Miss, what do I do next?'
Teacher: 'Where are you on the worksheet, Ryan?'
Ryan: 'I don't know – I can't do it, can't you just tell me?'
Teacher: 'Lets have a look – you've done really well on steps 1 and 2, I know you can do step 3, come on, I'll be back in a minute to check.'

Later, when the teacher sees Ryan using the worksheet, she returns for a quiet word.

Teacher: 'I think the way you are working today is spot on – I knew you could do it. I reckon you can get to step 5 by the end of the lesson.'

As pupils get used to using resources we can begin to gradually introduce language that they may find more challenging and as their ICT skills improve we can provide less explicit instructions. In this way we give them the skills to learn rather than just the skills to memorize and copy.

Building-in wider curriculum opportunities

In Chapter 3 we discussed how cross-curricular links could be used to provide an integrated context which makes sense to pupils. Of course, we need to plan this into our individual lessons. The next section looks at the idea of context in further detail and provides an opportunity to think through some possible cross-curricular links.

In Jason's example lesson we have considered additional learning that pupils may gain outside the ICT subject domain, specifically in literacy and through other cross-curricular links, for example the increasing use of robots in industry can lead to unemployment which may be a current theme in history or citizenship. See the weblinks at the end of this chapter for links to the numeracy and literacy frameworks.

Jason's example lesson lends itself well to building pupil's literacy skills, particularly in reading, speaking and listening. Using the *Framework for Teaching English: Years 7, 8 and 9* (DfES, 2001b) we can extract the relevant objectives. Giving all this information to the children in the form presented below would not be appropriate, Jason will use these objectives to focus the worksheets, key teaching points and assessment criteria he prepares.

Example lesson: literacy objectives

Text (reading)
R4. make brief, clearly organized notes of key points for later use

Word
W14. define and deploy words with precision
W21. read accurately, and use correctly, vocabulary which relates to key concepts in each subject

Sentence

S13. Stylistic conventions of the main types of non-fiction:
News report : c) Explanation, which maintains the use of the present tense and impersonal voice, and links points clearly;
Sales poster: e) Persuasion, which emphasises key points and articulates logical links in the argument.

Speaking and listening

SL3. Tailor the structure, vocabulary and delivery of a talk or presentation so that listeners can follow it.
SL4. Give clear answers, instructions or explanations that are helpfully sequenced, linked and supported by gestures or other visual aids.
SL5. Promote, justify or defend a point of view using supporting evidence, examples and illustrations which are linked back to the main argument.
SL6. Listen for and recall the main points of a talk, reading or television programme, reflecting on what has been heard to ask searching questions, make comments or challenge the views expressed.

Source: adapted from DfES (2001b).

Reflection Point 4.6

As you read the section 'Making lessons interesting, meaningful and memorable', try to identify possible cross-curricular links with other subjects.

Peripatetic staff

Teachers are frequently supported in class by a range of adults including teaching assistants, special needs assistants, classroom volunteers and trainee teachers. Forming a professional relationship is vital to make the best use of this invaluable resource. Spend some time ensuring you know when they will be available and what their skill-set is. In this way you can plan lessons which make effective use of their talents. Prior to the lesson discuss your plans and agree routines so that the lesson runs smoothly.

Evaluating the lesson

Reflecting on and evaluating the lesson shortly afterwards will help you at one level to remember the key points you need to cover next time and at a deeper professional level to become a better teacher. As with behaviour management, we must not fall into the could have, should have, would have trap – 'The pupils should have all taken part in that discussion, but it was chaos!' More productive to solve the problem, probably a combination of training individuals to take part in the discussion, a more structured format and, perhaps, an alternative activity. You can see Jason's evaluation of his lesson in the lesson plan in Figure 4.12 at the end of the chapter. These provide key teaching points for his next lesson. (See the video clips on the companion website, www.sage pub.co.uk/secondary, *Reflection, Improvements* and *Independence* for examples of Richard evaluating his lesson in detail.)

MAKING LESSONS INTERESTING, MEANINGFUL AND MEMORABLE

When you think of a favourite teacher, the chances are that you remember the stories that they told and the way that they enabled you to understand difficult concepts by relating them to meaningful real-world experiences. Having activities which meet learning objectives is all well and good, but a good context transforms a seemingly random set of exercises into a memorable learning experience for children.

In ICT we have some of the most exciting stories to tell in terms of ingenuity, progress and possibility. No other subject is transforming our world so rapidly and completely. And yet some ICT lessons are pedestrian (dare we say boring?) They miss the big picture and concentrate on skills without a context.

To make lessons meaningful and memorable, there are two key aspects to consider – first, the contexts you use within lessons that enable pupils to see why the current topic is important and second, the teaching techniques or devices to keep them interested and engaged.

Context: the big picture

A 'big idea' makes planning learning experiences straightforward. Although the major concept for every child is the same, you can easily plan several ways to approach learning the same concept. The context serves as an anchor for the unit or lesson you are planning to differentiate. Even if you decide to take different students on varying paths of learning, they will all end up at the same point with an understanding of the same major concept.

Throughout this chapter we have tried to describe and exemplify how teachers can use a context to make learning meaningful and interesting. Many example lessons use ideas which are not interesting or realistic to children.

Reflection Point

Reflection Point 4.7

Look at the example lessons for unit 7.4 published as part of the Key Stage 3 National Strategy (see weblinks at the end of this chapter). In lessons 1 and 2 of 'Spreadsheets and modelling', pupils create a times table square, investigate the cost of feeding animals in a zoo, the cost of producing biscuits and the way in which a football league operates.

Consider:

What is the big picture context behind these lessons?
Are there too many contexts in two lessons?
Are all (or even a majority) of children interested in these topics?
Are they realistic models?
How could the real-world examples mentioned in the unit be used to produce more meaningful and memorable lessons?

In asking our trainees what contexts they might use in ICT the topics of football and pop groups are typically some of the first ideas to come to mind (usually aimed stereo-typically at boys and girls). Perhaps this partly reflects the IT lessons our trainees had as children and their own generalized view of what school children as an amorphous body would like. When they begin to consider individuals' interests within their own classes however, their views often change. Football and pop music may be interesting to some (perhaps the majority) of pupils, but what if you are a pupil who has no interest – is there scope to do something different (and will you be singled out because of it)? They can also reinforce gender stereotypes and, in terms of realistic aspirations, how many of our pupils will be employed by the football or pop industries?

Projects that involve children as stakeholders in issues they care about can provide excellent alternative contexts for learning ICT capability. Children are curious about a whole range of topics; these might include environmental issues, self-awareness, iden-tity, communication, relationships, poverty, aspirations, learning and entrepreneurship. How do you find out what contexts will most engage your pupils? Why not ask them? Find out their aspirations, the issues that concern them and the ways in which they use (and would like to use) technology. In fact, this can become a context in its own right – use a collaborative tool to record the ideas of all pupils. Then, either use the common themes as contexts for further work, or, if there is disagreement, split the class into groups and ask each to produce a time-limited presentation to state their case, or host an online debate, followed by a class vote.

Ideally all our contexts will suggest an output that will be of interest to a real audi-ence such as teachers, politicians, other pupils or business people. Although it will not always be practical to seek the intended audience's opinion on the finished work, we should try to do this wherever possible.

Figure 4.8 demonstrates how an initially IT-focused activity has been broadened using a more interesting and relevant context. All of these activities provide pupils with

Original activity	Contextualized
Researching the law about copyright.	Sharing or stealing? Preparing for a court case or televised debate where half of the class represent the music industry who want to prosecute the other half of the class who have downloaded material via peer to peer sites.
Producing a website and animated logo advertising our school.	Be a games designer In teams, produce a hypertext-based adventure game with branching choices to be used for Year 6 open evenings. Each page should contain a simple animation to set the scene along with story text and links to other pages for each choice to be made.
Produce a survey of pupils' hobbies, analyse the results and produce a report.	Train the teachers Survey and analyse the ICT skills of our teachers. Plan an after-school club for a one-hour session to teach them the essential skills they need in a new technology, e.g. blogging, podcasting, SMS texting.
Make a cars database, feed in some data and then answer these queries …	Be a campaigner Produce a database of environmental issues within your town, e.g. a wildlife survey, identifying pollution hotspots, litter issues or availability of recycling facilities. Pupils collect data from their local areas, input to a database and extract key statistics to form a persuasive case for change for a councillor or MP. Could also export the postcodes and descriptions as Google Earth Placemarks and plot these on a map.
Use the Internet to research and produce a booklet about the solar system.	Be an expert educator Plan a 10-minute video-conferencing activity which will teach Year 5 pupils about the solar system. Either record and edit an offline version or perform the event to a live audience via a video link.
Collect data about height and shoe sizes. Produce graphs.	Be a researcher Look at how a real context affects pupils then extend this to look at local and global impacts. So, for example, taking the environment as a context, they could examine their own energy use, carbon footprint, quantity of waste produced or water use. They could then extrapolate the class data to look at total impact by the developed world and take a global viewpoint by examining data/case studies and debating an issue, e.g. implications of frequent flooding.

Figure 4.8 Contextualizing activities

a *real* (or realistic) context, a clear *role* to play which relates to the world outside school and an *audience*.

All the above ideas are quite ambitious and it may not be possible to show all the final products to a real audience, but even the idea of a simulated context is a powerful motivator for children – they understand why they are doing the learning. Collaboration is a focus of all the contexts because children need this skill and they can achieve much more when working together than duplicating each other's efforts. It does matter that you can distinguish their individual contributions through self, peer and teacher assessment, and you need to think this through carefully before setting off on a project, but this does not mean they all have to hand in the same six-page report at the end of the topic (see Chapters 6 and 7 for more ideas).

A strong advocate for using real-world contexts in ICT lessons is Alex Savage. His CommunICTy website, wiki and blog provide inspiring real classroom examples that integrate ICT capability, global citizenship, environmental issues and self-reflection. See the companion website, www.sagepub.co.uk/secondary for links.

> Instead of creating a model for an imaginary zoo, our students research all the ways they use water during an average day and calculate how much they actually use ... We then tell them that the water budget for a child at our link school in Malawi is only 20 litres. They then interrogate the model to find out ways to reduce their water budget. This really engages the students, as they are keen to find out how much water they use and the importance of using less. (Savage, 2007a)

Alex has also re-contextualized existing lesson plans so that, for example, students do not merely produce the sometimes bland 'All about me' presentations so ubiquitous in Year 7. Instead the work is embedded into the Social and Emotional Aspects of Learning (SEAL) curriculum. First, using a strong visual cue – the Emotions Tree – children consider how their attitude and character is made up of strengths and weaknesses (see Figure 4.9). Through a collaborative blog they share their thoughts with others and then use the results to create an interactive presentation using a common template. To add an international dimension the school twinned with Apeejay School in New Delhi who also undertook the project and contributed to the blog.

> You can imagine the cries of excitement when my students were reading their comments and found phrases written by Nikita, Dhruv, Eashan and their classmates in India! They were also surprised to find out how similar they felt about school life in both countries ... There has been a marked difference in the engagement of my students in creating presentations about their emotions towards school life rather than their families and hobbies ... Often in ICT, we concentrate more on how to create a product rather than the message that it is trying to communicate. However, I am convinced that allowing students appropriate time to generate quality content on a theme that is relevant to their own lives leads them into producing a better end product and consequently better progress. (Savage, 2007b)

Teaching techniques

When you picture a teacher, they are probably stood at the front of a room, telling a class something interesting. Perhaps this is how you imagine yourself in the classroom.

'When I'm with my friend I feel really happy and enjoy myself loads.

I love being around my friends because I trust them and they know loads about me.'

Figure 4.9 The Emotions Tree project – Year 7. Each set of characters on the main page is hyperlinked to a zoomed-in view and pupils' comments such as those on the right

Instructing, telling, showing or demonstrating are certainly important techniques. How you convey information is as important as what you say, as in this example:

As part of a lesson about the impact of technology Yasmin (an NQT) displays and reads out a slide (Figure 4.10).

The class seem to be listening – at least they're all looking in her direction. However, she's unsure whether they have really understood the concept. Her head of department suggests a different approach which she tries out next lesson using an adapted quotation (Figure 4.11).

Reflection Point 48

We hope that you agree that the second approach is both more engaging and memorable; you may even feel like telling someone else this amazing fact. Why is this? You could argue that the first approach gives more information in a more concise form.

Spend a few moments now reflecting on why the second approach is more successful.

Reflection Point

> **Technology – the pace of change**
>
> These things double approximately every 2 years:
>
> - the number of transistors on a chip
> - the amount of computing power for the same cost
> - the amount of storage capacity for the same cost.

Figure 4.10   Yasmin's original approach

> **Technology – the pace of change**
>
> Suppose for a moment that cars had developed at the same rate as computers over the last 30 years.
>
> - What would be different about the cars we use today?
> - You have 30 seconds to think about this question on your own.
> - You have 1 minute to discuss it with your partner.

Yasmin collects the class' feedback on the board and then reveals her answer.

> **Changing technology**
>
> - **For the same price, computing power and storage capacity double every 2 years. This means …**

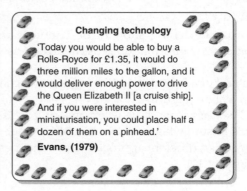

> **Changing technology**
>
> 'Today you would be able to buy a Rolls-Royce for £1.35, it would do three million miles to the gallon, and it would deliver enough power to drive the Queen Elizabeth II [a cruise ship]. And if you were interested in miniaturisation, you could place half a dozen of them on a pinhead.'
>
> **Evans, (1979)**

Figure 4.11   Developing an idea to make it meaningful and memorable

Yasmin uses a number of techniques to make this learning memorable. The combination of these techniques moves the teacher's role from being a provider of facts to being a facilitator of learning. The class moves from relying on being told information to actively trying to work out the implications of the question. Yasmin does this by simplifying the original information and then using an analogy with a real-world context (car production) to help pupils grasp the concept. She adopts a question-based approach, structured to give all pupils time to think, and she tells the class something amazing and memorable which will help them remember the key idea. The next section presents these and other common techniques that you can use in combination when planning and teaching a lesson.

A common theme that runs throughout is the idea that we are trying to help children make sense of a complex world by constructing a narrative, experience or example which links their current knowledge with the new information or skills. If we do not bridge this gap effectively they learn facts or skills in isolation that they may be able to repeat, but cannot make use of in new situations. There is a continuum of practice when linking our teaching to everyday experience. At one end of the spectrum we will literally be talking about a situation that is familiar to them, for example visiting a supermarket. At the other end of the spectrum are highly imaginative, role-play activities such as Newspaper Days where pupils assume the role of editors, journalists and typesetters.

Simplify layers of complexity

Most learning is sequential – we need to understand one concept before we are ready for the next (and we probably need some time in between to internalize the concept and test it in the real world). In the previous example we see how Yasmin simplifies the complexity of the pace of change in technology by using a headline example. In fact the picture is much more complex. She could have explained that computing power is closely related to the number of transistors packed onto a microchip and that the architecture of the circuits is also a major factor. She could have gone on to discuss the implications of parallel or distributed processing, developments in organic computers and the fact that the rate of change is not smooth over a short time period. Clearly this would be too much information in a short space of time for the class; at the moment, knowing a little about the rate of change and possible implications is sufficient. Over the years in which Yasmin teaches these children she will expand and modify the original description.

Often it is useful to tell pupils when you are simplifying a complex concept: 'This isn't quite how it works in the real world, but it will help you to understand for now.'

We must be wary of *oversimplifying* a concept. For example, beginning teachers may say that good web-page design is merely choosing the right colours, fonts and images. In fact we can show pupils some initial design concepts (using the language of visual design) and then ask them to evaluate existing pages and use the principles in their own work.

Build from basic principles

Pupils can often tell you some facts about a topic, but may not have the underlying concepts to really understand what they mean. Using questioning we can take them back to the basic concepts and lead them to tell a story that links what they know with what it means. Here is Yasmin again teaching about data storage media:

Scenario

The whiteboard contains the title 'Measuring Memory'.

Yasmin: Can anyone tell me what these two objects are? Hands up. (She holds up a floppy disk and a CD)

Luke: Miss, is it a DVD and a floppy disk?

Yasmin: Well done, Luke, in fact this is a CD, but they do look identical. Now a trickier question – approximately how much information can the floppy disk hold?

After various guesses, the class settle on about 1 megabyte.

Yasmin: OK, it is about 1 megabyte, but what on earth does that mean? What does 'mega' mean – it is a number?

Derren: Is it a million, Miss?

Yasmin: Excellent answer, Derren, so a floppy disk contains a million bytes, now who can tell me what a byte is?

Asif: Is it a bit?

Yasmin: No, though a byte is made up of bits – we won't worry about that for now.

Jane: Is it a memory?

Yasmin: It is a way of measuring how big memory is, but there's an easy way to think about how big a byte is. I'll give you a clue – there are 16 bytes on the board.

Asif: It's a letter.

Yasmin: Excellent, a byte is equivalent to a letter, or a …?

Jane: A number.

Yasmin: Exactly – a letter or a number, or a punctuation mark or any key-press – what do we call those things altogether?

Luke: A character, Miss.

Yasmin: Brilliant! So a byte is equivalent to a character and a floppy disk holds a million bytes – that means you could sit at your keyboard and type a million letter 'A's and they could comfortably be saved on a floppy disk.

Something amazing

There are many amazing stories to tell and things to show pupils in ICT if you look for them. The earlier section on generating ideas and subject research provides some starting points. Yasmin extends her discussion on storage capacity by illustrating just how much information can be stored in a very small space.

Scenario

Yasmin: OK, so we know a floppy disk can hold about a million bytes of data. All of the seven Harry Potter books put together have about 6.5 million characters (letters and spaces) in them. How many floppy disks would I need to store them electronically?
Jane: Seven, Miss.
Yasmin: Exactly, Jane – that would be a bit more portable than the actual books. Now let's think about the CD – how many floppy disks worth of information could I fit on here – have a guess, let's go around the class?

After a game of higher and lower, the class come to a figure of 650 floppy disks.

Yasmin: That's right – a CD can hold about the same as 650 floppy disks or 650Mb. That's the same as a stack of floppy disks about 2 metres high – taller than me. Or put another way, a CD could hold 100 sets of all of the Harry Potter stories – a stack of those would be 30 metres tall, about the same as seven double-decker buses!

Analogy

Sometimes the concept we are trying to explain does not relate directly to previous experience. Analogy allows us to show how an unfamiliar concept is similar to an idea we do understand. We can use analogy in different ways, first to present an idea:

Yasmin: A database is like a filing cabinet, all of the information, the FILE, is the same as the cabinet. A RECORD is all of the information about one person or thing, like opening my filing cabinet and pulling out a criminal record. An individual piece of information like 'Surname' is held in a FIELD in my database.

Secondly, we could ask pupils to construct their own analogies:

- How is a hard-drive like a library?
- How is a computer network like a road network?
- How is a program like a recipe?
- How is a database like a filing cabinet?
- Describe encryption using locked boxes.

Analogies have their limitations and will usually break down as pupils scrutinize them – point these limitations out to children as necessary. Finding the weaknesses in an analogy is a great way of identifying real understanding in your pupils:

- How is searching a filing cabinet different from searching a database?
- How does a recipe differ from a computer program?

Embed the knowledge in the task

You can create a powerful learning feedback loop by asking pupils to transform what they have learned so that it can be understood or used by others. For example if you want pupils to learn some hypertext mark-up language (HTML) commands you could get them to create a web page (using HTML) which describes to someone else how to use those HTML commands. So the finished page might begin with:

> **My HTML guide**
>
> Writing HTML web pages is easy provided you know the commands – here is a list of the ones I know about:
>
> <B> makes text **bold**
> <I> makes text *italic*

The output of these tasks makes it easy for teachers to assess both skills and understanding, particularly if the page goes on to describe why you might choose to use HTML over other web-page creation software.

Other ways that you can embed the knowledge in the task include:

- writing a user guide.
- recording an animation demonstrating how to do the task
- making a quiz or game that tests others on the topic studied.

Personify the process or idea – anthropormorphism

Attributing human characteristics to a computer, device or process can help children understand difficult concepts. Jason uses this idea when he asks pupils to imagine they are the computer inside a washing machine. The following are examples of teachers using anthropomorphism:

- 'Kevin is the LOGO turtle. We are going to give him instructions to walk around the classroom in a square. What commands might Kevin understand?'
- 'Someone has pressed the WAIT button at the pelican crossing. What will the computer think next?'
- 'Imagine you are going to do the job of a temperature sensor in an arctic weather monitoring station, you have a thermometer, a notebook and a watch.'

- 'Imagine you are an email message about to be sent around the world. The user presses send – what happens to you next?'
- 'When I fill the formula down into the cells below they all go horribly wrong – why? What is the computer thinking?'

Role play

This is a very similar technique to anthropomorphism. Whereas anthropomorphism asks children to imagine they are objects or processes, role play asks them to imagine that they are taking on the role of another human being, usually with a specific job. Role play does not have to involve dramatic performance. The simple idea that today we are going to act like programmers, web designers, scientists or hackers is enough to change the tone of a task. Of course, you may at times want to include an element of drama, for example when having a debate about an issue. Teachers can also play a role as in this example:

Yasmin: 'Good morning. Before we start today, I thought you might like to see this.' As she opens a folder on the computer, she draws attention to a file 'Headteacher's star pupils'. 'Oops, Mrs Marshall must have put that in the wrong folder, shall we have a look?' She opens the document but it is password protected. 'Shall we have a guess, what do you think the password could be?' After several guesses the pupils hit upon the correct answer – the school name backwards. A list of pupil names appear. 'How come none of your names are in this folder? Do you think we should add one of you to the list as a joke?' Having done this, she pauses dramatically. 'How many of you have heard of the Computer Misuse Act – do you know how many years we could spend in jail for doing what we just did?' She then explains that this was a simulation and gives the class enough information for them to calculate the potential fine and jail sentence.

Mysteries and problem-solving

Mysteries can give children a chance to exercise their creative thinking skills. Typically, children are presented with stimulus material which is incomplete, ambiguous or both, and asked to infer a solution to an open-ended problem or question. As a teacher you can vary the parameters of the task such as the source material, the opportunity for further research and the openness of the question. Mysteries are a good way to allow a class to explore the complexities of an idea in detail. They require careful management to ensure that individuals do not dominate the discussions and to refocus the class if they become overly involved in peripheral issues. Examples include:

- *Why is Frances Clipper losing money?* Pupils are given some incomplete information about an apparently successful hairdressing salon and propose answers to the question using spreadsheet modelling.

- *Why did the traffic accident occur?* Pupils are given contradictory eyewitness statements and access to some traffic-light control flow charts and have to figure out what went wrong.
- *Is Mrs Evans a fraudster?* Pupils are given an electronic trail to follow of sales receipts, credit card transactions and Mrs Evans' testimony, and have to figure out whether she is a victim of identity theft.
- *Who committed the crime?* Pupils compile a suspects database and conduct queries to solve a variety of crimes from evidence collected at the scene.
- *'What if' scenarios.* What if an electronic pulse bomb disabled all the microchips in our town?

Of course, we can set smaller problems than the above in any ICT lesson, where we work with children to solve the problem or answer the question rather than telling them the answer:

- 'Why is an international phone call expensive and an email virtually free (regardless of size)?'
- 'Why does more RAM make a computer operate faster?'
- 'Does a flash drive have a battery?'
- 'How can a jpg be physically larger (height and width) than a bmp image but smaller in memory size?'

Reflection Point

Reflection Point 4.9

Which teaching devices or techniques are used in the example lesson?

PLANNING AND MANAGING PROJECT WORK

This chapter has focused on a particular style of lesson which is commonly used in introducing topics and teaching theory-based content. However, much ICT work is project based. In these sessions children spend a considerable period of time, often several weeks, applying practical skills to solve a problem or produce an output. The degree of direct whole-class teacher input in these sessions varies, but is likely to be shifted towards more individualized target-setting and support.

As projects progress, the differences in support needs and rates of progress made by individuals can mean that it is more appropriate to plan on an individual pupil basis rather than for the whole class. This does not mean that you need to produce individual lesson plans, but you will need to provide feedback to each pupil about what they have achieved and what their next target is. Chapter 6 provides further guidance on how you can achieve this.

Project-work lessons place a greater reliance on the use of resources to support learners so that they can move on when they are ready. You will need to employ strategies to manage individual targets and deadlines, so good record-keeping is essential. Most children do not have realistic time management skills, so you will need to help them with this, and direct them to out-of-class opportunities such as lunchtime computer clubs. It can be useful for pupils to have a log on the desk as they work so that you can record agreed actions and timescales as you support individuals.

Be aware of your use of time when supporting practical work. In a one-hour lesson with 20 pupils you only have three minutes per pupil on average and if pupils monopolize your time every lesson this is clearly unfair. It can help to have a rota system so that you aim to spend a longer period with a different subgroup of pupils each lesson. Also consider making use of pupil expertise in the class so that they are enabled to help each other (make the rules clear – they can help, but they must not do the work).

Whole-class teaching can be more ad hoc in project-based lessons so that as the teacher realizes there is a common issue they may pull aside a subgroup of pupils or stop the whole class for some direct teacher input.

Is there a place for a tripartheid lesson structure in project-based lessons? This is a matter for your professional judgement. The best use of time may be to get pupils working individually as soon as they enter the room, then set targets, support and monitor them throughout the lesson. If there is common learning happening in the class then it will probably be appropriate to make use of a starter, main and plenary style structure.

Keeping pupils motivated and on track is hard work; do remember to make full use of rewards and sanctions that may be available. Smile, cajole and drive pupils towards the goal. They are learning a very important skill that will stand them in good stead for the rest of their lives.

Planning checklist

The following list contains the most commonly overlooked items by beginning teachers. You may like to check your plans against it.

Subject knowledge – have you checked definitions and descriptions against a reputable source, for example an ICT textbook?

Context – does the lesson have a *big* picture, real-world context or is it skills based with no context?

Challenge – do you know about the class (class lists, CAT scores, reading ages, SEN)? Are the objectives and tasks too challenging/not challenging enough?

Are your instructions planned out and clear, so that you can, for example, display them on the board?

Have you provided clear assessment criteria (what good looks like) with examples?

Have you planned to share WALT and WILF?

Have you provided examples and visual cues – instead of 'So remember I'm looking for good use of frames, colour, contrast, and no Word Art etc.', show them two examples

Have you planned your questions, both in terms of phrasing and how you will structure and capture pupil responses (see chapter 6)?

Are there appropriate (not too many) transitions from one activity to another?

Have you prepared a seating plan and checked lines of sight, so that everyone can see the board?

Does your plenary link back to your objectives and outcomes (WALT and WILF)?

Have you checked the National Curriculum level descriptors to ensure that pupils can reach the higher levels?

What the research says: Pupil generated contexts

In this chapter, we have advocated the use of contextualized learning opportunities. Futurelab in partnership with Microsoft are currently developing and evaluating a curriculum model (Enquiring Minds) which takes the idea of pupil-generated contexts even further. The project seeks to create curriculum space so that pupils can learn through contexts they choose themselves. The evaluation for the pilot year (Williamson and Morgan, 2007) provides interesting insights into the benefits of this approach. The teachers involved concentrated on pupil negotiated project work rather than upfront teaching.

Some of the main findings are summarized below:

- Teachers had to shift their focus from information and subject delivery to the learning process.
- Pupils liked the idea of change, but some had quite fixed (narrow) ideas of the teacher's role which did not encompass this kind of collaborative working.
- When teachers initially tried to find out about pupils' own lives and experiences, pupils could not understand why teachers were interested (and were sometimes hostile). A less personal approach in asking what they would be interested in learning was more successful.
- Choosing areas of study can be challenging:

Some children's interests simply appear superficial, depthless and offering no opportunities for intellectual advancement. [T]his needs to become the focus of evaluation so that students know how to go about things better on subsequent occasions. It may also require teachers to do a little bit of research themselves, in order to identify some points of interest and possibility in children's ideas. (Williamson and Morgan, 2007: 26)

- but ultimately worthwhile:

[A]t times for some of the staff, students came up with fascinating ideas for exploration, on subjects as varied as medical breakthroughs, aspects of cosmology, 'fake' hauntings, memory and the brain, climate change, the links between bullying and teenage suicide, Japanese animation, the design of football boots, and the popularity of cosmetics. [M]any of them had clearly enjoyed exploring these ideas thoroughly, and were enthused by how much they felt they had expanded their prior knowledge. (Williamson and Morgan, 2007: 12)

- Flexibility in time management, classroom layout and grouping were important.
- An overarching project structure is important and this is balanced against the choice of context. Routines are also important such as agreeing deadlines and using proformas to track progress.
- Many students claimed that classroom behaviour was improved.
- Many students responded well to the method of assessment (mostly ungraded).
- Teachers were encouraging of pupil work, but sometimes did not provide the depth of feedback required to move the work on.
- In comparison with other pupils in the same school, pupils were more interested in their lessons, felt these were more relevant to their lives and a significantly higher proportion felt they had more control of their learning.

Subject: ICT	Date/time: 23/1/09 9:35	Sequence: Lesson 1 of 7	Class: 7GT (20 pupils)	Ability setting: Mixed	Room: 36

Topic learning aim:
To understand the basic concepts of computer control and programming. Pupils can understand and design basic control systems. They select appropriate input and output devices and use flow-charting software to create control programs. They can identify relative advantages and disadvantages of computer-controlled devices.

Learning objectives (in terms of skills, attitudes, concepts, knowledge):
By the *end* of this lesson:
1 Pupils can apply the terms input, process, output and feedback to describe how real-world systems work.
2 Pupils can use the idea of a computer program to invent instructions which control a device or process. They can deduce the effect of imprecision in computer instructions.
3 Pupils can explore the relative advantages and disadvantages offered by independent robotic devices.

Previous knowledge: Last lesson, most pupils said they had some limited experience of using LOGO – about half have used a roamer but only with simple, direct commands.
Key issues (based on last lesson evaluation/administrative points): Reinforce seating plan as pupils enter. Reminder – Computer Club. Write WALT on the board prior to class entry.

SEN/IEP interventions for this lesson:
S1: Learning support assistant – to support the 5 pupils identified in the register.
S2: (Hearing impaired): Collect and wear radio transmitter.

Differentiation strategies for this lesson [Grouping : Outcome/outputs : Tasks/worksheets : Graduated tasks : Support (LSA/teacher/peer): Resource]:
Support – during main phase, offer specific coaching to identified individuals. Use phone-a-friend during feedback.
Grouping – mixed ability groupings during programming activities.
Graduated questions during feedback

Resources required:
Seating plan
20 dry wipe boards and pens
Y7 control presentation. ppt
WALT and WILF on the flip-chart
Sandwich stuff – tray, knife, margarine, jam, loaf of bread, tea towel [on front desk, covered with tea towel]
Two part homework sheet – 'Input, process, output' and 'Thinking about robots'
Lesson concept map.

(Continued)

Figure 4.12 (Continued)

Subject: ICT	Date/time: 23/1/09 9:35	Sequence: Lesson 1 of 7	Class: 7GT (20 pupils)	Ability setting: Mixed	Room: 36

Numeracy/literacy opportunities:
R4.   make brief, clearly organized notes of key points for later use
W14. define and deploy words with precision
W21. read accurately, and use correctly, vocabulary which relates to key concepts in each subject
SL4.   give clear answers, instructions or explanations that are helpfully sequenced, linked and supported by gesture or other visual aid
SL5.   promote, justify or defend a point of view using supporting evidence, example and illustration which are linked back to the main argument.

Cross-curricular link opportunities: English – writing for an audience. Design and technology – control technology

Time	Pupil activity	Teacher activity	Learning outcomes/ assessment
9:00	Lesson entry – collect wipe board at the door.	• Welcome class • Slide 1 – 'What do these devices have in common?' • Probe answers – reveal 'They are all controlled by a computer microchip' • Show WALT and WILF on flip chart • Questions to ask [HANDS UP with WAIT TIME]: 1. **What do we need to know in order to do number 1?** 2. **Has anyone here written a computer program?** 3. **What does 'justify' mean in point 3?**	
9:10	Record answer to question on dry wipe board and hold up. Answer questions. Work in pairs to solve each example, be prepared to feed back. Record homework in planners.	• Slide 2 Input/output • Washing machine. '30 seconds – on your wipe boards write down the inputs and outputs for this device.' **Start on-screen timer** • Pupils hold up their boards. Probe – **capture** key answers on the board – mixture of whole system and computer control responses • Thought experiment – 'Remember the things we are interested in are those that the computer inside the washing machine 'knows' about – INPUTS and the things it can directly control – OUTPUTS. Close your eyes. Imagine you are the computer that 'lives' in the washing machine – your job is to get the clothes clean. Think about what senses or sensors you have that tell you what's going on in the washing machine and what devices you can control in order to wash the clothes.	LO1 and homework

(Continued)

Figure 4.12   (Continued)

Subject: ICT	Date/time: 23/1/09 9:35	Sequence: Lesson 1 of 7	Class: 7GT (20 pupils)	Ability setting: Mixed	Room: 36
Time	Pupil activity		Teacher activity		Learning outcomes/ assessment
			• Feedback from class – volunteer updates list on the board so we are only left with computer-controlled inputs and outputs. Save the slide. • Slide 3 – Think–Pair–Share for remaining examples, collate feedback on slides 4–6 and save updated slides. • Ask a pupil to distribute the next activity sheet and the homework sheet – describe. Ask a pupil to explain back to the class what the task is.		
9:20	Log on. Complete web-quest individually.		Show picture of robot glider – Introduce robots web-quest Check understanding of task Transition to main phase Support – coach Kieran and Suzanne to be able to say answers during the feedback.		LO3 and homework

3:35	Feed back answers.
	Participate in discussions.
			Monitors-off **[CHECK – esp. Kieran's at the back]**.
			'NO hands-up – I expect everyone to have an answer – Phone-a-friend is active.'
			• **What do you think this is? (Robot glider)**
			• **Now you know the job it does, what kinds of sensors do you think it has?**
			• **Display robots vs. humans table**
			  ○ 'Robots are better than humans at … because … .'
			  [prompts: dangerous environments, strength, long hours, repetition]
			  ○ 'Humans are better than robots at … because … .'
			  [prompts: making complex decisions, using judgement, flexible thinking, interacting with people, solving problems]
			• How do these robots make decisions?
			• Who writes the instructions for computers and microchips?
			• What is a computer program? [compose a definition on flipchart]
					LO3 and homework

(Continued)

Figure 4.12 (Continued)

Subject: ICT	Date/time: 23/1/09 9:35	Sequence: Lesson 1 of 7	Class: 7GT (20 pupils)	Ability setting: Mixed	Room: 36
Time	Pupil activity		Teacher activity		Learning outcomes/ assessment
9:45	Writing a list of instructions. Testing instructions. Thinking about why the activity is so difficult.		So now we know a little about computer programs, I want you to have a go at being computer programmers! Sandwich-making task: • Display slide showing photograph of the sandwich tray and a description of the task rules • Check understanding Set on-screen timer – 3 minutes 'While we do the task, I want you to think about why each group is successful (or not)'. Feedback from each group		LO2
9:55	Discuss and complete the concept map for the lesson.		Refer to the learning objectives Complete the broken concept map Homework reminder.		LO1, 2 and 3

Lesson evaluation

What went well?
Most of the class enjoyed the topic and worked throughout.
They had got the point after the first input, process, output example – so didn't use the last 2.
On the whole they met the learning objectives, their individual understanding will be more apparent during the next activity.

What could be improved?
Perhaps too many transitions – could these be reduced?
Smoother handing out of material – have it on the desks ready next time – TA could help.
Balance of teaching and learning time – still lots of me talking, how can I get them doing more of the work?
Swap the sandwich making and feedback activities?
Timings were very tight, will need to finish off the concept map at the beginning of next lesson.
Forgot to ask them to record the homework in their planner.
DH and CP were absent – will need catch-up activity next week.
The extension task was too vague – need to give them something more structured next time.

Figure 4.12 Jason's example lesson plan

Further reading

Please see the website, www.sagepup.co.uk/secondary, for a list of books to help improve your ICT subject knowledge.

Anderson, L.W. and Krathwohl, D.R. (eds) (2001) *A Taxonomy for Learning, Teaching, and Assessing: A Revision of Bloom's Taxonomy of Educational Objectives.* New York: Longman.
An in-depth discussion of the refinement of Bloom's original taxonomy with useful vignettes to illustrate the taxonomy in use. Also considers the limitations of the model.

Cohen, L., Manion, L. and Morrison, K. (2004) *A Guide to Teaching Practice.* London: RoutledgeFalmer.
A useful all-round text with specific chapters that discuss and illustrate the planning process.

Petty, G. (2004) *Teaching Today – a Practical Guide.* 3rd edn. Cheltenham: Nelson Thornes.
Geoff Petty writes about teaching and learning with clarity and passion. In this book, he effectively illustrates the planning process through a variety of scenarios.

Williams, R. (2008) *The Non-Designer's Design Book.* 3rd edn. Berkeley, CA: Peachpit Press.
An excellent introduction to page design and typographic principles. This book will help you diagnose your own design strengths and weaknesses and will help you to introduce the language of design into your own classroom.

Weblinks

Live links to each of these websites can be found on the companion website, www.sagepub.co.uk/secondary.

CommuniCty – http:// communicty.org/. Alex Savage's website which links to his blogs a resources wiki and a social networking website. Many good resources here for lesson planning.

Futurelab – www.futurelab.org.uk/. Provides information about a range of innovative education projects including Enquiring Minds.

Key Stage 3 National Strategy: Year 7 Sample Unit – www.standards.afes.gov.uk/secondary/keystage3/all/respub/ ictsampley7.

Teach-ICT – www.teach-ict.com/. Lots of useful resources and links for lesson planning. (Note: critically evaluate any resources you select.)

5 MANAGING AN ICT LESSON

This chapter covers:

- positive behaviour management as an important professional competence – which can be learned
- the importance of teaching a behaviour curriculum in parallel with the ICT curriculum
- how a framework of rights, responsibilities, rules and routines can help you lead and manage a class
- the importance of attention in understanding children's behaviour
- strategies for managing a class in an assertive and positive manner
- health and safety and e-safety considerations for ICT teachers.

If you turned to this chapter first then you are not alone. Most beginning teachers rank 'classroom management' as their single biggest source of uncertainty and, often, anxiety. In many aspects of teaching and learning, we have some form of personal experience to draw from, we have planned activities or events, played and worked with children as individuals and maybe prepared presentations and done some public speaking. However, the act of managing the learning and behaviour of 15–30 individuals, of engaging them, keeping them on track and moving them all from one activity to another is outside the experience of most people. I do not know of any teacher who was a complete natural, who walked into a classroom for the first time as a teacher feeling comfortable and capable. I do not even know anyone who did not feel anxious to some degree. I distinctly remember being one of a group of students arriving for my first teaching practice and being told by our mentor that after a few days' observation we would be working with classes and 'taking control as soon as we felt comfortable, probably within a week'. Our calm smiles and nods masked our churning stomachs and racing hearts.

In fact, through a series of small steps we actually enjoyed our time, each small triumph built our confidence and even the setbacks were learned from and laughed at in the staffroom afterwards. The steps we went through were typically:

- observing
- working with individuals

- working with groups
- leading a section of teacher-initiated activity (lesson starter)
- delivering a lesson from start to finish with decreasing support from the class teacher.

The anxiety we felt was actually helpful, it ensured we were focused and prepared. Walking into a classroom knowing you have a fully prepared plan with (hopefully) engaging activities decreases anxiety a great deal and reduces the degree of uncertainty in the classroom. In fact, having interesting things to do is half the battle and most children will want to work with you provided you are fair, consistent, set clear boundaries and are (at least moderately) interesting.

Teaching ICT offers opportunity and challenge in just about equal measure. Many pupils are motivated to study ICT and this can make your classroom one of the most positive environments within a school. On the other hand, distractions in an ICT room can be enormous. The magical box which sits in front of your pupils can play music, videos and games, and provides a window to the entire world – most people would find that pretty distracting, especially if they are disengaged with what is happening in the classroom. In fact, ICT teachers have to manage two learning spaces, the physical classroom and the virtual environment.

In our experience many beginning teachers tend to think of classroom or lesson management in terms of 'controlling behaviour' – and negative behaviour at that. This is entirely understandable, but over-focusing our efforts on negative behaviour and feeling that we have to 'control' others is debilitating and makes for high levels of stress and frustration. Effective teachers use a mixture of explicit expectations, appropriate (though not indiscriminate) praise and clear choices with associated consequences to help children manage their own behaviour.

There may be a link between how you think about behaviour management and your confidence in schools. Gutherson et al. (2006) have correlated beginning teachers' self-rated confidence in behaviour management with the terms they use to describe it and found that teachers who use terms like 'control' and 'discipline' had the lowest level of confidence in their ability to manage behaviour. Conversely, those who describe the concepts of consistency, fairness, boundaries, rules and understanding individual needs had the highest levels of confidence going into schools.

Beginning teachers forging their teaching identity and skills understandably want answers to 'What should I say and do if … happens?' type questions, and are not impressed with 'Well it depends' … type answers. However this is really the only truthful response as so much depends on the situation specifics, school rules, the relationship between teacher and child, and the personality and style of the teacher. We can, however, move from the situational specifics (exactly what you should say or do) and zoom out to examine a set of generalized principles and techniques that most of us can use within our own personal style – that is the aim of this chapter. We hope to boost your confidence by examining how managing the physical classroom environment and the people who use it can lead to a learning environment which is a positive place for most pupils (and teachers), most of the time.

Clearly within the limitations of a chapter we cannot examine all facets of behaviour management in detail and so will focus on practicalities within an ICT classroom. See the list at the end of the chapter for more general further reading.

CAN CLASSROOM AND BEHAVIOUR MANAGEMENT BE LEARNED?

The *Discipline in Schools* report (Department for Education and Science, 1989) (commonly referred to as the Elton Report after the Committee of Enquiry's chairman) published two decades ago remains a landmark document in this field. The report soundly rejects the notion that classroom management skills are simply a 'natural gift' and that teachers who have difficulty in this area are in some way personally inadequate. There will be a small number of teachers who come to teaching with most of the skills already in place and will need very little additional training, equally there will be a small minority whose personalities do not match the job where training cannot be effective. However, the vast majority of teachers can learn and improve these skills through practice, training, observation and experience.

Certainly our own experience of working with beginning teachers is that forward planning, mentor feedback, and knowledge and practice of a range of approaches can enable almost all trainees to improve their classroom management from one lesson to the next.

The personality you present to a class will not be the personality you present to friends and family, or even peers in the staffroom. It is wise, for example, to maintain some professional distance between yourself and your charges, being careful about how much you reveal about your personal life. This is usually the intention behind the 'Don't smile before Christmas' advice that most beginning teachers hear, but is too simplistic. In fact, smiling communicates confidence and we need to appear confident (even if we do not feel it). (See companion website, www.sagepub.co.uk/secondary, video clip, *Organized and confident*, to hear about Richard's personal approach.)

Be wary of using 'personality' as an excuse to continue doing what you have always done (or what was done to you). Learn from experienced colleagues and be open to new approaches. It is unwise to mimic a teacher directly, but you can take the key principles they use and make them work for you.

Just as we can learn classroom management skills, we may need to unlearn some unhelpful language or behaviour. Be careful you do not perpetuate the phrases and actions that you may have experienced as pupils and children. These can slip out so easily when we're not conscious of the language we use. Statements like:

> 'Would you do that at home?'
> 'How dare you?'
> 'Do you think I'm stupid?'
> 'You've wasted my time, so I'll waste yours.'
> 'Perhaps you would like to teach the class?'
> 'How many times have I told you?'

probably did not help us control our own behaviour and they probably will not help you as a teacher either.

THE BEHAVIOUR CURRICULUM

As beginning teachers you are rightly concerned with how you teach and assess the ICT curriculum. You will spend hours crafting learning objectives, writing lesson plans and producing worksheets, presentations and other resources. Equally important, but sometimes neglected, is the idea of a curriculum for behaviour.

In order for pupils to learn in a typical lesson they need to:

- focus their attention
- take turns
- listen and participate in class discussion
- ask questions appropriately
- maintain focus as they work towards a target.

Some pupils need practice at these skills and most need to hear the explicit expectations that teachers have about how to behave. Note also that there are a whole set of sub-skills underlying each of the above – for an excellent overview of the behavioural skills pupils need to survive in school (and life) see the 'Positive Behaviour Curriculum (secondary)' report commissioned by Cumbria County Council (weblink at the end of the chapter).

It is natural as a beginning teacher to feel that pupils should already know how to behave, and we frequently hear comments like 'Why won't they listen to each other? They should be quiet, why must I tell them every time?' or even 'I shouldn't have to provide a pen, it's not my job!' There are two aspects to consider here. First, we need to recognize that behaviour is learned and can change – although it takes explicit teaching, time and persistence to do so. Secondly, if we say to ourselves and our staffroom colleagues 'but they *should* just …' without coming up with a strategy or solution 'they' never will change. Perhaps they should, but the reality is that they have not done so yet, and so we need to find a way of changing the environment or our practices in order to elicit the behaviour we want to see.

Sometimes beginning teachers plough through the ICT curriculum without ever addressing the behaviour curriculum. With classes which have typical mixed levels of interest, experience and expectations, this is unsatisfying for all. Teachers feel they are constantly going over old ground, activities tend to emphasize skills-based individual work while group work or discussion is sidelined because unclear expectations can lead to chaotic classrooms.

Commit time to planning your approach to behaviour management, setting expectations and teaching a curriculum of behaviour alongside ICT work and uncertainty is reduced, classrooms are calmer places and productive learning can happen.

It is likely that you will have to devote more time to the behaviour curriculum during the establishment phase of working with a class, with typically the first lesson being dominated by setting expectations and teaching explicit routines. Figure 5.1 illustrates how the behaviour curriculum runs alongside the ICT curriculum. The first few lessons will feature opportunities to practise and positively reinforce these routines. As routines become embedded you can spend more time on your ICT teaching. Whenever a new way of doing things is introduced there will be a need for additional teaching of routines, for

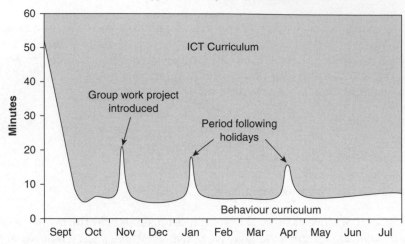

Typical time spent each lesson

Figure 5.1 Showing how the time requirements for the behaviour curriculum might fluctuate during a typical year

example introducing group work. Also routines need regular reinforcement, particularly after holiday periods.

It is worth noting that the establishment phase is easier when you are starting with a class at the beginning of a year than when you are parachuting into a teaching practice placement. Notwithstanding this you must establish how things will work in your lessons (your rules and routines) during the first lesson with a class. The following sections provide an overview of this establishment phase.

THE SCHOOL FRAMEWORK

As a beginning teacher you do not operate in a vacuum. All schools will have a policy which describes the school ethos and how classroom and behaviour management is to be implemented. We always advise new teachers to obtain this document on their first day in school, not least because it will describe how to get help from colleagues when necessary. The amount of detail specified in these policies varies from school to school (for examples, see the companion website, www.sagepub.co.uk/secondary), but they will set out some minimum standards of conduct and define specific behaviours with serious, non-negotiable consequences, for example regarding possession of drugs or weapons. Many go further than this and offer useful and detailed advice for classroom teachers.

Individual departments within a school often build upon this whole-school framework to meet their particular needs. For example, an ICT department will set out how work is celebrated and praised as well as rules in an ICT room and a description of how incidents are referred to within the department. Sometimes these rules are not formally documented, relying on custom and practice. It is helpful for departments to agree and write down their classroom management practices to help ensure consistency across teachers. This consistency in our approach across the school, departments and individual teachers is probably the single most important factor in effective behaviour management.

RIGHTS, RESPONSIBILITIES, RULES AND ROUTINES

Rights, responsibilities and rules in a secondary school are often decided and published at a whole-school or department level, so it is likely that you will adopt these alongside a set of specific rules and routines for your classroom. When you take on a new group at the beginning of a year it is good to have a school and subject approach to introducing rights, responsibilities, rules and routines. You will typically spend most time focusing on rights and responsibilities at the beginning of Key Stage 3 and again at Key Stage 4 where working practices are significantly different from previously. It is useful to explicitly explain your rules and routines with every class you meet for the first time – with frequent reminders in lessons.

Rights and responsibilities offer a useful framework for beginning a class discussion with pupils about owning their behaviour. Pupils readily understand that they have rights. For example, when asking a class about their rights, they will often say 'I have a right to have my viewpoint heard'. Pupils can suggest the personal responsibility that follows, for example, 'Therefore, I have a responsibility to listen to other peoples' points of view'.

Rogers identifies three key areas where pupils have rights:

- to be respected and treated fairly
- to be safe – physically and emotionally
- to learn (Rogers, 2002: 28).

Rights and responsibilities are the 'big picture' – they help pupils understand why we need rules and routines in the classroom and wider life.

Rules protect everyone's rights and encourage pupils to take responsibility for their actions. They also provide us with a shorthand way of reminding pupils of our expectations, for example instead of 'Carly, when we're discussing in a group I need to hear only one voice, the rest of us should be listening. If you want to speak next, please raise your hand and wait to be asked', we could say, 'Carly, remember our rule for class discussion?' We may even simply point to the rule on the wall poster. This reduces our intervention time and we're giving Carly less attention so that the discussion can continue.

Wherever possible rules should:

- be developed with pupils using inclusive language such as 'our' and 'we'
- be few in number
- have a positive behavioural focus describing what pupils should do. (Sometimes the phrasing becomes so clumsy that the alternative is preferable – see the food and drink rule in the following example)
- be displayed in the classroom.

Example rules for an ICT classroom

In our classroom we will treat each other with respect. We will:

1. use manners and polite language
2. not use 'put downs' or bully others
3. respect other people's differences and opinions.

To stay safe we will:

1. wait outside the room for the teacher and then walk to our seats
2. keep our belongings under the desk
3. stay in our seats, unless asked to move by the teacher
4. keep our hands away from wires and tell the teacher if we see anything dangerous
5. follow the safe email and chat room guidelines and the Acceptable Computer Use agreement
6. not eat food and drink in the IT room.

So that we can all learn we will:

1. stay focused and try our best in every task without disturbing or distracting others
2. listen to each other and give everyone a fair chance
3. use the computers and internet only for our school work
4. ask for help by raising our hands when we are stuck.

Note that most schools require all pupils (and often parents) to agree with an acceptable use policy (AUP) which deals in detail with safety and technical issues (see 'Health and safety' section in this chapter).

Rights, responsibilities and rules provide structure in our classroom. *Routines* reinforce our classroom rules and other day-to-day practice. They make everyone's lives easier and free-up your most precious asset – thinking time. Routines are especially important in an ICT room where there are frequent transitions between teacher instruction, different computer-based activities and group work or discussion. You can plan many of these routines in advance; some will only become apparent when you reflect on how your lessons are going. For example, when you have had to ask the tenth child to sit down rather than rushing eagerly to the printer, it is time for a routine about collecting printouts.

Routines need to be devised, explicitly taught and practised. Work hard at these during the establishment phase with lots of reinforcement. Sometimes beginning teachers know what they want, but do not spend time teaching and reinforcing, then give up because they think the routine cannot work. It can take several weeks to have our class use a routine say for entering a room (a single line, bags down with room for the teacher to get in first), but if we are persistent then we can get this routine to work and then move on to other things. A bit of time and consistency early on will pay dividends over the long term.

Once inside the classroom we can use a variety of verbal and non-verbal cues to 'telegraph' an upcoming routine. Using the same off-pat phrase or gesture with a particular class each time helps reinforce the routine. Note that cues may need to be age or situation specific, so for example a countdown or hand-clap to initiate whole-class attention with

12-year-olds may not be appropriate with 15-year-olds where a simple instruction may be sufficient. Figure 5.2 describes common areas where teachers use routines and some of the issues you will need to consider.

Reflection Point 5.1

Our goal in using routines is to minimize teacher talk and time.
   For each of the previous routines:

1.   Plan the cues you will use – short phrases and/or non-verbal cues.
2.   Practise the language you will use.
3.   Decide how you will teach these routines to your classes during the establishment phase.

So far we have looked at a framework to establish positive working practices. In the next section we look at the kinds of interventions that teachers make on a day-to-day basis to reinforce desired behaviour and to correct or manage inappropriate behaviour.

WHAT DO CHILDREN WANT?

As discussed previously most children want to learn in an environment which provides structure, consistency and fairness. They also need to feel a sense of belonging to a class or peer group. We play a big part in creating this for our classes through our personal interactions, the activities we plan and the language we use – hence the focus on inclusive language in our classroom rules.

Children want to work in a calm environment. You play an enormous part in communicating calmness through your management of transitions and general use of voice and body language. Have you ever sat in a classroom where the teacher speaks constantly in a raised tone of voice (bouncing their voice off the back wall)? In these circumstances children get excited and unsettled and their behaviour can become agitated and disruptive. If the teacher responds to this by further raising their voice (and making expansive gestures, or striding around the room) the classroom dynamic becomes locked into a spiral of increasing volume and disruption. To calm the class, effective teachers pause, modulate their voice (initially raised, then dropping to a normal level) and avoid too much movement. (See companion website, www.sagepub.co.uk/secondary video clip, *Remaining calm*, to hear about this in practice.)

Most pupils also want attention from their peer group and teacher. Pupils will strive for attention in a whole variety of ways from the wholly appropriate like raising a hand, through to the entirely inappropriate such as swearing, grandstanding and teacher-baiting. For some pupils the attention we provide reinforces that behaviour – *even if the*

Routine	Consider
Entering the room	Will the room be unlocked? If not, who has a key? Where should pupils initially sit – at their computers or at desks?
	When introducing or reinforcing a seating plan, numbering the desks/computers and sticking a pupil list near the door is fast and effective. Stand near the door to greet pupils and control flow.
	How will you deal with latecomers?
Settling/securing pupil attention	***Always*** take the time to secure attention before addressing the class rather than giving instructions over working noise.
	This usually requires an audio cue – verbal instruction, countdown or repetitive noise (tapping a cup or ringing a bell). It is often most effective when combined with a visual cue, e.g. a simple raised hand or a visual cue or picture projected onto the whiteboard to focus attention.
	Sometimes stopping and waiting with an expectant expression is sufficient or try punctuated speech where the teacher speaks each word of an instruction clearly with a pause, until all pupils are focused: 'In … five … seconds … I … would … like … everyone … looking … this … way … thanks.'
	Where pupils are sat at their computers – monitors must always be switched off, with hands away from equipment and chairs turned around to face you.
	Class control software (for example, where the teacher can blank or freeze all pupil screens) can be useful, but always give a warning/countdown and remember that ultimately we want them to control their own behaviour rather than relying on teacher/computer control.
	Younger children respond well to 'follow-me' clapping games where the teacher claps a rhythm and the pupils have to follow it – this has the added advantage of moving hands away from keyboards and mice!
Releasing pupils on-task	Check pupil understanding of the task. Asking 'Do you all understand?' rarely results in any dissent. 'Any questions?' is marginally better. A more robust approach is to ask a pupil to tell the class what they have to do next; you can repeat this with a number of pupils to ensure most questions are cleared up prior to the on-task phase.
	Set a timed target for the task – what must they do and how long do they have to complete it? There are some excellent (free) on-screen timers that can help you and the pupils monitor this together and inject some pace into lessons (see companion website for links).
Logging on	Time taken to access a network varies enormously from school to school – where this is problematic, consider making pupil log-on a part of the entrance process so that the process is complete by the end of the starter.
	Forgotten passwords – how is this resolved? Do teachers have a master list? Does CAPS-LOCK matter?
	Where there are more children than computers, how can you ensure fair access? Who logs on and how will they be assessed? This will require a rota system rather than having the same pupils always sharing.

(Continued)

Figure 5.2   (Continued)

Routine	Consider
Transitions between	Transitions are challenging to manage, especially where pupils are activities expected to move around the classroom. Try to avoid unnecessary transitions in your lesson plans between teacher explanations and computer activities. Where transitions are necessary: • Start by securing all pupils attention. • Explain the transition, beginning with 'In a moment …' or 'When I tell you …', otherwise they will start moving straight away. • Phase pupil movement, for example row by row. • For complicated instructions, bullet point the steps on the board.
Movement	Do pupils have to ask permission to be out of their seats? How do pupils collect printouts? How is peer support encouraged and monitored, for example when pupils complete their work, may they act as teacher helpers?
Appropriate noise levels	It can be useful to define several appropriate levels of classroom noise: Active listening Group/partner discussion On-task working noise Remember to tell pupils which is appropriate for the next task. How will you monitor this and convey to pupils without constant teacher talk? Some teachers make good use of a noise-meter visual cue, which shows an acceptable noise level. These can be simple cardboard indicators, projected images or even a microphone hooked up to a computer with a visual output. Sometimes the simpler versions are monitored and changed by pupils themselves. Examples can be found on the companion website, www.sagepub.co.uk/secondary.
Distributing and collecting resources	Lessons tend to lose focus when teachers break off to distribute material. Make this a routine using a rota of pupil helpers. Where are pupil folders physically stored? Is this likely to cause a bottleneck of pupil traffic?
Saving, logging off, tidying up and exiting the room	Allow sufficient time for this, usually around 5 minutes. Procedures for saving work need to be made crystal clear – check their understanding. Should pupils power-down their computers? Spend time checking the room (computers, litter and tidiness) before dismissing and as with all transitions allow movement in batches, e.g. row by row.

Figure 5.2   Typical routines in ICT

behaviour and attention is negative. Providing appropriate attention when pupils are on task and responding to inappropriate attention-seeking with the least attention possible can, over time, modify behaviour. A common phrase in behaviour management textbooks is 'catch them being good' and this is certainly a useful phrase to have in mind whenever you are in the classroom. The type of attention you give is as important as when you give it. Praise does not have to be effusive and public, often with adolescents this can work against you; they like your genuine personal attention but do not want the spotlight turned upon them. A quiet comment – 'I really liked the way you've approached the task today, you're well on with things', or a subtle non-verbal signal such as a smile, wink or thumbs-up is often all that is required. Many schools also make use of a 'postcard home' system to praise pupils in a private, but very effective way.

If we aim to reward appropriate behaviour with positive reinforcement, how should we deal with inappropriate behaviour?

'MANAGING' VS 'CONTROL'

Just about the only actions you can 'control' in the classroom are your own. When Robert puts his MP3 ear buds in his ears we cannot physically control him. Seizing the offending item (while tempting) puts us in a morally (if not legally) intolerable position. We can, however, control our own actions (our body language, positioning and carefully chosen words) and manage his behaviour by offering clear choices with sensible consequences. This might seem like semantics, but there's a whole different mindset behind feeling as if you have to *control* someone and feeling like you are *managing* their behaviour. From a pupil's point of view this feels very different too. Think about how you would feel when a teacher towering over you, hand moving towards the MP3 player (given as a birthday gift) shouts 'Give me that MP3 player right now. How dare you have that thing out in my lesson? I've warned you about your behaviour all lesson, now I've had enough' compared with a teacher who while angry and frustrated says in a calm but firm manner' 'Robert, the choice is, put that in your bag where it stays or we're having a discussion after the lesson' and then moves away. The first situation will most likely result in a battle of wills and, equally serious, the alienation of many class members who see an adult who has lost their temper using belittling language to 'put down' a fellow classmate. The second situation takes more work, and certainly more practice, but the pupil is left to 'control' their own behaviour. Ultimately the choice is theirs, the majority will comply, classmates see an adult in control of themselves, managing the situation. Note that where compliance does not occur or behaviour is repeated over time there *must* be an appropriate consequence. Consistency in this approach is the key. Remember that our central aim here is that *pupils ultimately take control of their behaviour in the classroom and throughout their lives.*

AWARENESS IN AN ICT CLASSROOM

Successful teachers know what is going on in their classroom. They scan the class during teacher explanations and on-task time to identify pupils who need support and potential disruption hotspots. While they are explaining a point to the class they may be simultaneously using non-verbal signals such as eye contact or moving next to a daydreaming pupil. Dividing attention in this way is a skill that takes time to master. Beginning teachers are very focused on what they will say and do next, particularly in relation to their subject material. As you become more confident you will find that you have freed up enough mental space to be able to scan, talk and use non-verbal cues at the same time. The classroom management theorist Jacob Kounin (1970) neatly encapsulated these two ideas in the concepts of 'withitness' and 'overlapping'.

'Withitness' is most frequently described as appearing to have 'eyes in the back of your head'. If we examine this idea further, there are two important components: first, regular scanning of the class and, second, making your awareness apparent to the pupils or 'letting them know that you know'. Some teachers make great use of a short pause between spotting a potential incident and responding to it so that it really does appear that they are omniscient. For example, having spotted which child is making their computer beep during a teacher explanation, a teacher waits until the next time it happens and says without turning towards the pupil or making eye contact, 'Michael, if I hear that again, we'll be having a conversation after the lesson'. Withitness shows pupils that you care about their progress and that they cannot get away with procrastination or off-task behaviour.

'Overlapping' is the ability to handle two or more events at the same time. A key skill here is the ability to detach yourself from the immediate situation and take a step back so that you can think through actions in advance – more on this in the next section.

The ICT classroom presents a number of specific challenges to maintaining teacher awareness. Most ICT teachers enhance their explanations by using a combination of software, projectors, interactive whiteboards and wireless presentation gadgets. This can be distracting for teachers and pupils; it is all too easy to lose awareness of the classroom while you try to deal with a technical glitch. Our best advice here is to have everything prepared in advance – easily accessible from the desktop. Copy files from removable media onto the desktop to avoid pauses or jerky video and do not forget to check the audio volume. Embed screenshots within presentations rather than switching between lots of applications. Position yourself so that you do not have to turn your back on the class or bend down to a computer screen. A wireless mouse, trackball or pointer can really help here – you may want to consider investing in a USB version that you can take into each classroom you use. If you have an interactive whiteboard, ensure that it has been properly oriented (and do not forget to use it – it is easy to forget and dash from the board to the computer to advance slides when you could use the board controls).

When pupils are using computers their actions can be hidden. Smaller pupils can disappear altogether behind computer monitors. It is also easy for pupils to hide their on-screen actions by minimizing windows whenever a teacher is near. Combined with this, teachers regularly need to sit next to pupils to work through a problem and so become invisible to the class. Classroom layout is a key factor here and although you may not be able to do much to change this in the short term, you can work out the best strategy to use in any particular layout. Most classrooms have one or more zones where you can stand and see the majority of the screens. Aim to spend any 'down time' (when you're not working with individuals) in these zones, scanning the screens. Some classroom control software allows you to remotely monitor pupils' computer activity – here the threat of surveillance is often more effective than the practicalities of using this as a regular tool. When working with an individual, position yourself at an angle so that as far as possible you can see their screen and the majority of the class. (See companion website, www.sagepub.co.uk/secondary, video clips, *Control software* and *Dealing with complexity*, to hear about this in practice.)

Seating plans can simplify life in an ICT suite, they allow you to learn names more quickly and address individuals rather than using less effective generic terms like 'girls' or 'you'. They are also a useful tool for reflection and action, where you can identify groupings that are not working and re-seat pupils in a more productive area. Although many pupils will complain at being moved, the results can be surprising. For example, one Year 8 pupil 'playing' to his peers was moved next to the teacher's desk; on being offered the chance to return to his previous place, he said, 'I think I worked better here, I'll stay here next week'.

Teaching assistants (TAs) are a valuable asset in maintaining classroom awareness. They are a useful second pair of eyes and ears in terms of both class behaviour and spotting pupil misconceptions. They also often know of incidents from the informal school grapevine that affect an individual's or class's mood. It is useful to agree beforehand the routines and signals you will use when interventions are needed. For example, when the teacher is explaining at the front, the TA can manage a range of low-level disruptions and keep individuals focused.

Many teachers benefit from having their lessons video-taped to reflect upon the degree to which they identify and deal with classroom incidents. While this can be uncomfortable, it very often provides insights into specific areas to improve. Brief case studies of teachers who have used video to improve their skills can be found through the companion website, www.sagepub.co.uk/secondary, links.

CHOOSING WHEN AND HOW TO INTERVENE

Teachers make hundreds of decisions a week about when and how to intervene to reinforce or correct a pupil's behaviour. For experienced teachers – most of these decisions and subsequent actions have become habit – they have developed a number of approaches that work and only unusual circumstances require them to stop and actively consider their next response. Beginning teachers are in the process of learning what works for them through a process of trial and reflection. This section introduces some important concepts to help you through this formative process.

> ### Scenario
>
> As Suresh moves around the class he scans the screens and notices that Nick has a computer game in progress. Suresh approaches Nick who responds to a classmate's nudge by closing the game window with a keystroke, revealing today's (largely incomplete) work.
>
> 'Nick, why are you playing games in my lesson?'
> 'I wasn't, Sir.'
> 'I saw you from the back of the class.'

Nick smiles, 'I was just researching the 'net to do with this work sir.'

'Nick, I'm not stupid – I saw what you did.'

Nick acts aggrieved, 'I'm not stupid sir, why are you always picking on me?'

'I do not always pick on you, and I didn't call you stupid. Now if I see any more games today you'll be in detention. Understand? Let me see where you're up to. [Reads the screen]. You've hardly done anything, Nick – why have you done so little?'

Nick whines, 'I've had my hand up for half an hour, Sir; you've been too busy with Katy.'

'Now that's not fair, the lesson only started 25 minutes ago and I haven't seen your hand up once. You know I try to get around everyone. Now will you please get on with your work?'

As Suresh starts to move away, Nick mutters 'It's sooo boring anyway.'

Suresh turns back and raises his voice. 'What did you say?' (Now the class are really taking an interest.)

'Nothing, Sir.'

'I distinctly heard you say something. What was it?'

'I was just asking Adam what to do, Sir.'

'You said this is boring (sniggers from around the class) – how dare you? What do you have to say for yourself?'

'Sorry, Sir. It's just we did all this last year with Mrs Henderson.'

'Well, if you've done it before, it shouldn't take long to finish, should it? In fact, you can stay behind through break to finish off.'

Nick is genuinely angry now. 'That's not fair, I'm ahead of loads of people and you said we had two weeks to finish off.'

'Well, you should have thought about that before you started answering back.'

What a lot of teacher and peer attention Nick gets. Perhaps Suresh is tired or simply having a bad day and is being entirely reactive. Perhaps Nick is difficult with most teachers or is genuinely just bored with the material. The underlying reasons are worth reflection (after the lesson), but in the moment of intervention what matters is giving Nick the opportunity to change his behaviour, without escalating the level of conflict. See the companion website, www.sagepub.co.uk/secondary, video clip, *Remaining calm* to hear a teacher discussing his experience of handling low-level inappropriate behaviour.

Reflection Point 5. 2

Before reading ahead think about how you would have handled the interaction differently.

Pausing

When an incident happens it is all too easy to react immediately, guided primarily by our emotions. The most important thing we can do, however, is to pause and think. As with good question and answer technique, good behaviour intervention requires a little thinking time for both parties. Stopping and thinking if only for a couple of seconds gives us a chance to take a mental (and emotional) step back and to think about the situation, the emotions we are feeling and the best approach to take. This simple act is a learned professional skill, and is much more easily done prior to an incident than when we are in the thick of it.

Once we have assessed a situation we need to decide on our course of action. The idea here is that we have a menu of responses up our sleeves – a repertoire. We choose the lowest level response that could change the behaviour. In doing this we are seeking to deny inappropriate behaviour the oxygen of our attention.

One of the most basic choices we can make is to ignore the behaviour. 'Tactical ignoring' (Rogers, 2002) of low-level attention-seeking and secondary behaviour can be very effective at showing pupils that they can only secure your attention in appropriate ways. Note that tactical ignoring is a deliberate choice and where behaviour does not change we need to select another approach. Tactical ignoring is most useful in sending a clear message to individuals that behaviours like calling out and inappropriate asides ('Sir, did I see you in the supermarket with your girlfriend last night?') do not warrant your attention – where behaviour persists we can follow up with a rule reminder or direction – 'I'll help you when you're sitting quietly with your hand up' or 'Now isn't the time to discuss that, but we can talk about it after the lesson if you like'. The other area where tactical ignoring is of primary importance is in managing incidental or secondary behaviour.

Secondary behaviour

In the previous example, Nick has developed a set of diversionary skills which he uses to draw Suresh away from his main point into an argument of Nick's choosing. Many children learn this skill early on – distracting adults is a great trick for avoiding or minimizing blame and consequences while simultaneously 'saving face'. These secondary behaviours – eye-rolling, muttered comments, diversionary questions and 'It's just not fair!' last-word type comments – can take up most of your time if you over-attend to them in class. Some individuals are particularly adept at identifying insecurities and pushing teachers' buttons. Notice how Nick does this in suggesting that he was not getting the help he deserved and that the work is boring.

Some hyper-vigilant teachers see secondary behaviour as a personal attack, feeling that they must win every battle and follow up every incidental behaviour (often by using aggressive or sarcastic language). The working atmosphere in such classes is tense and unpleasant. Frequently, pupils in these classes actively seek ways of baiting the teacher. The irony is that teachers do not need to seek power in this way – they already have it. They are adults with a set of well-developed (hopefully) interpersonal skills and the fluff and nonsense of secondary behaviour should not overly concern them.

How should we handle secondary behaviour? In most instances we can tactically ignore it. In the case of non-verbal behaviour (slouching, eye-rolling, tutting, sighing and puffing) or muttered comments at the end of an exchange we can give the pupil some 'take-up time' (Rogers, 2002) simply moving away and giving the pupil the chance to respond to our expectations. Where a pupil makes a direct challenge we ignore the content of what they say and assertively re-state the behaviour we are looking for. Staying focused on the primary behaviour and ignoring secondary behaviour is perhaps the most frequently used technique of effective classroom teachers.

Another useful tactic in diffusing secondary behaviour is to partially agree (Rogers, 2002) with a pupil's statement and then refocus on the primary behaviour. For example if a pupil says 'But Mrs Henderson lets us play games'. Our response might be 'That may be true (partial agreement), but right now I need you to focus on completing the worksheet'. Notice how this exchange avoids the trap of getting into a pantomime style, 'Oh no, she doesn't/Oh yes, she does' interchange or, even worse, the temptation to undermine a colleague – 'Then I'll have to have a chat with Mrs Henderson'. The situation is effectively diffused, there is no naturally flowing argument because we did not flat out disagree with the pupil's premise.

Aggressive, assertive or passive?

In the last section we used the terms 'aggressive' and 'assertive'. Before we look at some other interventions it is worth examining these concepts and taking a moment to consider the impact of our own personal teaching style.

When we are aggressive we try to win by disregarding the other party's rights. We use the power we have *over* someone to achieve our goal. Aggressive behaviour aims to threaten or hurt the other party. Aggressive teachers shout, use sarcastic language, personal comments and physical proximity to 'show who is boss'. They combine an ever-alert attitude with high-level responses such as shouting across the class or an immediate consequence like detention without warning. They will seek to *make an example* of a pupil to show the class that they *mean business*. They may also use whole-class consequences as a punishment. Pupils in these classes rarely have a right of reply.

When we are passive we allow others to abuse our right to be heard and treated fairly. Passive teachers tend to ignore incidents in order to avoid confrontation. They may talk at the same time as class chatter is happening, ploughing through explanations as quickly as possible. Passive teachers may threaten consequences, but avoid following up in a consistent manner, for instance where a pupil does not turn up to detention. Passive teachers are often led into following up secondary behaviour and end up being defensive of their own practice. They may try to befriend a class in order to avoid conflict. Passive teachers are often reluctant to seek help through school policies and systems. Where conflict occurs and is not resolved, passive teachers may label themselves a failure, or blame external factors (for example 'lack of effective punishments' or 'the senior management') outside of their control.

These descriptions are generalizations and most of us can think of incidents where we have responded aggressively or passively (and sometimes both at the same time). However, the characterizations are useful when reflecting on incidents – were you passive, or aggressive and how would you change things?

When we are assertive we are clear about our own rights and seek to achieve our goals without trampling on the rights of others. Assertive teachers try to empathize with the other parties' position – even if they do not agree with it. They work with children in a respectful manner – even if that respect is not reciprocated. Assertive teachers address the behaviour – not the person. 'Sam, when you want to speak, raise your hand, thanks' versus 'Why are *you* always shouting, what's wrong with you?' Assertive teachers are aware of what's happening in their classroom, choose when to intervene and choose their language and actions carefully so as to change behaviour with the least amount of teacher intrusion or attention.

Correcting behaviour

Let us assume you have identified an incident that requires your attention, paused, got into an assertive frame of mind and recognized that tactical ignoring is not appropriate (all within the space of about three seconds). Now what will you do?

There are broadly four levels of response that we could consider (Figure 5.3).

Relection Point

Reflection Point 5. 3

What logical consequences would you apply in the following scenarios? A pupil:

- regularly swears at the computer in frustration
- jams the printer after ignoring your instructions
- switches off the power to a classmate's computer resulting in lost work
- hands in an assignment copied from the Internet
- disconnects network leads
- accessses unauthorized chat rooms.

General principles when correcting behaviour:

- Wherever possible the interaction should be private not public, defer the interaction if necessary – 'I'll talk with you in a moment/after the lesson'.
- Consequences should be known in advance and applied after pupils have had the opportunity to correct their behaviour (with some take-up time.)
- Avoid the temptation of points scoring. 'I'm fed up of having to see you in this detention. Didn't I warn you all the way along that this would happen? Why do you never listen? What do you have to say for yourself?'
- Avoid whole-class consequences. 'Punishing the innocent with the guilty is always seen as unfair by pupils and their sense of grievance damages the school's atmosphere. ... We recommend that headteachers and teachers should avoid the punishment of whole groups' (Department for Education and Science, 1989: 101).
- In one-to-one discussions always try to ensure another teacher is within earshot, preferably within the room, particularly for longer discussions. At the very least ensure that the door is open. Alternatively reschedule the meeting.
- Re-establish the working relationship as quickly as possible. We are the adults in this relationship, it is unlikely that adolescents will come to us and say, 'You know I was thinking about what happened yesterday and I realize that I was a little over-emotional so I'd like to apologize'. It is our responsibility to approach them and give a little encouragement – 'I know you're going to do some brilliant work today'.

Response level 1	Observation and behaviour narration
When to use	Where we are trying to demonstrate to an individual or class that we trust them to take responsibility for their own actions with minimal implied direction.
Examples	'I notice that there's a lot of people around this printer.' Smiles and waits – giving take-up time.
	'I can see Michael looking at me ready to listen – and Emily and Noreen. Iqbal's ready, Karen's looking this way, thanks …' Continues until all are ready.
	'Nice work today you two, listen I notice there's some bits of paper under your desks there, I'll be back over in a minute.'
Notes	If pupils don't take up (or choose to ignore) your implied direction, move on to level 2 quickly or you'll appear ineffective, but keep persisting week to week. Practice an expectant expression – they will get there eventually!

Response level 2	Direction/re-focus
When to use	The most used teacher intervention, but there's a hierarchy of ways of giving directions – remember we're giving the least attention possible for off-task behaviour.
Examples	**Non-verbal cue** Finger on lips or hand behind ear to indicate listening. Raised hand to stop interruption. Miming chewing gum thrown in the bin. Open palm towards seat to indicate sit down. **Behavioural direction** 'Eyes and ears looking this way, thanks' 'Monitors off, chairs turned around, looking this way' 'Darren, headphones away, thanks.' **Rule reminder or question** 'Our internet rule is school work only, Nathan.' 'Remember our hands up rule?' 'What's our rule about drinks, Jenny?' **Refocusing question** 'What are you doing, Simon?' 'How much do you have left to complete?' 'What should we be doing?' 'Can you think of a more appropriate word to use?'
Notes	Remember when issuing directions to individuals to move close so that you are not shouting over the class.
	Using 'Thanks' conveys greater expectation than 'Please'.
	When using questions, avoid 'Why?' – it leads to secondary behaviour and at this point we're more interested in refocusing the primary behaviour. For example, the possible responses we might get from 'Simon, why are you spinning on your chair?' range from 'My foot slipped', through 'I was trying to raise it up a bit', to 'Because it's fun, Miss', all of which require further teacher attention and time.

Response level 3	Offer a choice with possible consequence
When to use	Most often for repeated inappropriate behaviour, or where a direction has been (or is likely to be) ignored.
Examples	'If you continue spinning in your chair, you'll have to use a chair with fixed legs.'
	'If you touch anyone's keyboard but your own, I'll be asking you to work with pen and paper.'

Figure 5.3   (Continued)

	'If I see any games on your screen, we'll be having a conversation after the lesson.' 'Your choice is to complete Task 3 now, or you can come back tomorrow for detention.' 'Put the phone away, or on my desk – it's up to you.' 'When you have completed Task 1 then you can start the internet research.' 'If I have to stop again and wait for you to be quiet, I'll be moving you to work at my desk.' 'You can choose to move to the timeout desk or I'll have to call your Year leader.'
Notes	These consequences are all spelled out in advance – there are no surprises here for pupils. They have the choice to modify their behaviour and we will give them a little take-up time to do so. The *inevitability* or certainty of any consequence is more important than its perceived severity. The fact that all pupils know that you chase up those who have skipped a detention with a letter home and a visit to their form room next day is what makes pupils turn up (or hopefully make the right choices and avoid detention altogether). The range of consequences that classroom teachers can apply is relatively small – but that doesn't mean that they're ineffective. In a typical school they include: • Re-seating pupils • Withdrawing computer access for a short period (this is often very effective – but you need to adapt the current task to be a paper-based activity) • Discussion after the lesson. See Rogers (2002: 71) for an excellent framework you can use for post-lesson discussion. • Detention • Parental notification (telephone or letter) and possible further involvement • Time-out – either in the room if you have space or to a pre-arranged place outside the classroom, or to a colleague's room • Escalation/referral – using the school's behaviour policy, e.g. calling for a colleague to withdraw a pupil from the lesson. It's important that we as class teachers follow up with such pupils afterwards. Ultimately, after subsequent escalations, the ultimate consequence for repeated highly disruptive behaviour may be exclusion from the school. Wherever possible, we should try to link the consequence to the incident, so for example where a pupil makes a mess, the consequence will be to clean it up. Where there isn't such an obvious choice, you may need to invent an activity which demonstrates why the behaviour is inappropriate, such as a reflective piece of work or working with the ICT technician. For example, when one pupil used expletives in a personal web page design, they were asked in a detention to write a page-long explanation of the potential dangers of publishing this to the World Wide Web.
Response level 4	**Command**
When to use	Where we need to stop a behaviour immediately in order to protect pupils or property.
Examples	With direct eye contact 'Bradley, put the chair down now.'
Notes	Once we have the pupils' attention our goal is to calm the situation. Call the pupil's name then gradually drop the volume of your voice. Be aware of body posture – assertive (not aggressive), feet planted firmly, direct eye contact, open palm gestures (not pointed finger or fist). You may need to repeat the command several times.

Figure 5.3   Correcting behaviour – response levels

Putting it all together

Reflection Point S. 4

Read the following scenario and identify the techniques Sarah uses to manage the class.

1. What preparation did she undertake?
2. What use does she make of rules and routines?
3. How does she handle secondary behaviour?
4. How does she correct inappropriate behaviour?
5. How do the structure of activities and the instructions help her manage the class?

Scenario

Year Group: Y8 Group Size: 25 (mixed ability)
Topic: Science poster – research and design
Room layout: Horseshoe – computers around the edge, tables in the centre

At 9:05 Sarah arrives at her classroom, the door has been left unlocked; most of her class are waiting outside. Inside the room Ryan, Nathan and Asif are sat at the back of the room clustered around one computer, obscuring the screen.

'You three out now and line up, come on you know the rules.'

Ryan moans. 'Awww Miss we were just getting logged on, Mr Daniels lets us come in at lunchtime before he arrives'.

'That might be so Ryan, but before my lessons you wait outside, now please.' She moves towards them, palm extended toward the door, the boys move reluctantly outside.

Outside the room she addresses the class. 'OK, listen please. Your number is on the door – check it and sit at that seat.' She stands in the doorway to check their entry, smiles and welcomes them to the class.

The class enter and log on to their computers. Sarah approaches Ryan who is chatting to a friend.

'Bag please, Ryan' she points under the desk. 'What are you doing next?'

'Logging on, Miss'

'Excellent – I know you're going to do some brilliant work today'.

Moving to the front of the room, she scans the screens. Most pupils have typed usernames and passwords – she knows that the log-on process can be slow at this time of day.

'OK, you know the routine, log on then join me in the centre.'

Natalie chips in, 'Miss, Amanda in 8H changed my password last week – I can't get in.'

'OK, Natalie come and sit at the front and we'll sort it out later, thanks.'

'Right, I'm ready – Paula, Tom, Asma, Harry – join us now, thanks'

Sarah introduces the lesson through a class team game to identify the topic keywords. She explains today's task and finishes by displaying an example of the work they are to produce.

(Continued)

(Continued)

'Right, we're going to work on the computers using a program called …'

A number of the class begin to stand and move toward their workstations.

'Whoa there, sit back down, thanks – let me start again. *In a moment*, when I tell you, we're going to work on the computers using a program called (she explains today's task). OK, Asif, can you tell me what we're doing today?'

Asif recounts the task.

'Great, thanks. Ryan, how long do we have to do this?'

'35 minutes, Miss'.

'Any questions?'

Natalie asks, 'Shall we print it?'

'Great question, thanks for asking before doing. We're not printing this week, because next week we're going to add some diagrams.

'I'm setting the on-screen timer – keep an eye on it folks – off you go. Natalie, can you come and see me about the password, please?'

As this is a new topic, Sarah spends a good deal of time checking progress and giving pupils positive feedback, though she expects them to use the worksheet she has spent time preparing.

'Miss, I'm stuck – what do I do next?' cries Tom across the room.

'Tom, remember our rule for getting attention?'

Tom raises his hand, in a moment Sarah looks over, 'Thanks, Tom, I've seen you and I'll be over once I'm done with Amy. In the meantime try to use the worksheet.'

Later when she goes over, Tom says, 'It's OK, Ryan helped me, I'm up to step 6.'

'That's great – thanks for helping Ryan.'

Part-way through the on-task phase, Sarah gives an update, '15 minutes left guys'. Scanning the screens she notices that many of the class have not used linked text frames. 'Don't forget everyone that you can link text frames by …' Twenty of the class are so focused on the task that they have not heard her. 'OK, eyes and ears looking this way, chairs turned around and monitors off in 5..4..3..2..1' She scans the room, asks individuals to turn monitors off and waits until all are facing her. Sarah projects the worksheet onto the board and draws their attention to the point that explains linked frames.

'If you can come up here and explain to me how to do this, thumbs up, if not thumbs down. OK, people with their thumbs up can resume work, the rest of you join me at the front please.'

Sarah gets the subgroup around the interactive whiteboard and uses a volunteer to show how linked frames can be used. She frequently scans the classroom and spots Hannah using her mobile phone to text. 'Excuse me one second.' She goes over and says in a quietly assertive voice, 'If I see that out again you'll be seeing me in detention tomorrow.' She moves away before there is a chance for secondary behaviour. Returning to the group she checks understanding – 'Lucy can you run through it for us again please … Any questions? OK, 10 minutes left – get to it.'

Hannah has begun to re-engage with the task. Sarah goes over, 'How's it going Hannah, can I have a quick look? It's great to see that you've used the colour scheme guidelines, now think about proofreading.'

With most pupils reaching the end of the task and two minutes to go on the timer Asif cries out in frustration, 'This machine's crap – it's lost my work!' Sarah moves next to him and pulls up a chair. 'Listen, I know you're frustrated and I'll help you, but do you think that language is appropriate in our classroom?'

'No, sorry, Miss, but it's just disappeared!'

'Can I borrow your mouse a second?' Sarah scans the desktop and determines that this isn't a problem that can be resolved quickly. 'I think we're going to need some help – please take this support card to the technician.'

The timer alarm sounds. 'OK, eyes and ears looking this way, chairs turned around and monitors off in 5..4..3..2..1' Sarah points to a set of instructions written on the whiteboard. 'When I tell you and not before – I need you to: (1) save your work in your OWN network area; (2) log off and turn off your machines; (3) leave your belongings where they are and sit in the middle. Nathan, can you collect worksheets in please?'

When all pupils are seated in the centre, Sarah uses questioning to assess today's learning, identify misconceptions and then sets the homework.

'OK, as usual you have 60 seconds to tidy your work area, tuck your chairs in and stand behind them.' Sarah scans the classroom and dismisses the class a section at a time.

HEALTH AND SAFETY

Most teacher training courses expect beginning teachers to explicitly identify health and safety issues and teaching points within their lesson plans or schemes of work. The British Educational Communications and Technology Agency (BECTA) have produced some excellent guidance and resources which will help you both manage the risks and teach children about health and safety and e-safety – see the weblinks at the end of this chapter.

Up until the late 1990s, the emphasis on safe use of ICT within the classroom was on the physical environment, particularly safe workstation use and ergonomics. Increasing Internet access in schools gave rise to the need for consideration of e-safety. Increasing use of mobile technology and social network sites has led to the phenomenon of cyber-bullying, while back in the physical world, new devices such as classroom projectors and Wi-Fi equipment have raised some new safety concerns.

Reflection Point 5.5

What role does an ICT teacher have in both managing classroom risks and teaching children about health and safety?

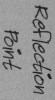

While 'the employer' has the legal duty for ensuring the school is a safe place to be, everyone who uses the school is responsible for the safety of themselves and others. Classroom teachers have a specific duty for:

- the day-to-day management of health and safety in accordance with the school's policy
- checking classrooms/work areas are safe

- checking equipment is safe before use
- ensuring safe procedures are followed
- bringing problems to the relevant manager's attention.

Teachers are responsible for identifying possible hazards and taking action to reduce risks to an acceptable level. Physical hazards are often fairly obvious, for example:

- loose bags present a trip hazard
- electrical equipment should be in good condition and safely powered, from separate switched wall sockets
- leads should not trail on the floor
- screen glare caused by inappropriate screen position or lighting can cause eye-strain
- ensuring fire exits are accessible
- inappropriate chairs or desks can cause musculoskeletal problems.

The UK's Health and Safety Executive's *Working with VDUs* (HSE, 2006b) leaflet contains further useful advice for those using computer equipment.

Teachers are also responsible for educating pupils about specific risks related to the physical and virtual aspects of ICT. This need not be just a list given to pupils, you could for instance use a spreadsheet model to demonstrate how we can assess levels of risk by multiplying the probability or likelihood of an event by the severity of its outcome to rank activities from 'most risky' to 'safest'. Pupils can then understand that no activity is risk-free, but that some have an unacceptable level of risk which can be reduced. You could extend this work by asking them to identify hazards in an ICT classroom and online, then use this to produce a basic risk assessment.

Where new hazards are identified, such as mobile phone or Wi-Fi radiation it is important for the classroom teacher to research the issue, take a balanced view of the evidence and present this to children so as to reassure them, or take appropriate remedial action. Organizations such as the Health Protection Agency, BECTA and teaching unions are sources of advice and guidance.

E-SAFETY

The UK Children Go Online (UKCGO) major research project set out to explore use of the Internet in a large cohort of 9–19-year-olds. Its final report (Livingstone and Bober, 2005) offers a useful set of key findings which can inform ICT teachers about how children and their parents view the opportunities and risks offered by the Internet. The statistics presented in this section are drawn from the report and except where stated represent the responses of frequent (at least weekly) Internet users aged 9–19.

Most children in the UK have access to the Internet. 75% of all 9–19-year-olds have home Internet access, 92 per cent at school. Nineteen per cent have Internet access in their bedroom. While most children want access to the Internet and use it appropriately,

48 per cent worry about 'being contacted by dangerous people', and 38 per cent worry about 'others finding out things about you'.

Most schools require pupils who use the Internet to agree with an acceptable use policy (AUP). This seeks to protect the school and individuals from potential risks and usually covers:

- types of acceptable Internet use
- viewing inappropriate content
- preserving personal privacy
- inappropriate or illegal activities
- plagiarism and copyright infringement
- arrangements for school monitoring of Internet use.

As an ICT teacher it is important that you understand the AUP and teach children why it is important and how it applies to them.

Internet literacy

Children who have a high level of Internet literacy are more likely to make good use of the opportunities the technology offers and, while they are more likely to come across risks, they are better equipped to handle them appropriately. Yet 30 per cent of all pupils report having received no lessons at all on using the Internet.

Thirty-eight per cent trust most of the information on the Internet. Thirty-three per cent felt they had been taught how to judge the reliability of online information. Similarly, only 41 per cent of parents are confident that their child has been taught this skill.

Internet literacy is more than being able to use applications to view and create content. It is about a set of more general, critical competencies including:

- a recognition of the benefits and limitations of the Internet compared with other media
- effective research strategies to find, corroborate and use information appropriately
- evaluating the value, reliability and potential bias in any information source. The Quality Information Checklist (QUICK) website is a very useful starting point – see link on companion website, www.sage pub.co.uk/secondary
- understanding the relative risks of Internet use and how to safeguard themselves, their computer systems and their data.

Inappropriate content

Sixteen per cent of parents think that their child has seen pornography on the Internet; 57 per cent of children and young people report having done so. Most is viewed unintentionally, for example through pop-ups or unsolicited junk mail. Among teens (12–19 years) the figure rises to 68 per cent with 20 per cent seeing pornography 'many times'.

Twenty-two per cent have accidentally viewed a site with 'violent or gruesome pictures' and 9 per cent a site that is 'hostile or hateful to a group of people'.

Most schools use filtering software to detect and block content which may be inappropriate, or alternatively only allow access to specific sites. Neither solution is perfect and as an ICT teacher you will probably have some control over how this works in practice. Creating an environment where children can report accidental access with no value judgement made is as important as controlling access through software. ICT teachers can take practical steps to help avoid accidental access:

- Most search engines have a safe search option which filters much inappropriate content – check this is turned on by default.
- Check websites before use with a class and search terms that may be used – both for appropriateness and to check that legitimate sites are not blocked by the school's filter.
- Where appropriate, limit searches to a specific domain, for example gov.uk or ac.uk.
- Ask pupils to apply the 'parent looking over my shoulder' test to judge appropriateness.
- Explain that their activity is logged and so it is best to tell if something goes wrong.

Interacting: email, Internet messaging (IM), chat rooms and virtual worlds

Most children do not use the Internet to access strangers. Most online communication is with local friends. Nevertheless, a significant minority, 30 per cent, have made an online acquaintance, while 8 per cent have had a meeting with someone they first met on the Internet.

A significant proportion of regular users have had a negative experience – 31 per cent received unwanted sexual comments, with 33 per cent receiving nasty comments (bullying) online or via text message. Parents significantly underestimated the scale of the problem, their estimates were 7 per cent and 4 per cent respectively.

Many children are not sufficiently cautious in protecting their personal information from someone they have met on the Internet. Twenty-four per cent have provided their full name, 9 per cent the name of their school and 7 per cent their phone number. Seven per cent have provided a photograph to someone that they met on the Internet. Only 5 per cent of parents think their child has given out such information.

It is important that children have an opportunity during ICT lessons to explore the implications of sharing personal information online with strangers. Areas important to cover here are:

- an online persona can be very different from the real person
- the small, but very real risk of possible physical harm or abuse
- the increasing dangers of phishing leading to identity theft
- how responding to unsolicited email can lead to spam and malware propagation
- the dangers of running executables from an unknown source.

Prevention is key in this area, actions teachers and children can take include:

- never sharing personal information with strangers
- using only teacher-moderated chat rooms in school, with logs kept of activity
- limiting or denying access to IM applications, although we need to recognize that children use these in the home and so will need to know how to manage privacy settings and 'buddy lists'.

Where children have received unwanted attention or are bullied online they need to feel comfortable in immediately reporting this to an adult. They should not make any response to the message and should also be made aware of the need to keep evidence such as text messages, emails, chat-room logs or screenshots.

Electronic communication has a different tone to face-to-face communication. It is usually briefer and sometimes the immediacy of being able to reply leads to a reactive response. For these reasons, sometimes individuals may make others feel bullied even where this was not the intention. Children need to be aware of the implications of their own actions and should be introduced to the idea that sometimes face-to-face contact is far more appropriate.

Publishing: web pages, blogs, podcasts and social networking

While a minority of pupils do publish web pages, blogs and podcasts, it is the rise of social networking sites such as Facebook, Friends Reunited and MySpace which has provided the motivation in addition to the tools to self-publish.

All the guidance from the previous section applies to these applications. In addition the potential audience of the pages generated is much wider, literally worldwide, and many have search capabilities and may be indexed by popular search engines so that individuals can be easily found. Pages can be copied locally, mirrored on another site or cached by a search engine – so even if you remove the original, what you have written or posted may still be accessible elsewhere. Text, images and video can also be manipulated in inappropriate ways.

Children need to be aware of all of the above before publishing any material on an Internet page. If they would be unhappy with parents or prospective employers viewing their pages or profiles, they should not publish. In addition, comments perceived to be defamatory, abusive or libellous could result in legal prosecution.

This is an area which many schools are struggling with – where a class or individual has produced a set of web pages, collaborative blog or Wiki and understandably want it to be published to show parents and seek broad feedback. There is no reason this should not be possible provided individuals are not identifiable, perhaps using a generic school email for feedback.

When incorporating photographs or video into such content, or on school web pages, ensure you obtain permission from parents in advance – state the ways in which the images may be used and only use the material for the purposes stated. Avoid identifying individuals; use the generic 'pupils' or first names only (with permission).

Internet dependence

Finally, talk to children about how to use the Internet appropriately and to be critically aware of their own use. Where they feel the need to check messages several times a day (or an hour) or spend longer on social networking than talking face to face, it is probably time for them to disconnect, unplug and (our favourite teacher cliché) get some fresh air!

What the research says: Lessons from psychology

An understanding of psychology can help us understand the ways in which individuals and groups behave in schools. Psychology can also inform the choices we make in behaviour management and help explain why some strategies do not work (such as corporal punishment), while others have greater success (such as certainty of consequences).

Obedience to authority – Stanley Milgram

Milgram's classic (and controversial) experiment (1963) will be familiar to all students of psychology. Volunteers participated in a laboratory experiment at Yale University on the premise that the study was examining the effects of punishment in teaching and learning. In the experiment, pairs of volunteers would play a teacher or learner. The learner was strapped into an 'electric chair apparatus' in one room; the teacher would then ask a series of questions in another. Whenever a learner was incorrect the teacher administered an electric shock which increased in intensity with each question. In fact only the 'teacher' was a volunteer, the learner was a stooge and the chair was not connected up to deliver electric shocks. Milgram was interested in how high an intensity of shock the volunteers would be prepared to administer. The volunteer could select shocks ranging from 'slight shock' to 'severe shock' and 'finally' 'XXX'. As shocks apparently increase in intensity, the learner pounds the wall between the rooms and eventually becomes silent.

Milgram polled psychology Yale seniors to predict how many of the 40 volunteers would administer the maximum shocks, their estimates were very low with the mean at 1.2 per cent. The actual number of volunteers who administered the highest shock was 26, or 65 per cent, with all administering shocks above the 'very strong' category.

The majority of volunteers showed extreme signs of anxiety and many protested verbally. Nevertheless, they continued at the insistence of the technician who used four 'prods' such as 'Please continue' 'The experiment requires that you continue' (Milgram, 1963: 374).

Milgram identified a number of factors that combined to produce such a high rate of obedience. Those of most interest as teachers are:

* background authority – the setting at Yale university created a perception of authority, legitimacy and competence upon the experimenters
* the request is perceived as legitimate – in being part of a scientific study
* the volunteers must respond in a specific and visible way (it is obvious if they have not complied).

Milgram's experiment highlights a potentially dark aspect of humanity, but as he points out in the paper's introduction: 'Obedience serves numerous productive functions. Indeed, the very life of society is predicated on its existence. Obedience may be ennobling and educative and refer to acts of charity' (1963: 371).

Milgram's experiment has lessons for us as classroom teachers. First, it highlights the potential power that teachers have and the responsibility that follows from our perceived authority: 'It would be interesting to repeat the experiments today and to see whether the results are as dramatic, in an age which we fondly believe is less in thrall to authority. Nevertheless, the authority of the teacher in the classroom tends to be preserved, amplified by a culture of dependence' (Atherton, 2004).

The appearance of legitimacy amplified the authority effect, this is to some extent why appearing confident is so important in establishing your authority, also why things are easier when you are no longer a trainee teacher (and to some extent as you appear older). The verbal protestations made by the volunteers did not prevent them from carrying out the actions, provided they were given straightforward prompts which did not engage with their protestations. This can be paralleled in a much milder form when we see secondary behaviours from pupils which can be overcome simply by re-stating our request.

Cognitive dissonance – Festinger and Carlsmith

In 1959 Leon Festinger and James Carlsmith set out to test a theory of cognitive dissonance by examining the level of reward necessary to persuade someone to change their opinion. A group of volunteers were asked to perform a boring, repetitive task (stacking cotton spools and turning pegs) under experimental conditions. They were then (unbeknown to them) assigned into one of three groups. The control group took no further action.

The other two groups were both asked to tell a lie to another volunteer who they believed would be doing the task after them (this person was actually a stooge). The lie was that the task was interesting and fun. The second group were paid 1 dollar if they lied, the third group received 20 dollars for their lie.

After a short interval all three groups were asked to rank how interesting they honestly found the task. The statistically significant results reveal that on average the control group and 20-dollar group rated the tasks in a similar way – slightly less than neutral. However the 1-dollar group on average rated the task as interesting, why should this be?

Festinger and Carlsmith theorize that when two cognitions do not fit together psychologically (for example, when you hold a private belief but act differently publicly) a state of cognitive dissonance (or discomfort) is created which individuals seek to minimize (in the same way that we seek to minimize thirst or hunger). This dissonance is reduced if external factors can explain the discrepancy (such as punishments or rewards). If the dissonance is great, one way that it can be reduced is to change their private belief. In the experiment, the 20-dollar group could justify their lying behaviour by the fact that they received a large reward. The 1-dollar group could not; a dollar was not sufficient for them to publicly act against their beliefs – they therefore changed their own attitude about the task.

Carlsmith and Festinger summarize as follows:

1. If a person is induced to do or say something which is contrary to his private opinion, there will be a tendency for him to change his opinion so as to bring it into correspondence with what he has done or said.
2. The larger the pressure used to elicit the overt behaviour (beyond the minimum needed to elicit it) the weaker will be the above-mentioned tendency. (1959: 210)

The implication for teachers is that pupils will modify their *behaviour* for a variety of sanctions and rewards (both groups told the lie). However, teachers can potentially modify pupil *attitudes* by using the minimum reward or sanction needed to illicit the change.

Further reading

BECTA (2007) *Signposts to Safety – Teaching e-safety at Key Stages 3 and 4.* Coventry: BECTA. An essential resource for all ICT teachers. Highlights benefits and risks of ICT, includes case study material, National Curriculum links and references to other resources.

Department for Education and Science (1989) *Discipline in Schools: Report of the Committee of Enquiry chaired by Lord Elton.* London: The Stationery Office.
The Elton Report – a comprehensive and influential report which draws evidence from classrooms and experts. It remains very relevant to teachers today.

Livingstone, S. and Bober, M. (2005) *UK Children Go Online: Final Report of Key Project Findings.* London: London School of Economics and Political Science.
A comprehensive investigation into the use of the Internet by a large cohort of 9–19-year-olds.

Ofsted (2005d) *Managing challenging Behaviour.* London: Ofsted.
An account of behaviour in UK schools based on national evidence.

Rogers, B. (2006) *Classroom Behaviour.* 2nd edn. London: Paul Chapman Publishing.
Bill Rogers's excellent book provides a comprehensive, readable and very practical guide to effective behaviour management regardless of subject specialism.

Weblinks

Live links to each of these websites can be found at the companion website, www.sagepub.co.uk/secondary.

Becta – http://schools.becta.org.uk/. For an excellent range of advice on health and safety and e-safety see the 'Security and safety' section within 'Leadership and management'.
Cumbria County Council Education Service (Positive Behaviour Curriculum) – www.cumbria.gov.uk/childrensservices/behaviour/resources.asp. Contains sample pages from a collaborative project to explore and develop the idea of an explicit behaviour curriculum.
UK Children Go Online – www.children-go-online.net/. Research website from the London School of Economics and Political Science. Contains the *UK Children Go Online: Final Report of Key Project Findings* as well as interim reports and media coverage.
WikEd – http://wik.ed.uiuc.edu/index.php/Kounin,_Jacob. A useful general education wiki site hosted by the University of Illinois – these pages detail the ideas of Jacob Kounin.

6 ASSESSMENT IN ICT

This chapter covers:

- the various uses of assessment in schools
- the principles of formative assessment (Assessment for Learning)
- preparing pupils for summative assessment
- considerations in tracking pupils and record-keeping.

In the recent past, ICT was arguably the least often formally assessed subject in school. While other subject teachers heaved suitcases of workbooks home to mark each night, some ICT teachers (and we include ourselves here) argued that we could not rely on pupils having access to a computer and that the homework we set (if we set it) was generally preparation for the next session. Much of the work in class time was project work of relatively long duration (five to seven weeks) and while ICT teachers ran around the class like a manic plate-spinner trying to keep the network from crashing and pupils on task, there was relatively little time for formative assessment and target-setting.

When the projects were complete teachers might first establish a ranked order and then begin to allocate (fairly arbitrary) marks along with written feedback which perhaps tended to emphasize presentation and quantity. Then it was time to move on to the next project. Learning happened in spite of these practices, and many pupils did very well in the high stakes world of GCSEs. And yet the profession has recognized the need to change for a number of related reasons.

First, there is strong evidence that effective assessment helps all children to learn and that its effect is disproportionately large when compared with other teaching innovations such as 'setting' or 'computers in classrooms' (Hattie, 1999). In addition, not only does it seem that all children benefit, but that children at most risk of failing have the most to gain from effective assessment practices.

Second, while it must be the case that there were pockets of excellent practice in ICT assessment, there had been issues raised over time at a national level, highlighted by the implementation of the Key Stage 3 National Strategy: 'Assessment in ICT, both formative and summative, is a weakness. It is unsatisfactory in two thirds of the schools. ... Assessment is often cursory. Teachers do not, in the main, have good systems for monitoring the progress of pupils or involving them, actively and positively, in developing their capability' (Ofsted, 2004: 46).

Undoubtedly assessment in ICT has moved on and there is some excellent practice in schools. This chapter aims to give beginning teachers the tools to continue this improvement in their own classes.

USES OF ASSESSMENT

All assessment should enable us to measure our performance against a target standard. The idea of 'assessment' for most of us probably means some kind of examination, either written or practical, like a driving test. The image that comes to mind when you think of teacher assessment may be those red-penned comments 'V. Good' or the neat rows and columns of a teacher's mark-book meticulously filled with indecipherable codes. As ICT teachers we may also think of assessment in terms of computer-based tests and tasks. More important than these visible manifestations of assessment are the day-to day and sometimes minute-by-minute assessments that teachers use to inform their teaching, such as questioning and verbal feedback.

In Chapter 4 we discussed how Benjamin Bloom sought to move assessment away from directly comparing people's performance against other people in a cohort, instead comparing them against a set of objective criteria. The former situation uses norm-referenced criteria and the latter criterion-referenced criteria. In the world of work, these distinctions can be blurred – think of a job interview, applicants are judged against a person specification which is (mostly) criterion referenced, but the final decision is usually made by comparing applicants against each other which is a norm-referenced (competitive) process.

The term 'assessment' is so broad it can be difficult to tackle the subject meaningfully. Therefore let us subdivide the world of assessment into the areas of summative and formative assessment.

Assessment which takes place at the end of a learning experience and summarizes our attainment at that point is usually referred to as 'summative' assessment. This kind of assessment often will not tell us how to improve our performance (think of GCSE results – a single grade with no meaningful feedback). In general terms, summative assessment is useful to people who are external to the learning process; for example, employers, or university admissions tutors who take grades into account when making decisions about a candidates 'suitability' for a role or course. They may also be used as a controversial mechanism for judging the effectiveness of organizations like schools.

In contrast 'formative assessment' is a form of feedback loop which takes place during the learning process. It provides information about what we need to do to achieve a learning objective and how to progress once we have met it. Formative assessment takes place in the minute-by-minute interactions which take place in the classroom. Figure 6.1 illustrates the differences between these two forms of assessment.

Type of assessment	Formative assessment	Summative assessment
Examples	Sharing criteria Questioning Teacher feedback Self-evaluation	Coursework Examinations
Purpose	Helps children: • understand how to do well in a task • understand how to improve their performance • set targets and keep on track with their work. Helps parents understand how to help their child. Helps teachers: • understand children's needs • improve their lessons.	Helps employers/admissions tutors judge competence in a subject. Helps school managers/governors compare their relative performance against other schools. Fulfils statutory reporting requirements. Provides information at transition points, e.g. Year 6 SAT results moving into Year 7. May form the basis of streaming and setting.

Figure 6.1 Distinctions between formative and summative assessment

FORMATIVE ASSESSMENT (ASSESSMENT FOR LEARNING)

the process of seeking and interpreting evidence for use by learners and their teachers to decide where the learners are in their learning, where they need to go and how best to *get there*. (Assessment Reform Group, 2002: 2)

Transforming recommendations informed by good research evidence into almost ubiquitous classroom practice is difficult if not impossible. Yet the practices embedded in formative assessment are on the right path to achieve this. While the central ideas have been described before this period, the work conducted by the Assessment Reform Group (ARG) and particularly the publication of 'Inside the black box' (Black and Wiliam,1998) served to provide a unified, coherent and lucid message which spoke to educators and policy-makers alike. The document does such a good job of defining the issues and summarizing the findings that we will not repeat them here – see References. The overwhelming weight of evidence by many researchers including Black, Wiliam and Hattie indicates that formative assessment can produce some of the most powerful positive learning effects of any intervention we may choose to make as teachers.

Subsequent work including that by members of the ARG and teachers in schools shows how the recommendations have been developed into practical classroom strategies (see Black et al., 2003).

Reflection Point 6.1

Read 'Inside the black box' (Black and Wiliam, 1998).

1. What methodology was used?
2. What is an 'effect size'?
3. What value of effect size has a significant impact upon learning outcomes?
4. What are the key recommendations of the report?
5. What are the most significant deficiencies in 'current practice'?
6. How persuasive do you find the report? Have key decision-makers taken notice?

Formative assessment is fundamentally concerned with teaching children how to be independent learners and to move the balance away from teacher-talk and towards learning. Given a situation where an expert is on hand, most of us will take the easiest route and rely on the expert to tell us what to do. If you do not believe us imagine you are trying to assemble flat-pack furniture, the instructions are nonsensical and your next-door neighbour is an expert at DIY – what would you do? In your classroom your pupils are faced with the same situation: they can figure out how to sort out the problem themselves (eventually), but there is the expert standing right over there! How tempting to just put a hand up and call for help, especially if the teacher always tells us what to do, rather than say asking a question. We need to encourage pupils to understand the task, ask questions, self-assess their work and act on feedback. See the companion website, www.sagepub.co.uk/secondary, video clip *Independence* to hear a teacher discussing his experience of this.

In this section we look at four of the key principles behind Assessment for Learning and how they can be used by ICT teachers.

Agreeing and sharing assessment criteria

In Chapter 4, we discussed the problems of embarking upon an activity without being clear about what you are looking for in pupils' work (and how this meets the learning objectives). Not only do all children perform better when assessment criteria are clear, those pupils who would be lower academic achievers make even greater gains than their peers; for example, see White and Frederiksen (1998).

Why do pupils who are potentially lower achievers stand to gain so much? Simply put, all pupils need to understand what is required to do well in a task ('the game we are playing'). Potentially higher achievers can make inferences about this from past work and clues the teacher offers, sometimes without thinking. They are also more likely to be confident in questioning the teacher to clarify assessment requirements. Potentially lower achievers may not yet be able to make these links and stand most to gain when we take what is implied and make it absolutely explicit.

ICT tasks can offer pupils a huge range of choices in how to carry out their work. Imagine a science lesson where pupils have free reign of the laboratory, can choose any apparatus, chemicals and so on in order to do an experiment – most likely chaos would ensue. Yet this is analogous to the situation in ICT where we provide complex software with many functions which are redundant to the task in hand. One reason why defining and sharing assessment criteria is so important in ICT is that it gives pupils a sense of how best to spend their time – instead of changing the colours of their fonts, they may be more likely to be successful if they printed and annotated their spreadsheet formulae.

Let us turn our attention to practicalities. Imagine you want to assess this learning objective:

1. *Pupils can identify a range of web page design features and can explain why the designer has chosen to use them for the target audience.*

We will give pupils a number of website addresses and ask them to take and annotate screenshots. They will then label the features they think are important and suggest a justification of why the designer used them for their anticipated audience.

Working through a task before giving it to children can illuminate what is most important in terms of assessment criteria. Another helpful strategy is to look back at work that previous groups of children have produced on a similar (or the same) task.

If you run this task with a class with no assessment criteria or guidance, you will encounter a whole range of responses. Figure 6.2 demonstrates the different ways in which responses may vary, providing examples from both ends of the potential ability spectrum.

What we have done here is to identify the criteria that we might use to judge whether the learning objective has been met. In fact, the same kinds of criteria can apply in many ICT projects, although we may weight the importance of the elements differently (see Chapter 4 for the same types of criteria in a different context).

This idea of using contrasting examples is very powerful in illustrating to you and your students what is important in a task – and, consequently, how to do well. In fact, in the previous task we can use the idea of contrast in two distinct ways. First we can present pupils with contrasting examples of websites (good and poor) so that they can begin to understand the design, function and content requirements for a website which meets the needs of an audience. Second, we can give them contrasting examples of previous pupils' responses to the task – we can show a low-quality piece of work (with all the responses shown in the second column in Figure 6.2) and a high-quality piece of work (with the third-column's responses). If we ask them to say why one is better than another, they will come up with the same kinds of assessment criteria we have identified – what is more, they will genuinely *understand* the assessment criteria – they will know what 'good' (and 'poor') looks like.

Variations in...	Example response – least successful	Example response – most successful
Volume / completeness	Single word answer	All features identified, labelled and justified
Subdividing content, design and functionality as three separate elements	'I like this website – it's all about my football team.' (content only)	'On the first screenshot I have labelled all of the design features. On the second screenshot I have labelled how the navigation works. This list shows the content covered and what I would add ...'
Use of subject-specific terms	'It's really eye catching and full of bright colours.'	'The designer used white space to separate the three main ideas on the page.' 'The graphic logo is repeated on each page in the same location for consistency ...'
Awareness of audience	'It's good because it tells you everything you need to know about gardening.'	'Features important for gardeners would be: Design: Photographs of plants – so they can make choices about what to buy. Content: Information about planting conditions and how big they grow. Functions: A way to search for plant names. Links to shops which sell seeds.'
Balanced thinking – evaluation	'I think it's really good.'	'These elements match the needs of the audience ..., but there could be these improvements ...'
New thinking/ research/ creativity	Response does not go beyond the teacher's direct guidance.	I found out that this site uses animated GIFs – these can be displayed in any browser, without installing plug-ins.

Figure 6.2 Possible variations in pupil response

In setting assessments, be mindful that there are two categories of information that children need. The first, 'What do I need to do?', is the one that they will ask readily; this is the detail of what to produce, how many pages, deadline date and so on. The second, 'How do I do well in this task?', is much less frequently asked, and usually only by potentially higher-achieving pupils. This *quality* criteria needs to be our focus (and makes up the majority of what we have identified in Figure 6.2).

Now that we have identified, agreed and shared our assessment criteria with children, we need to publish it in a way that makes it accessible throughout the project. Posters and/or worksheets are good ways to do this (alongside reminders on the whiteboard at key points during our lessons). In this way we are constantly referring back to the criteria and, alongside informal feedback, children can readily see what they have achieved and how they can improve – the beginnings of self-assessment. If we have done this correctly there should be no surprises when we come to formally assess the work, for them or us.

To summarize the steps we have described in sharing assessment criteria:

1. Work through the proposed task to identify what is important in achieving the learning objective. It helps to imagine a 'best' and 'worst' response (Figure 6.2). Look at examples of how pupils have performed on this task previously.
2. Prepare contrasting examples to help pupils understand the criteria, usually:
   (a) example pupil responses – best vs worst
   (b) where appropriate, you can also use real-world examples, for example a good website vs a poor website.
3. Give pupils an activity which asks them to identify the differences between the results.
4. Take and clarify their feedback, and fill in any gaps so that you produce a set of defined quality criteria.
5. Clarify the production criteria – hand in requirements, deadlines and so on.
6. Publish the production and quality criteria – handouts, displays, slides.
7. Constantly refer back to criteria through peer/self/teacher feedback.

This basic approach can, of course, be refined to present students with a broader range of possible responses to a task, this can be particularly helpful in explaining differences in grade boundaries in summative assessment, for example National Curriculum attainment levels or examination board coursework criteria. In these cases, it helps to provide a table of the level or grade boundary descriptors and ask pupils to apply a 'best-fit' model for a given piece of work – they can then moderate grades in small groups (also see 'Coursework', in this chapter). See companion website, www.sagepub.co.uk/secondary, video clip, *e-portfolio,* to hear a teacher's analysis of how he might improve a lesson using this approach.)

Questioning

Teachers spend a great deal of their working lives asking questions. The most obvious reason we do this is to assess pupils' knowledge and uncover misconceptions. Effective questioning engages pupils and improves their achievement. Teacher questioning is not just concerned with finding out what pupils already know – it is a teaching technique which can help children integrate new knowledge with their pre-existing experiences as in this example:

Scenario

Teacher: Displaying a picture of a basket of supermarket products. 'Hands-up, can anyone tell me what the packaging of these products has in common?'
Pupil: 'They are all colourful.'
Teacher: 'True, think about the information they have.'
Pupil: 'Ingredients.'
Teacher: 'Many do, but only the food. Think about what helps the checkout person. Hands up, remember.' PAUSES until almost all hands are up.

(Continued)

(Continued)

Pupil: 'The stripy pattern – code thing that they scan.'
Teacher: 'Excellent – anyone know it's proper name?'
Pupil: 'Bar code, Miss.'
Teacher: 'Well done. Bar codes have a scanner-readable stripy pattern which represents the number printed underneath. There are four pieces of information coded into that long number; for example, the first digits tell us which country the goods were packed in – 50 is the UK; when you go home tonight, have a look in the cupboard and see how many begin with 50. What do you think that the other three pieces of information are that you could read from a bar code?'
Pupil: 'How much it costs.'
Teacher: 'OK, Kevin, you've suggested that price is included in the product bar code – can you tell us why?'
Pupil: 'Miss, the cashier scans the product and the price appears on the till.'
Teacher: 'That's exactly how it works, well done, but think about this – if the price was coded in the bar code, what would the store have to do when the price of beans is reduced from 29p to 27p?'
Pupil: 'They'd have to stick new bar codes on. Doesn't the till look up the price from a computer?'
Teacher: Writes 'Lookup' on the board. 'Kevin, you are a genius! Lookup is exactly the term that computer programmers use.'

The idea that price is coded in the bar code is a common misconception, it is almost always the first guess pupils make. Anticipating this, the teacher in this example does not correct the answer – they use it to pose another question which leads to understanding. This embedding or integration of new knowledge with existing experience is more meaningful and memorable than teacher talk per se – 'Bar codes contain four pieces of data, they are country code' (and so on).

Questioning is also often used as a low-level behaviour management technique to refocus individuals who are not participating fully – this is a very useful technique. However we must be wary of the perception that we are 'picking on' pupils. If they cannot answer we should scaffold the questioning so that they can arrive at a response. Consider the difference between the following interactions aimed at a distracted pupil:

Scenario

Teacher: 'Kelsey, what kind of validation could we apply to Date of Birth?'
Pupil: 'Don't know, Miss.'
Teacher: 'Why don't you know?'
           Pupil shrugs.
Teacher: 'I'll tell you why young lady, you weren't listening when you should have been. Now let's ask someone who was listening.'

Kelsey may be repeating this kind of interchange in all of her subjects, and her strategy of avoidance works. She would rather be seen as 'difficult' than 'stupid'. In this next example the teacher gives Kelsey a concrete example, time to think and most importantly has an expectation that she will answer. A behaviour intervention thus becomes a learning intervention.

Scenario

Teacher: 'Kelsey, what kind of validation could we apply to Date of Birth?'

Pupil: 'Don't know, Miss.'

Teacher: 'OK – remember that validation means "reasonable". Imagine a new member wants to join our gym, and you are taking their details and typing in their date of birth. What kinds of errors might you make which the computer could detect and beep to warn you?'

Pupil: 'I might accidently type a letter.'

Teacher: 'OK, so it could check that the type of data is correct – only numbers are allowed. Anything else?'

Pupil: 'I might put in the wrong date.'

Teacher: 'That's true, and validation won't detect all dates that are wrong, so what kinds of dates of birth would be UNREASONABLE?'

Pupil: 'If it was a date that made them a young kid – they have to be 14 or older to join.'

Teacher: 'Excellent – that would be a range check. We can apply those to numbers – including dates. Can anyone expand on Kelsey's answer by giving some other examples of unreasonable dates?'

Kelsey is left in no doubt that, first, she will always be expected to come up with an answer – there is no easy way out. Second, it is OK to be unsure or wrong – the teacher will help her through it. In the second example, Kelsey receives immediate positive feedback, not only has she participated, she also experiences satisfaction and is more likely to participate next time.

Creating an atmosphere where children feel they can 'have a go' and make mistakes is critical to effective learning. Overuse of (factual) questioning to confirm (mis)understanding and as a behaviour management technique combined with the uncertainties of adolescence can lead to avoidance of participation. This can be exacerbated where teachers rely on 'hands-up' as a questioning technique where questions become predominated by a vocal and confident minority. Therefore we must understand and plan the structure of **HOW** we ask questions (the structure) as well as **WHAT** we ask – the content.

Question content

This section concentrates on the second most common teacher activity after teacher explanation – oral questioning. Planning and analysing the questions we want to ask is time well spent. It is impossible to plan every question you will pose during a lesson, but key questions can be mapped out in advance. Clear and precise language is important. Common pitfalls in the phrasing of questions include asking and answering a question, allowing insufficient time to answer, rephrasing or switching questions part way through and playing 'guess what I'm thinking' – all of these are embodied in the following fairly typical example: 'When computers are joined together, it's called a [pauses] n, n, net. Nobody? It's called a network. So why would we want to join computers together? What ways might we use to communicate?'

Many teacher-training texts advocate asking 'higher-level' questions more frequently in order to elicit higher-level thinking. There is undoubtedly merit in this approach. However, as Cotton (1988) and others have pointed out what makes a type of question work is highly dependent on context, both in terms of the subject matter and the learner's background. What is most important is matching the question content to the subject and the learner's needs, while striving to move their thinking on to higher levels. So for example younger (or less advanced) learners who need some factual knowledge before they can begin a topic may demonstrate good achievement through the use of closed, recall-type questions before they can tackle some higher level discussion-type questions. Very often we will want to use a combination of graduated question levels. Chapter 8 explores the typical issues and question types you may want to consider for each broad age range. 'In most classes above the primary grades, a combination of higher and lower cognitive questions is superior to exclusive use of one or the other' (Cotton, 1988).

What does 'higher level' actually mean? Many authors use Bloom's taxonomy (Chapter 4) to illustrate the progression from factual recall questions which tend to be closed through to more speculative or evaluative open questions. There is certainly good evidence that increasing the use of higher-level questions has a number of significant benefits, when learners are ready and the subject material demands it:

> For older students, increases in the use of higher cognitive questions (to 50 per cent or more) are positively related to increases in:
>
> - on-task behavior
> - length of student responses
> - the number of relevant contributions volunteered by students
> - the number of student-to-student interactions
> - student use of complete sentences
> - speculative thinking on the part of students
> - relevant questions posed by students. (Cotton, 1988)

Be aware that your own perception of pupils can influence the kinds of questions you ask – which in turn can feed back into your perception of that pupil. Typically children identified as having lower potential academic achievement are those most likely to be asked low-level questions. Yet when these pupils practise higher-level questions the self-fulfilling prophecy is broken and teacher expectations increase.

As an example of the different levels of questions, Figure 6.3 identifies some questions which could be asked during an ICT lesson and how these might be arranged against Anderson and Krathwohl's (2001) update of Bloom's taxonomy.

Bloom's taxonomy	Question strategies	Example questions
Creating	Hypothesizing about an unfamiliar scenario. Drawing together several strands of information. Making cognitive jumps from specific instances to generalized principles. Identifying what's important and prioritizing.	An electromagnetic pulse bomb stops all computers working in your town. What are the effects today, in a week, in a month? Looking at the data we've collected using the simulation, the Internet information and eyewitness reports explain why you think the rocket exploded. Given that we know how to draw a triangle, square and hexagon, write a general procedure to draw any polygon. In pairs, decide on the features which should be included in our website. We'll then discuss and compile a storyboard as a class. Be prepared to justify your decisions.
Evaluating	Asking a question from an unusual standpoint. Asking pupils to identify and then apply criteria. Justifying decisions made. Evaluating peers'/own work. Seeking additional evidence.	Many hackers think that they provide a valuable service – why might this be? Looking at leaflets you have collected, produce a list of criteria for judging their effectiveness ranked in order of importance. Given the survey responses about your website, what would you change and why? What would you do differently given more time/resources? Rank your sources of information from most to least reliable and explain why. Explain what information you did not have that would have been useful.
Analysing	Providing evidence to support a statement. Asking pupils to analyse real-world situations. Explaining the advantages and disadvantages.	'Computers have improved our lives.' Explain how you would persuade someone to your point of view. Given the user's list of needs, produce a specification. Looking at the data you have collected, explain what kind of graph will be most useful. Change the temperature variable in the model then note down what other values change – now can you work out the rule?
Applying	Explain how to: demonstrate to the class. make appropriate choices. write a user guide. predict what would happen if . . .	Choose the most appropriate software for producing a poster. How could you change your web page so it is suitable for parents? Explain what we would have to change to make the turtle draw a pentagon. What would happen to water consumption in the model if we switched from a 20-minute bath every 4 days to a 10-minute shower every 2 days?
Understanding	Transforming information into another form. Tell me in your own words. Is this the same as . . .? Choose the best definition. Summarize this paragraph. State in X words. Which statements support . . .?	Using these keywords, write 5 reasons that explain why we might choose a desktop publishing package to produce a leaflet. Explain in your own words why a plain, coloured background is better for our audience than a patterned one. From the list of software features, choose those that are important for a flight simulator.

(Continued)

Figure 6.3   (Continued)

Bloom's taxonomy	Question strategies	Example questions
Remembering	Closed questions Who? Where? Which one? When? Multiple choice Closed exercises	Which software creates records? How often should we save our work? What is a 'turtle'? Come up to the front and label the key features.

Figure 6.3 Relating the question level to a taxonomy of learning

Reflection Point 6.2

Using one of your lesson plans, identify opportunities for using questioning to enhance learning. Consider the questions you might ask and try to match them against Bloom's taxonomy.

Alternatively during an observed lesson ask the observer to count the number of questions you ask in each category of the taxonomy.

Use Bloom's taxonomy resource on the website to help you (Chapter 4).

Higher-level questions provide opportunities for (and are enriched by) classroom discussion. These questions and the ensuing discussion enable pupils to begin to construct their own learning, as in this example:

Scenario

Pupils searched the Internet for information on current environmental issues. They then formed a hypothesis that they and their peers are more concerned about global warming than adults. Pupils designed questionnaires and used these to collect data from family and friends on environmental issues. They have collated the results using a database and have produced reports analysing the results.

Teacher: 'Everyone should have created their reports and you should have completed the worksheet with your results. I want you to think back to our original hypothesis which is on the board. Now, looking at the data we've collected using our questionnaires, how does this data support or disprove our original hypothesis which was based on the information we found on the Internet? Take five minutes to look at your results and report and then discuss your thoughts with the person next to you about whether there is sufficient evidence that our hypothesis was correct.'

Five minutes later, the class feed back:

Teacher: 'Right, Sharon and Thea, what are your thoughts?'
Sharon: 'Well, my data supports what we thought at the start, but Thea's doesn't.'
Teacher: 'Why might that be? Thea?'
Thea: 'Erm, I don't know, I guess maybe my family are more worried than Sharon's.'
Sharon: 'Yeah, it's not really enough, is it, Sir? I mean, I've only asked a few people, the same as Thea. If I asked more people I might get a different answer.'
Thea: 'Right! We need to know what everyone else has found out too.'
Teacher: 'So, what may be the best way of doing that?'
Thea: 'Don't know ...'
Teacher: 'Have a think about it and we'll come back to it in a few minutes.'

This question enables pupils to engage on a number of levels: initially pupils may just look for the answer (is the hypothesis supported or not?), but through discussion with peers and further questioning by the teacher, they can start to analyse and evaluate both their results and the information on which their original hypothesis was built. They can then identify methods to strengthen their research. Key to this process is the teacher asking the right question and then allowing pupils time to think.

Not all higher-level questions fit neatly into a structure like Bloom's taxonomy. As with planning objectives, use your own professional judgement and the views of your teacher colleagues to guide you. Here are some examples of the big questions you can use to spark discussion in ICT:

- How will ICT change our lives over the next decade?
- Should all information be available to the public? If not, who should decide? How can information be kept private?
- What are the differences between online and physical communities?
- Is artificial life possible? Can computers think/learn?
- Why is communicating via the Internet so much cheaper than communicating via telephone?
- Does ICT create a digital divide between rich, poor, educated, uneducated?
- Where has all the processing power gone – processing power has grown exponentially, what are people using all this extra power for?
- How have computers changed the entertainment industry?
- Does ICT help people be better citizens?
- Does computer-controlled surveillance help keep us safe or invade our privacy?

Question structure

In trying to manage behaviour, remember your place in a lesson plan, deal with unanticipated questions and engage children – this is a tricky task, even for experienced teachers. The more you can plan in advance, the better. Many beginning teachers do plan the content of their questions, often highlighting them on the lesson plan. Yet sometimes the level of response to their well-planned questions can be lacklustre. The temptation at this point may be to move towards more teacher talk and less discussion. In our experience, however, the solution is to plan the structure of questioning in terms of how you will ask the question, what you will ask pupils to do and how you will take the feedback.

There are specific questioning strategies you can use to increase participation (Figure 6.4). Alongside these there are some general techniques and principles that you can use in any question sequence.

Wait time

The average time which teachers wait between asking a question and either moving on or answering it themselves is less than a second. This is an astonishing fact. We need to train ourselves and our pupils that questioning is not like other social interactions where a silent pause may be uncomfortable or awkward; in fact, a pause affords valuable thinking time.

For low-level factual recall questions a wait time of around three seconds is correlated with optimum performance. For higher-level questions there appears to be no upper limit – the longer you wait the more frequently pupils generate a better quality, more considered and complete answer (Cotton, 1988).

Increasing wait time is yet another strategy which particularly helps potentially lower-achieving pupils. Typically, teachers allocate less wait time to such students (perhaps because they do not want them to feel uncomfortable). Yet when wait time is increased these pupils participate more and teacher expectations of them also increase (Cotton, 1988).

When teachers increase their wait time they can feel uncomfortable at first. Time perception shifts when you are the centre of attention and three seconds can feel like 15 seconds for both the teacher and the student. You can manage this transition to longer wait times by explaining to children how questioning is going to be a little different and why. You could even ask for their help in reminding you and each other of the three-second-plus rule.

There are two components of wait time – the pause between you asking the question and the pupil formulating an answer. Then there is the time between their response and your reaction and feedback. Give yourself a few seconds to pause, consider their response and formulate what you will say.

Fielding responses: probing, redirection, praise and coaching

The most important advice we can give in responding to questions is to listen, really listen to pupils' responses. There are many occasions when we have observed beginning teachers who have missed a pupil's interesting, often insightful comment because it did not match the answer they were expecting. First, use wait time to understand their response. If there is any possibility of misunderstanding, repeat your interpretation back to them. If things are still not clear, ask for them to use different words or give an example. Once you (and the class) are clear, consider your response. If your question

Strategy	Uses	Watch out for
Handsup The most ubiquitous questioning technique – a default which is easily over used.	When gauging whole-class and individual understanding and participation levels. Voting for options.	Accepting calling out – insist on handsup. Fairness in selecting respondents. Non-participation.
Targeted Pupils do not raise their hands, but are selected by the teacher – often paired with other strategies in this table.	You want to increase class engagement – pupils expect to be asked. You want to target an ability range of pupils in order to gauge the understanding of the whole class.	Over-targeting stronger (or weaker) pupils. Avoidance tactics – *'I don't know'* is a cue for teacher scaffolding, not moving on to someone else.
Think – pair – share Pupils are given time to answer a question on their own, then to share their answer with a partner, finally feedback is taken from one or more of the pairs.	Introducing group work in a manageable and structured way. Giving pupils an opportunity to practice their answers before speaking to the class.	Jumping straight to paired talking without the initial (silent) individual thinking. Do not overestimate the time required – 1 minute for a straightforward topic can be sufficient. Longer periods can lead to unfocused discussion.
Round-robin Teacher asks each member of the class in turn. E.g. *'I will be the turtle – each of you in turn will give me an instruction so that I walk in a complete square.'*	Where answers are short and there are many possible answers or where you need to develop a sequence of instructions.	Overlong responses – a class of 30 with 30 second responses uses up 15 minutes.
Hot-seating and role play One or more members of the class answer questions in character (often as an expert). They may be supported by a team of pupil 'advisers' who can pass notes or help prepare an answer. Questions may be prepared and given to the 'expert' in advance. E.g. *'Grace is our Internet safety expert today and she'll be answering your questions about how to stay safe online.'*	Fostering a collaborative working atmosphere. Providing strong motivation for in-depth research, both for the 'expert' and the 'audience'. Summarizing learning.	Lack of participation by those not in the hot-seat – ask everyone to prepare a question. Pupils who like the idea, but find the pressure uncomfortable – coach, support and be prepared to end the exercise if they show signs of discomfort.
Snowballing As with think-pair-share, but then pairs link up to agree a composite answer, groups can continue to combine as appropriate.	Summarizing and sharing the whole-class learning. Can be used to uncover areas of disagreement or pupil misconceptions.	Movement issues – it can be a good idea to use collaborative software to produce a virtual snowball. Can become repetitive if answers are straightforward. Manage timings carefully.

(Continued)

Figure 6.4 (Continued)

Strategy	Uses	Watch out for
Experts Each pupil, (or small group) is to become an expert, answering a particular question. Groups first record their own thoughts, then visit every other group to both seek answers to their own question and to offer their perspectives on the other groups' questions. Each group reports back to the class.	Splitting up a complex task into manageable sub-areas. Providing focus and sustains interest during feedback because each group has a different area or task. Encouraging the ability to sift and summarize information.	Each switch should become progressively faster as groups discount duplicate ideas.
Jigsaw/combination questions Different groups are given different questions, or different aspects of the problem to examine. This approach works well when combined with Edward de Bono's 'Six-thinking Hats' technique or Tony Ryan's ' Thinker's Keys'.	Encouraging balanced analysis and debate, e.g. where one group look at positive opportunities whilst others look at negative aspects and potential pitfalls.	Feedback from groups will take time – may be a good idea to span two lessons and ask them to prepare a visual cue, e.g. presentation slide or flipchart page to provide a focus.
Individual white boards Pupils record their answers on an A4-sized plastic board using dry-wipe pens. They hold them up for all / the teacher to see.	Ensuring full participation. Allowing the teacher to take feedback without necessarily attributing it to a pupil –'I can see 5 or 6 of you have the wrong end of the stick about this…' Providing a level playing field – all answer the question without having to speak out.	Can be difficult to summarize very different responses. Handwriting needs to be legible. When asking several questions, don't forget to provide cloths to wipe the boards in-between.
Quick quiz **True or false**	Confirming factual understanding, establishing baseline knowledge. Often most effective part-way through a topic, to inform future learning.	In a verbal quiz, be aware that the pressure of Q&A can cause individuals to under-perform, don't pounce – always use thinking time. In a written quiz – over-reliance on a mark to represent learning – pupils should have an opportunity to repeat the quiz or do follow up work to demonstrate improvement.
Sequencing/ranking/categorizing Pupils are given terms (usually on card) to sequence, rank or categorize.	Can be used for a range of questions from simple (single correct answer) through to complex evaluative questions with many possible responses.	Pupils copying each other's responses (because responses are visible on desks).

Figure 6.4 (Continued)

Strategy	Uses	Watch out for
Opinion line Teacher gives two ends of a spectrum of opinion and places these at two points in the classroom. Pupils place themselves on a line between these points to represent their personal opinion. The teacher asks individuals to explain their position and 'undecided pupils' can swap places on the line as they are persuaded.	Refreshing attention spans – everyone gets up and moving. Developing evaluative skills and ability to justify and persuade – provides a very visual way of experiencing how persuasive you have been. Alternatively, teacher can present new material to see if the class can be persuaded to move from one position to another.	Teacher positioning – it can be difficult to see the whole line at once. Pupils standing in friendship groups – probe their opinions and move them if necessary.
Traffic lights/thumbs up Pupils indicate their response by holding up a traffic light colour or thumbs up/down or to the side.	A quick way of gauging whole-class confidence or progress in a task. Helps when forming mixed-ability groups – 'Greens and ambers work together, reds work with the teacher.'	Using this method exclusively – use follow up questions to confirm whether individuals' confidence is well founded and also to identify why pupils are indicating a lack of confidence.
Games-based questions There are many templates available for traditional games such as crosswords as well as those based on board games (e.g. Taboo) or television quiz shows (e.g. Family Fortunes, Countdown and Who Wants to be a Millionaire?)	Motivating and reward a class. Asking pupils to make their own from the blank template to provide good opportunities for further research and demonstrating subject understanding.	Overuse – pupils do enjoy these games, but unless they make their own, they are probably only providing recall level questions.

Figure 6.4 Strategies for structuring questions

has only a correct or incorrect response, your opportunities for feedback may be severely limited. In this example, the structure of the question and the way the teacher responds puts the pupil in a position of 'guess what I am thinking':

Scenario

'So can you tell me, Michael – is a 'range check' validation or verification?'

'Verification?'

Teacher raises eyebrows.

'I mean validation.'

'Excellent, a range check is a type of data validation.'

The teacher could of course have probed Michael's understanding further, to understand whether he understands the terms and has mixed them or has a misconception:

> **Scenario**
>
> 'So can you tell me, Michael – is a 'range check' validation or verification?'
>
> 'Verification?'
>
> 'OK, can you tell me what the difference between the two is?'
>
> 'Verification is where you check the answer is realistic and validation is the one where you double-check the data.'
>
> 'You've done a really good job of explaining the difference, but you have swapped the words around. What did we say was an easy way to remember?'
>
> 'Not sure, Miss.'
>
> 'OK, I am going to give everyone one minute to come up with a way of remembering which way round they go.'

Notice how the teacher's probing of Michael's understanding is very focused, she is not just saying 'No that's not right, try again'. The teacher now knows Michael has the correct understanding, just incorrect recall. She uses praise to reinforce Michael's achievement and to signal to the class that a thoughtful answer is at least as important as being 'right'. At the end of the sequence she redirects the question to the class. We can also give the pupil the option to redirect – 'Would you like to ask a classmate to help you out?', although if we do this we need to ensure that the target pupil will be expected to answer the question later – perhaps in the plenary. Research suggests that redirection and probing are only effective when they are precise and focused as in this example.

Reflecting on this interchange the teacher could restructure the question for future classes to allow some thinking time, provide examples which do not rely on recall alone and use further questioning to clarify the answer.

> I'm going to give you one example of validation and one of verification. In pairs I want you to figure out in what ways they are similar and in what ways they are different then we'll work out a definition of each.

Alternatively, to provide a greater range of responses and good evidence of the depth of pupil understanding, the teacher could provide an even more open question:

> The answer is 'validation' so what is the question – I want three suggestions from each group.

Going back to the first example the teacher says Michael is 'Excellent'. What is she praising here – his ability to interpret not so subtle facial expressions? Frequent, vague or insincere praise devalues its use in pupils' eyes. There is a difference between being personable and approachable and saying that merely contributing is 'Excellent' or 'Brilliant' – save these superlatives for when they truly reflect what a pupil has achieved. Be specific in your praise so that they know what they did well – 'Sasha and Amy, I really liked what you said, instead of rushing to an answer you thought hard and balanced advantages with disadvantages.'

Opportunities for coaching (where we practise answers in advance) arise whenever a class have been asked to consider a question for a short period of time. The coaching can be subtle, as when a teacher listens to group discussion and helps clarify their thinking ready for feedback. Alternatively coaching can be explicit – working through an answer with an individual and practising the answer with them before asking them to respond a little later in front of the class. The latter approach works well with less confident learners as well as those with English as an additional language.

Body language

In the previous section we touched upon how teachers sometimes use body language and especially facial expression to communicate what they are really thinking. While we may seek to minimize those which give away an answer, there are a variety of techniques we can use to encourage responses:

- When a pupil is responding show attentive listening – smiling and head-nodding can be powerful signs of approval and encouragement.
- A palm held up or pointing to your ear can refocus a class who may be tempted to talk while a pupil is responding. The advantage here is you do not have to interrupt the pupil.
- Holding out both hands to indicate the whole class should respond or bringing palms together towards an individual you are targeting.
- Moving closer to an individual who is responding so that they do not have to raise their voice or repeat their answer.
- Pausing, nodding with a 'tell me more' hand gesture to indicate a more extended answer is required.
- Looking upwards to indicate that you are considering a response.

Summarizing answers

Usually, for anything more complex than routine factual questioning we will capture a summary of pupil responses. This communicates to pupils that their responses are valued and serves as a reminder of what has been said so answers are not duplicated. It also provides a visual cue we can use throughout the lesson and helps pupils whose attention may have wandered.

Where you are collecting together many responses you may like to try collaborative software such as discussion boards or shared applications such as Google Docs. Be aware though that there is a time overhead in setting up such systems, however, the end result can be excellent – especially where the results will be used by the class over several lessons.

Visual cues

Children's attention spans are generally shorter when they are asked only to listen to responses for an extended period. In the previous section we encountered capturing feedback as a visual cue to extend attention spans. We can use other cues to sustain attention:

- the question itself written on the board
- an associated image or animation
- flip-chart style feedback where groups hold up images they have drawn to help explain their answer
- relevant quotations
- graphs and charts
- interactive whiteboard tools – images to label, items to categorize or sequence, tables to populate with data.

Specific questioning strategies

Figure 6.4 outlines a small selection of specific strategies. There are many more excellent ideas (see the works of Petty, Ginnis and Ryan for more.) Whichever strategies you choose, it is important to know why that method is appropriate and to vary your choice to keep your teaching fresh. Do not forget to tell pupils the rules of the strategy, be consistent in applying them and clearly signal a change when switching from one strategy to another.

Reflection Point 6.3

Either take a topic you are planning to teach or choose one of these topics:

1. ICT allows the (fairly) unlimited copying of data. This raises new legal and moral issues and dilemmas.
2. Computer chips and their related information processing are embedded in every aspect of our lives.
3. ICT can reduce the amount of repetitive work people do – it can also create new tasks.
4. Computers can process data more quickly than the brain, but cannot (yet) replicate many of its functions.
5. ICT is integrated with and drives changes in society.
6. ICT allows people to work together in new ways.
7. Lack of access to ICT may result in inequalities.
8. ICT is a powerful tool, which allows people to manipulate information in ways that were previously impossible or time-consuming.
9. Modelling allows people to explore ideas and hypotheses.
10. Not all information is equally valid.

Plan a learning sequence which helps pupils understand the topic using *only questions* and visual cues. Your aim is that by the end of the activity you will ask 'what have you learned?' and pupils will tell you a version of the topic title (with examples).

Rules:

- Don't reveal the topic – start with a question.
- Make them think, no excessive teacher talk or telling – just guiding, probing, questioning.
- Use visual cues.
- Think about and plan the structure *and* content.

Reflection Point 6.4

Watch the Teachers' TV clip 'Too Much Talk'. List the questioning techniques that the teacher uses in the second lesson in order to promote and verify learning. What advice would you offer if he were to repeat the lesson?

Figure 6.5 shows how a teacher might construct a questioning sequence, taking into account the above factors.

Teacher talk/action	Rationale
Today we're going to answer questions in a different way. Reveal on board: • **10 seconds to think of an answer** • **No hands up – I'll go round the class in turn** • **Having a go is more important than being right**	Establish routine – wait time
Q. Why do the police store information about criminals? Q. Think about our local police station, before they had a computer, how did they store this information? Q. What problems may have been caused by having all criminal records on paper? *[record responses from all and list]*	Differentiated questions – varied challenge
OK, lets play higher or lower – Q. How many criminal records could we store on an average computer hard drive – say 200Gb? {A 800,000} Q. If a paper criminal file is 1 cm thick and we stacked them up, how far would they reach? {8000 meters – almost as high as Mount Everest!}	Change pace – increase participation
Reveal – 'Computer databases can store VAST amounts of information in a TINY amount of space.'	Exploration of possibilities through real-world examples
Q. What would be the best order to store this information so that they can find things quickly *[record responses from all: categorize and discuss – explain how the same information would have to be duplicated and categorized in different ways]*	
Q. Computers can perform complex searches – *show criminal database excerpt and pre-defined query* – Which criminals would be identified as suspects?	Identify limitations Widen context
Q. Did one of these criminals commit the crime?	
Q. What other databases do the police use to detect crime?	
Main task – constructing queries to solve crimes	
Plenary	
Q. Why might people object to their details being held by the police?	Contrasting viewpoint

Figure 6.5 Questioning in practice

Teacher feedback

In the opening paragraphs of the chapter we suggested that one of the images that may come to mind when considering assessment are those brief teacher comments, something like '10/10 V. Good' or '6/10 More detail next time'. In fact these comments are not effective in improving pupils' understanding and can actually be demotivating for all but the highest scorers.

Imagine for a moment that you are in a class learning to juggle in which the teacher demonstrates a juggling pattern and then asks everyone to attempt to duplicate what they have seen. What would the results be if the teacher simply allocated marks and gave vague messages – '6/10 Try harder', '7/10 Excellent effort', '4/10 Next time don't drop them'? Everyone might be interested in the rankings and those not scoring well would find their relative position demotivating – 'You got 8/10, why did I only get 6?' All but those with some prior knowledge or natural ability would very quickly become demotivated because there was no meaningful feedback which helped them close the learning gap between what they were doing and what they needed to do next. Much more useful feedback would analyse what they were doing and specific strategies in how to progress. 'You have the sequence right but are tending to throw the beanbags out in front of you, stand in front of a wall to practice.'

Ruth Butler designed a study (1987) which examined how pupils responded to different types of feedback in terms of their enjoyment and the assessed outcomes on a number of tasks. One group were given only marks, one group were given only comments and the third group were given marks and comments. You may expect the last group to have improved the most. In fact the counter-intuitive finding was that there was no effective difference between the first and last groups. In both of these groups those pupils with high marks said that they were interested in the tasks, those with low marks said that they were not. Overall both groups showed no learning gain. In the group which received only comments there was an average 30 per cent improvement in assessed outcomes and all pupils reported interest in the task. Why should this be? It is likely that groups that receive marks focus their efforts upon comparing their mark with their peers, the motivational impact this has (positive or negative) appears to overwhelm any positive effect the comments may have had. In short, if you are giving marks and comments on pupils' work (and expecting this to have an impact on their learning) you are wasting precious teacher time!

So far we have hopefully reached the conclusion that formative feedback is based around a comment or instruction which closes the learning gap between what a pupil can do at this point in time and what they need to do next to improve. What kind of comments should these be? Butler (1987) and Hattie and Timperley (2007) distinguish between feedback which is related to the task and that which is related to the person, self or ego.

It appears that feedback which focuses on the pupil rather than the task is least powerful and can have a negative effect where it is perceived as threatening. So comments such as 'Jason I know this isn't your best work, you need to come into class ready to work' can actually have the opposite effect. On the other hand, comments which focus on the task and process can have a powerful, positive influence on learning.

'Your spreadsheet produced the right answer and all the ticked formulae are correct, well done. Some of the formulae include values I'd like you complete the following –

1) My break-even point is _____
2) Change the price of a cup of coffee to 50p.
3) When I change the price of coffee my break-even point is _____
4) I therefore made this change to my formula in C2 _____
5) My break-even point is now _____.'

Write a sentence which explains why we use cell references in formulae rather than values.

Figure 6.6   Example of teacher feedback

Feedback becomes easier for the teacher when we have defined our assessment criteria clearly and we should make explicit links back to the criteria when feeding back on task performance. In addition to task performance it is also helpful to feed back on aspects of the process that the pupil undertook – what they did, how they did it and 'what next?' Feedback should usually direct pupils to do something specific; avoid the 'Think about …' opener, it is too vague. Putting this all together we may annotate a piece of work with a comment like that in Figure 6.6.

Writing good quality feedback is time-consuming. ICT teachers may see 300 pupils every week, so we need to be realistic in what we can achieve. Consider the following strategies to create some time for quality feedback:

- During on-task time give focused feedback and targets to a small group of pupils. Plan to focus on a different group each session.
- Use tracking systems to record targets from feedback – so that you can check that they have responded to what you have written.
- Use peer and self assessment alongside teacher assessment so that, for example, if you had three Year 9 groups you mark each groups' tasks in detail once every three weeks (in rotation). In between times you verify that they have completed peer or self assessment.
- Where many pupils are receiving the same comments and required improvements consider using pre-printed responses or task sheets.

Reflection Point 6.5

Many school marking policies require teachers to allocate an achievement and effort grade to all work. What is your view on this practice in light of the evidence presented in this chapter? Can an effort grade ever counterbalance a pupil who scores consistently poorly on achievement grading, and what might be the impact upon such a pupil's self-esteem?

Reflection Point

Peer and self evaluation

Giving children the skills to assess their own progress provides three significant benefits. First, knowing how you are doing and how to correct or improve your endeavours is a key skill in becoming an independent learner – once you can do this you are no longer wholly reliant upon the teacher. Second, you are engaged and focused upon the assessment criteria in a clear and explicit way. Third, as mentioned in the previous section, peer and self-assessment create space for the teacher to give focused assessment and feedback to individuals. The focus here is not on providing a mark. Instead, it is to help develop the skills to understand the assessment criteria and then use it to provide feedback which can be used to improve the work (see companion website, www.sagepub.co.uk/secondary video clip *E-portfolio,* to hear a teacher describing how this might be done).

Pupils need time to reflect on their work. In a busy curriculum it is easy to move swiftly from topic to topic without giving pupils adequate time to review and consolidate their learning, reflecting on what and how they have learnt.

Black et al. (2003) report that often when teachers tried to introduce self-assessment into their classroom the results could be disappointing. Partly this was because pupils did not have experience of using the criteria to think about what they needed to achieve and to plan next steps realistically. Also, even if pupils knew that there was a problem with the output, they could not necessarily diagnose where the problem lay in their thinking and how to correct it. Improving the clarity of assessment criteria and teacher feedback can help model to pupils the skills they need to self-assess. However it emerged that peer assessment is a significant route to, and possibly a prerequisite for, peer assessment.

We regularly see that our trainees are much better at critically evaluating each other's practice than their own. This is also true of children in school. This is partly because trying to perform a task and evaluate it at the same time is a difficult undertaking and because personality and self-image factors come to the fore when talking about ourselves. Peer assessment, carefully structured, is not burdened by these issues. Pupils who peer assess are generally honest and frank with each other, often in a way that teachers could not be! Some also find peer assessment less threatening than teacher assessment. The language pupils use with each other can seem more salient to them than teacher comments and so have a greater impact, and the rephrasing of assessment criteria in their own terms helps both parties' understanding. Pupils are also more likely to interrupt and clarify points rather than perhaps nodding along with the teacher. In addition, pupils are seeing the task from another's viewpoint which provides additional ideas and approaches for their own work.

 The following are the most common strategies used in both peer and self assessment; see the website for links to examples.

- *Traffic lights* – children label their work red, amber or green to illustrate how far they have travelled in meeting the criteria. Provides a quick means of identifying where teacher support is most needed, and is a useful precursor to more in-depth methods.
- *Learning logs or diaries* – there are many templates for these; some are generic while others are tailored to each activity. It is useful for pupil to always have them on the desks so that they, their peers and the teacher can record comments at key points.

- *Round robin* – pupils either pass printed work around in one direction or, more commonly, physically move from one computer to the next in unison. They record comments for each piece of work on a pre-prepared sheet – or even better on screen so they are not limited by the size of a textbox. This is repeated several times so that each piece of work has several comments.
- *Marking work* – against the agreed criteria, National Curriculum Attainment Targets or examination board specifications. This is an excellent way of ensuring pupils understand the criteria they are working towards.
- *Marking examination papers* – using a mark scheme. Often very effective part-way through a course – do not leave this until the end when there is not time for additional learning to take place.

Changing the ethos

Most ICT departments are implementing formative assessment practices. While the changes do take time to embed, you as a beginning teacher can contribute to this process. The change is one of ethos as well as practice, from infrequent summatively focused assessment to increasing use of planned collaborative in-lesson formative assessment. Teachers may worry about the views of pupils, headteachers, parents and Ofsted, for example in introducing innovations such as comment-only marking. Black et al. report that 'Students came to realize that the comments helped them in their future work' (p. 45). One teacher in the research commented: 'At no time during the first 15 months of comment-only marking did any of the students ask me why they no longer received grades' (p. 45) and furthermore,' […] neither parents, senior management teams nor OFSTED inspectors have reacted adversely. Indeed, the provision of comments to students helps parents to focus on and support the students' learning rather than focus on uninformed efforts to interpret a mark or grade and/or to simply urge their child to work harder' (Black et al., 2003: 46).

The evidence that formative assessment can have a powerful influence on learning outcomes is strong and robust. Teachers are developing approaches to harnessing the power of formative assessment in the classroom. Trainees who put this evidence to pragmatic use report learning gains for both their pupils and themselves, and in some cases are actually changing practices within schools.

SUMMATIVE ASSESSMENT

In this section we briefly look at summative assessment at Key Stage 3 before moving on to the high-stakes summative testing which typically occurs in secondary schools from ages 14 to 19.

Key Stage 3

At the time of writing Key Stage 3 is entirely internally assessed by teachers. Pupils are assessed against the National Curriculum (NC) Attainment Targets, taking into account a broad range of the ICT work they have completed. There is no requirement to report an attainment level until the end of the key stage, although some schools may choose to indicate a level on pupil reports each year.

How ICT departments generate these levels varies widely. In some schools a holistic judgement is made during Year 9, taking into account a portfolio of projects. This end-loads the teacher assessment burden and it may lead to key areas being overlooked which could have been rectified had they been spotted earlier. Another approach is to use a summative project alongside prior assessment records; this can be a good way of preparing pupils for Key Stage 4 coursework. It also gives them opportunities to plug any evidence gaps in their prior work. A final approach is to allocate a level whenever marking work throughout Key Stage 3 and then use a formula to aggregate these together. This is a thorough approach, but can be quite restrictive in terms of teacher flexibility. Also, it can become a tick-list type activity and is perhaps not in the spirit of the National Curriculum's holistic view of ICT capability. While it is essential that teachers plan with NC attainment levels in mind (see Chapter 4) it is not always useful to report a level when there may be wider learning issues for pupils to tackle.

Whichever approach is adopted in your school, the challenge remains that the attainment level criteria are open to a wide variety of interpretations and pupils' work is diverse in content, context and attainment. The QCA has published example pupil work in ICT for the 1999 NC programmes of study and will presumably do the same for the new programmes of study taught from September 2008 (levels first reported in 2011). It is good practice to moderate these grades across all teachers in an ICT department and, wherever possible, with other schools. Moderation is best tackled some time in advance of the reporting date so that, if there are differences of opinion, action can be taken to ensure groups are given equal opportunity to improve their level.

Key Stage 4

The qualifications picture in ICT is an ever-changing landscape. We here try to distil some practical advice based upon current qualifications in the full knowledge that such qualifications may have changed in a relatively short space of time.

All ICT qualifications include a relatively large component of coursework-based practice, with many also including an examination component.

Much emphasis is obviously given to preparing pupils for these high-stakes assessments, and because of this teaching key stage 4 and above can feel very different from teaching lower key stages. The teacher becomes something of an interpreter, translating the requirements of the course into activities which enable the learner to score well in examinations and coursework. Much has been written about how overemphasis on summative assessment outcomes can lead to surface learning or memorization rather than deeper understanding and integration. ICT perhaps has greater latitude than many subjects, with less focus on teaching to the test or ticking off very specific criteria because the idea of broad ICT capability often outweighs the need to know a body of specific 'facts' or very specific software skills. Much depends on the course chosen, with some offering open-ended assessment criteria while others use very specific competence-based work – we know which we prefer to teach!

Before we look at specific considerations in preparing trainees for summative assessment it is worth considering that summative assessments can be used as formative experiences. This can be by using past examination papers part-way through the course which helps reveal misconceptions and aids pupils in understanding the assessment criteria. The process of undertaking coursework offers many opportunities for peer and self assessment as well as interim teacher feedback – but always check the course regulations in advance, especially in 'controlled' assignments.

Just as pupils need to understand assessment criteria for a given project, so you as the teacher need to fully understand the assessment criteria applied by an award board. Published information is absolutely critical in this; all examination boards publish their course specifications (syllabuses) on their websites, together with other essential information. Sometimes there are several versions of these in use within one time period, so double-check the version that your pupils are entered for. Always go to the source, photocopies can have pages missing, or may have been updated and different teachers may have different interpretations of the standards, so do not rely on colleagues alone – but of course listen to their advice. You will find the following documents invaluable:

- course specification
- for examined subjects, past papers and mark schemes
- the chief examiner's reports – produced annually, particularly useful in highlighting what pupils have struggled with in the previous year
- example coursework projects – often with annotated marker's comments.

There is no substitute for attending award board meetings and training; here you will have the opportunity to discuss the course with examinations board staff who have written the specifications. These events can clarify questions about the syllabus and very often will provide you with sample material that you can use with your pupils to illustrate the differences between good and poor pieces of work. You will also have the chance to talk to fellow teachers, swap resource suggestions (hardware, software, websites and textbooks) and hear their ideas and approaches. These meetings inform your teaching practice and can make a difference to your pupils' final grades. It is also worth keeping up to date with online course forums where teachers share experiences of teaching and marking coursework, and any associated issues.

Examinations

Examinations are generally externally marked and so your role is straightforward in preparing pupils for the assessment. You can help pupils through your knowledge and interpretation of the examination criteria, teaching specific ICT theory and teaching revision and examination techniques.

In addition to the general preparation mentioned in the last section you can also do the following:

1. Plan specific revision sessions into your scheme of work.
2. Where there is more than one examination paper, be clear with pupils about what is tested in each part and what type of examination it is (multiple choice, short answer, extended answer or mixed). This is particularly important where the examinations are several days apart.

3. Prepare key definitions that the award board use/expect. Note that this can be very specific, some award boards may give marks for 'digital projector' and 'temperature sensor', but not 'projector' or 'temperature probe'. Be aware that brand names are *not* marked, for example, it must be 'spreadsheet' not 'Excel'.

4. Review any recommended textbooks.

5. Locate suitable revision sources including online and practice software (see website, www.sagepub.co.uk/secondary, for links).

6. Use past examination papers with mark schemes and examiners' reports in your revision sessions – it is often a good idea to try a past paper yourself before looking at the mark scheme. Peer marking of questions is a good revision technique.

7. Consider becoming an examiner – most boards require one to two years teaching experience.

8. Try to anticipate and teach how the same concept may be used in a variety of different contexts. Examinations often give scenarios such as a doctor's surgery, supermarket, cinema, theme park, school or hospital.

9. Make justifying their choices a part of every topic from Year 7. 'Quicker' and 'Cheaper' are never enough, their answer must be qualified with a reason and/or example.

10. Make it clear that examination contexts often lag behind current technology. So talking about topics like viral marketing via social networking sites, while accurate, may not gain marks.

11. Keep them interested – consider using pupil-generated quizzes and games.

There are specific revision and examination techniques which pupils may encounter across subjects and perhaps in PSHE or study skills sessions. Nevertheless, you can reinforce and broaden their skill-set here by:

1. Researching types of revision technique – concept maps, mind maps, index cards, learning posters, summary tables, explaining to others, practising past papers, study buddies. Remember your own personal preference will not work for all pupils, so it is a good idea to know a range.

2. Explicitly teach: the examination terms your award board uses (usually listed in the course specification). Examples include name, list, state, describe, with examples, explain. For example, 'Describe how "email" might be used to ... ' is different from 'What does the abbreviation email mean?'

3. Teach how to respond to specific question types, for example 'Features and Reasons' or 'Advantages and Disadvantages'.

4. Explain, how to interpret marks for a question – usually shown in a square bracket, for example [10].

5. Reiterate many times the importance of reading carefully – with examples (these are often highlighted in the examiner's report).

6. Explain how to manage time – for example, seizing the 'easy wins' (things they know) first and come back to difficult questions later.

Coursework

Managing coursework projects occupies the majority of teacher time above Key Stage 3. The role of the teacher is usually as facilitator, guide and examiner. This requires

Design – use of ICT tools	
Marks	**Description**
0	No consideration of hardware or software
1	Demonstrates knowledge of hardware and software
2–3	Selects appropriate hardware and software for task and describes alternatives
4–5	Justifies choice of hardware and software, comparing choice to alternatives

Additional guidance

For 1 mark candidates will state the hardware and software which will be used. They may only consider generic hardware and software.

For 2 marks the candidate will select appropriate hardware and software and will state alternatives which could be used for the solution.

For 3 marks the candidate will consider non-ICT solutions as well.

For 4 marks the candidate will compare the alternatives to their choice, describing the benefits and limitations of each proposed solution.

For 5 marks the candidate will justify their choice through discussion of ease of use and suitability of the solution for the end-user.

Figure 6.7 Example internal assessment criteria in a specification

professionalism in determining the amount of guidance you can legitimately offer and in dividing your time equitably across the class – not just to those who are most vocal, likeable or who need most help.

Specifications give grade descriptions for coursework. There will be a graduated range of grades. Figure 6.7 provides an example of how the grading criteria may be presented in a specification.

As teachers we can decide to either use the grade sheets as they are presented in the specification or we can alter them to suit our own classes. It may depend on the ability of the pupils within the class which we do. We would recommend that pupils should have some method of recording their own progress through peer or self assessment as well as teacher assessment against the grades.

The descriptors in Figure 6.7 may sit in a pupil resource grid, as displayed in Figure 6.8.

The following advice can help maximize pupils' success in coursework:

1. Emphasize the importance of documentation – justifying the decisions made is often more important than a technically complex project. Teach spell-checking and proofreading skills.
2. Where projects are relatively open-ended, stress the importance of simplicity and avoid approving overambitious projects which focus upon technical skills alone.
3. Subdivide large projects into manageable chunks. Select and create support material for each section of the work.

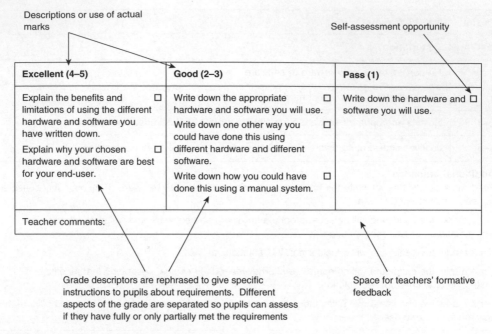

Descriptions or use of actual marks

Self-assessment opportunity

Excellent (4–5)	Good (2–3)	Pass (1)
Explain the benefits and limitations of using the different hardware and software you have written down. ☐ Explain why your chosen hardware and software are best for your end-user. ☐	Write down the appropriate hardware and software you will use. ☐ Write down one other way you could have done this using different hardware and different software. ☐ Write down how you could have done this using a manual system. ☐	Write down the hardware and software you will use. ☐
Teacher comments:		

Grade descriptors are rephrased to give specific instructions to pupils about requirements. Different aspects of the grade are separated so pupils can assess if they have fully or only partially met the requirements

Space for teachers' formative feedback

Figure 6.8 Pupil self-assessment

4. Build in self/peer assessment for each section. For instance, after completing the 'Analysis' and before moving on to 'Design', pupils self-assess their work against the grading criteria and then pass the work to the teacher for feedback.

5. Provide past projects or example work to mark.

6. Help pupils plan and manage their time. Set short-term goals and targets rather than a final deadline. Build in some flexibility for when things slip – use monitoring strategies to keep them on track. Stick to your own deadlines!

7. Use a tracking system which allows you to see if any pupils are falling behind, need additional support or have missed opportunities to maximize marks. In some cases it can be a useful strategy to share the tracking sheet with pupils; this can also introduce an element of competition and pace.

8. Make sure that everyone gets into the habit of evidence-gathering and annotation – often the final product is not as important as the process they undertook.

9. If using a systems life-cycle approach, ensure you use the model advocated by your awards board.

10. Consider creating posters of key points – with example work.

11. Be clear about the difference between offering support and doing it for them.

12. Mark the work at the right time. Sometimes it is essential to provide interim feedback on both a formative and summative basis. For example, one syllabus allows pupils to submit their 'Analysis' for initial marking so that any errors are not repeated throughout the work, resulting in multiple penalties.

13. Annotate the work when marking – many award boards require this and it is especially useful when explaining decisions in moderation.

14. Be aware that some teacher marking guidance may be confidential or embargoed to a specific date – keep this material secure.
15. Be prepared to offer support outside of scheduled sessions. After-school and lunchtime sessions are the norm in most schools, alongside extra sessions during holidays for many.
16. Standardize marking internally (moderation) – it is good practice to do this well in advance of the deadline (preferably at key points throughout) so that pupils can make any changes if teachers have had different interpretations of award board requirements.

SETTING TARGETS, TRACKING AND RECORD-KEEPING

Setting targets

We can set targets with pupils over a variety of timescales from 'By the end of this term I want to see you working at level 6', to 'By the end of this lesson I want you to be able to answer this question …'.

Recording all these targets is impossible, and not a good use of your time, but where a target will be monitored beyond the current lesson it is a good idea to note it in your recording system. Long-term targets set without interim steps tend to be fairly meaningless for pupils, but they can be useful for helping teachers work out the interim steps to reach the goal. So, for example, telling a pupil that they will reach a level 5 by January does not provide them with useful information or specific motivation, but the teacher can work backwards from this goal to make sure that the planned activities will enable the pupil to do this.

These long-term goals and targets are informed by prior attainment, either specifically in ICT or in more general baseline testing such as cognitive ability tests often combined with 'chances' graphs which indicate a probability that a pupil with a particular grade profile will achieve a grade or level in their next summative assessment. While this kind of data gives teachers a basis for target-setting, be aware that individual performance may be wildly different from that predicted – use your professional judgement and be aspirational but realistic. Remember data is the starting point, not the end result.

Target-setting on a day-to-day basis is really just a formalized form of feedback. It should be an opportunity for pupils and teachers to take a moment to agree the next learning steps. Setting a target does not guarantee success. Where targets are entirely set by the teacher, pupils will not have a personal stake and the target will have little impact. Targets set effectively can help to focus pupil effort and school resources (including teacher time). They should be specific and challenging. It can be helpful to refer to what the pupil is doing currently and how a change could result in a different result – 'If you carry on with your project in this way you will. … However with this specific work … you could achieve. What do you think you can do?'

Recording and monitoring targets requires a tracking system, let us now turn our attention to the other functionality that we would need from such a system.

Tracking

Reflection Point

Reflection Point 6.6

List the pupil data which is collected and recorded – daily, termly and annually.

Q. Who uses this data and for what purpose?

At a managerial, institutional, local and national level, data is collected to inform targets for the local authority, school and department. This data is often used to benchmark the school against similar schools, judge school effectiveness, identify issues and allocate resources. This data tends to be headlines – aggregate SAT results, absence levels, numbers of pupils in particular categories. The decisions this data informs impact indirectly on individuals over time. Teachers are responsible for feeding their own data into these systems, but of greater concern to us in this section is the information that teachers use to track and improve learning on a daily basis.

Lambert and Lines (2000) vividly describe how teachers can fall into an 'accountability trap' where they see their own tracking systems as being used to 'prove' their teaching competence to managers, headteachers, inspectors and the like. Accountability is undoubtedly important, but there are more important reasons to track pupils' progress in a formalized system:

- Assessment for Learning – as noted at the beginning of the chapter, tracking formative assessment is essential, particularly targets arising from teacher feedback, peer and self assessment.
- Informing curriculum planning and reflecting on your own practice through:
  - establishing baseline achievement
  - informing lesson evaluations
  - monitoring and modifying progress in the scheme of work based on pupil progress.
- Reporting to parents – parents' evenings and reports should provide parents with the information that helps them help their child. This can only be done if you have tracked their progress.
- Providing continuity if teachers change classes.
- Informing and tracking differentiation – pupil's current position helps set appropriate tasks for individuals and the system helps us track subsequent outcomes (also see Chapter 7).
- Identifying those who are achieving below their predicted potential or who are gifted and talented.
- Helping to identify special educational needs, where for example a teacher notices a pattern across a series of lessons or assignments.
- Target-setting at an individual level.

Reflection Point 6.7

Given the list of uses for tracking data (above):

1. What data will you capture/track for any given class?
2. For each item of data what will you record (for example, a grade, a comment, a code) and how often will you do this?
3. How will the above help you while you are teaching a lesson?

One of the difficulties teachers face in tracking pupil progress is that information tends to be decentralized. It is important to find a recording mechanism that works for you and the pupils. For example, we may give feedback which includes a direction or target; perhaps we record this by annotating the pupil's work or filling in a tracking form in their folder. Pulling together a class overview then becomes difficult and if the work or form is mislaid we end up relying on memory. A teacher's mark-book helps, but can result in a lot of duplication or transcription and we have to remember to update it when we update the target status. Electronic tracking systems can be an extremely useful solution in providing ways of sharing one set of data between the teacher and pupil. These may be specific tracking systems, or increasingly VLE-based components which allow pupils to view their own tracking data while at the same time allowing teachers to pull together an overview of class progress.

Whether we use a paper-based or electronic system we would expect its functionality to encompass:

*   storing baseline data – reading ages, cognitive ability tests (CATs) scores (or similar), SEN, English as an additional language (EAL), gifted and talented information, prior achievement in ICT.
*   recording progress against individual tasks – often a traffic-light system is employed.
*   recording scores or grades (note that we may choose not to share all grades with pupils – see 'Feedback', but it may still be useful for us to record a grade or coding to assist in aggregating progress reports).
*   space for detailed reminders/comments about individual pupils.

Reflection Point 6.8

Review the example mark-books link on the companion website, www.sagepub.co.uk/secondary.

1. To what extent do these mark-books approach the needs identified in this chapter?
2. What would you change/improve?
3. How might the mark-book interrelate with other data – marks on pupil work, learning diaries, parental reports, pupil targets and so on?

What the research says: Meta-analysis

This chapter asserts that there is a clear link between formative assessment methods (Assessment for Learning) and learning outcomes. How can we be sure of this when:

(a)   practice across schools and teachers varies so widely and
(b)   most educational research projects are quite small – perhaps a few classes in a small number of schools?

One answer is *meta-analysis*. Meta-analysis can be viewed in terms of a general idea and a specific technique (or more accurately a number of techniques). The idea is that the results of many separate pieces of research with a common theme or variable can be selected and synthesized together using statistical methods to give an overall result. Meta-analysis is then the analysis and combination of many separate analyses. Gene Glass first used the term in its current sense in 1976. In 2000 he published *Meta-Analysis at 25*, an interesting review of its use, development, weaknesses and possible future direction.

Statistical meta-analysis typically results in a combined *'effect size'*. This is a value which provides a measure of magnitude of the effect being studied. It allows us to compare the result of a particular innovation against a control group and, because it provides a 'common currency', we can directly compare the effect of one innovation against another. If we were studying educational attainment then the larger the effect size, the larger the impact on attainment of the particular innovation. Effect sizes which are negative indicate that the results of an innovation resulted in a negative effect on attainment.

Note that a meta-analysis will usually combine negative and positive effects to produce a mean effect size. This means in practice that we could boost the potential effect size if we could identify and eliminate a common factor in those studies with a negligible or negative effect size. For example, Black et al. (2003) refer to a study by Kluger and DeNisi looking at the effectiveness of teacher feedback which yielded 607 effect sizes. The average of the effect sizes was 0.4 – this is a significant effect (as we shall see in a moment). However approximately two-fifths of the 607 effect sizes were negative. By refocusing on only those studies which involved making use of the feedback for future improvement, all effect sizes were positive.

The effect sizes suggested by Black and Wiliam's research (1998) for formative assessment were between 0.4 and 0.7. If we could secure even the smallest of these effects in our classrooms they would improve the average GCSE performance of pupils by between one and two grades. Significantly these effects are so powerful because they have greatest effect upon the 'tail' of potentially lower-achieving pupils.

John Hattie effectively summarizes reasons why meta-analysis is such a useful tool in educational research (1999). He has reached related conclusions to Wiliam and Black, particularly in examining the role of feedback, target-setting and self-assessment. 'So far the prescriptions for influencing student learning are clear: dollops of feedback, specific and challenging goals, and a constant attention to asking, "How am I going?"' (Hattie, 1999: 14)

The scope of Hattie's examination of effect size is broad – 200,000 effect sizes covering many areas of possible innovation (not just formative assessment). His work can form a basis for deciding how to spend your precious time as a teacher, both in classroom practice and action research.

Reflection Point 69

Compare government priorities in education (for example, setting, use of computers in class) with Hattie's effect-size findings. To what degree is there a correlation?

Further reading

Black, P., Harrison, C., Lee, C., Marshall, B. and Wiliam, D. (2003) *Assessment for Learning: Putting it into Practice.* Maidenhead: Open University Press.
Introduces an overview of formative assessment research and reports upon the practices and results of teachers who put the ideas into practice.

Kerry, T. (2002a) *Explaining and Questioning.* Cheltenham: Nelson Thornes.
A highly practical textbook which provides both techniques you can use in the classroom alongside the rationale for why they are applicable. Encourages self-reflection and development.

Lambert, D. and Lines, D. (2000) *Understanding Assessment: Purposes, Perceptions, Practice.* London: Routledge Falmer.
Gives a considered view of current summative and formative assessment practices alongside teacher vignettes and case studies.

Weblinks

Live links to each of these websites can be found on the companion website, www.sagepub.co.uk/secondary.

The Association for Achievement and Improvement through Assessment – www.aaia.org.uk/. A comprehensive site which includes links to award boards. Has a large section devoted to formative assessment and includes links to the Assessment Reform Group's Assessment for Learning 10 Principles Poster.

Learning how to Learn – www.learntolearn.ac.uk/. Contains practical strategies for implementing the four strands of formative assessment in the classroom, alongside an excellent overview of the evidence base.

Te Kete Ipurangi, The Online Learning Centre – www.tki.org.nz/r/assessment/. New Zealand's Ministry of Education's website. Contains high-quality presentations which explore all areas of assessment for learning.

Tony Ryan's Thinker's Keys – www.thinkerskeys.com/. This site provides a useful set of resources and ideas for broadening your questioning repertoire.

7 LEARNING FOR ALL

This chapter covers:

- how differentiation can be used to enable all pupils to engage in learning
- how teachers can include all pupils within lessons, providing equal opportunities for learning
- how teachers can help pupils with additional needs learn, including pupils with special educational needs, English as an additional language and gifted and talented pupils.

Beginning teachers often find it helpful to imagine a class of average children when planning their lessons and activities. Of course, in reality there are no stereotypically average children who will match that image. This chapter looks at how we can develop strategies that will broaden our teaching repertoire and enable all children to make progress in their learning.

Teaching average lessons to notionally average children potentially excludes many from being engaged in learning. The National Curriculum in its statutory statement of inclusion sets out three principles for developing inclusive lessons which provide all pupils with relevant and challenging learning.

1. Set suitable learning challenges.
2. Respond to pupils' diverse learning needs.
3. Overcome potential barriers to learning and assessment for individuals and groups of pupils.

SETTING SUITABLE LEARNING CHALLENGES: DIFFERENTIATION

In Chapter 4 we dealt at some length with the issue of appropriate cognitive challenge in objectives and activities. In this section we explore how we can make the learning experience different to suit the needs of individuals in the class. Central to this is the idea that we don't just 'teach to the middle'.

A particularly attractive notion when faced with a diverse group of pupil experience and potential ability is to group children by prior attainment, usually in 'sets' that they stay in for a year. A great deal of research has been conducted into the effects of grouping pupils in this way and the debate has become somewhat polarized. On balance there is little hard evidence that homogenous ability groups directly result in higher attainment over and above the fact that schools may focus their resources and expectations upon such groups, perhaps to the detriment of others. Working from the medical principle of 'first do no harm' there is a wide range of evidence to suggest that when pupils are grouped by prior attainment, those at the bottom end of the potential-ability spectrum have a poorer view of schooling and lower self-esteem – wouldn't you if you were in the 'bottom set'? They also largely remain in their groups for the duration of their school life – are past results combined with teacher judgements really this accurate or, more likely, does teacher and pupil expectation have a large role to play? Another disadvantage of ability grouping is that it tends to limit the degree of social interaction within the school. Given the potential of ability grouping to create 'sink groups', the onus must be on those who advocate the practice to robustly demonstrate the benefits and to articulate how the most at risk are protected.

Mixed-ability grouping while it has advantages is not a panacea, nor is teaching in such an environment easy. There is a risk that when teachers teach the same curriculum in the same way to such classes, attainment suffers at both ends of the potential-ability spectrum. One solution (in fact a set of solutions) to these concerns is differentiation, where we change something about the learning activity in order to provide appropriate challenge and accessibility to all of our pupils. In the sections which follow we explore the various factors which can be changed, it would be unusual (and exhausting) to try to use all these methods in every lesson; you must choose the right mix of differentiation for your classes. Differentiation relies upon you knowing the children, not just baseline data (although that is important), but also what works well for them in terms of type of activity and how much choice they can sensibly manage.

Differentiation provides pupils with many different routes to reach the same learning objective. St. Mary's College of Maryland uses this powerful analogy throughout its excellent differentiation web pages (see 'weblinks'):

> We tend to choose paths of learning that make the most sense to us personally. In a classroom where there is only one available path toward learning, many students will feel lost, uncomfortable, or confused.
>
> If two students can reach the same understanding ... What does it matter if one student takes a shortcut and another takes the long way? Sometimes students are equipped with the prior knowledge that prepares them for the fast track toward understanding. Other times students will need to take the slower paced scenic route. Some may use maps & roadsigns, others will stop frequently for directions! (2005)

Reflection Point 7.1

Imagine you have been given a day to learn an unfamiliar skill (juggling is a good example). In a group discuss the different ways you might go about the task, including how you would spend the time. Are there general categories of ways in which your approaches differ? What kinds of support would you seek?

Reflection Point

Differentiation by outcome

There are several interpretations of the term 'differentiation by outcome'. In some cases the notion is closer to differentiation by product (see below). Alternatively, and probably the most widely accepted understanding is that pupils all do the same work (usually an open-ended task) and then have different outcomes which are assessed. This seems to rather evade the issue – doesn't this happen by default anyway? In fact wouldn't it happen even if the teacher left the room? Our contention would be that if your version of differentiation by outcome involves little teacher input (beyond assessment), then it probably is not really differentiation at all. Imagine a gym where everyone's personalized exercise plan was the same along with the support they had from trainers, would we be surprised if the differentiated outcomes were that some people got a little fitter, some a lot, some gave up and one had a hernia? If we have not convinced you, it is also worth noting that Ofsted are increasingly critical of lessons which rely on differentiation by outcome as a method of setting suitable learning challenges.

Differentiation by process and support

Process (the way children undertake activities) and how we support them are interwoven and so we will consider both together. In this section we are assuming that pupils are aiming to produce the same output (or product), but that how they go about the task may be different.

Perhaps the most obvious use of differentiation is the way that we divide our time differently between children in the class. We will often choose to provide additional support to struggling learners and to stretch the most able, while those in the middle are supported in other ways, for example through resources we have created. Teacher support is important, but as noted elsewhere it is a markedly finite resource and in ICT our flexibility may be limited, especially with large classes and a short period of time each week – a class of 20 children have three minutes of our time per week if we divide our hour up evenly. There are, however, other resources we can draw upon to provide differentiated support.

Peripatetic staff such as teaching assistants are an invaluable source of support for pupils. By working with them we can plan to target support to individuals (record this on your lesson plan).

Peer support can be very useful because it provides learning gains for the most able and creates time for teachers to work with those in most need. The traffic lights system is really useful in creating peer supported subgroupings. This is where pupils rate their understanding from red to green. The teacher then pairs each green with an amber and supports the red group directly. The advantages of this kind of temporary subgrouping are explored further later in this section. It is important to set ground rules for peer support; there will be a temptation for pupils who have completed work to 'show' others how they did it and in the process actually do it for them. All must be made aware that the teacher will expect everyone to be able to answer a question, justify a decision or demonstrate a skill. The onus is then on those being supported to ensure they understand.

The above approaches focus on who can help in supporting children, we can also differentiate the task itself, particularly the degree of structure or scaffolding. Differentiated worksheets provide one way of doing this. At its simplest we could produce a worksheet which is detailed enough for pupils who need the most guidance and then produce less specific worksheets by removing steps or levels of detail. More useful still are worksheets which allow all pupils to complete the same output in the same time, but provide different levels of challenge and guidance.

For example, suppose our assessed outcome was a data capture form to survey the quantities of water used by individuals in a week. We may need three levels of worksheet at various levels of Bloom's taxonomy:

At the *comprehension/application level* of challenge, our most detailed worksheet would provide a list of question types, example questions, layout guidance or a template and a set of steps to work through with appropriate comprehension questions built in.

At the *application/analysis level* our worksheet may give pupils an overview of the task and generic information about common question types. The task would be written in broad terms with specific assessment criteria.

At the *synthesis/evaluation level* our worksheet may be a task brief with points for consideration and assessment criteria. The worksheet may ask pupils to test, evaluate and refine their form and also perhaps to compare this method against say using a data logger which could measure water use at the mains.

A word of caution is needed here. Where pupils are provided with different worksheets they very quickly work out which ones are lower level and which higher, and while we may have allocated them using our best judgement many will see this as a label, be it 'stupid' or 'bright'. When this happens those at the lower potential-ability end of the spectrum lose motivation and self-esteem. Sue Hall provides a vivid account of this experience in 'The problem with differentiation':

At the end of the lesson, the students engaged in a discussion with the teacher about the cards. Their reactions were mixed:
Jane: I thought [the cards] were brilliant.
Phil: You would.
Teacher: OK Phil ... you didn't rate them then? (long pause)
Joseph: He thinks you think he's thick.
Phil: No I don't ... it's just ...
Debbie: Why should we have stuff for kids with pictures and not words – it's stupid. [...]
Jane: I just liked filling in the missing bits and thinking about it ... it was good.
Debbie: That's 'cos you're the boff and you get the best.
Teacher: Would you have liked the card that Jane had then?
Debbie: No point 'cos I'm too thick to do it.
Paul: Everyone says we're useless and now you're saying it too.

Again, the pattern was clear: those receiving the high-ability workcards were encouraged; those receiving the low-ability cards were discouraged. Peer attitudes, which are powerful influences in adolescents, also contributed to the plummeting self-esteem of the low ability students. (1997: 96-7)

It is important to note that Hall does go on to say that this group did subsequently respond well to differentiation through collaborative peer support. There are no easy answers to this dilemma. In some cases it may be possible to be explicit about the levels of challenge in different worksheets and offer pupils a choice, but this can be problematic if pupils continually opt for low-risk, low-challenge activities. We can also emphasize to pupils that the decisions we make about 'appropriate level' are temporary and will change as they progress, but this can be disingenuous where the gap in ability range in the class is unlikely to be closed in the short term. Other less overt ways in which we could seek to structure the task at different levels are through graduated tasks and additional support materials.

In graduated tasks all pupils receive the same worksheet (or a series of worksheets), and the tasks become more challenging as they work through them. The obvious disadvantage of this approach is that if pupils regularly expect to complete all tasks and repeatedly do not manage this, their self-esteem can be damaged. Therefore, it is important to agree with pupils a realistic personal target for each set of tasks. We can also offer branching tasks within a graduated worksheet where one set of activities is more challenging than the other and the pupil has an element of choice – sometimes guided by the teacher through target-setting.

We can also offer additional supporting resources as pupils work through a task. For example an additional worksheet or textbook exercise for any pupils who find a particular concept difficult (for example, absolute and relative cell references). Of course, the activities can also be extensions for those who have completed a section of learning. This is perhaps the best compromise between different worksheets for different ability ranges and graduated tasks – in effect we are doing both, but not in an overt fashion. A small bank of these activities also helps reduce teacher repetition.

The degree of intervention and feedback the teacher gives is also a form of differentiation. In the examples above the degree of autonomy and frequency of checking with the teacher could be incorporated into the worksheet; for example: 'Once you have completed step 4, please show your list of questions to your teacher.' Remember in all feedback we are seeking to help pupils learn, not spoon-feeding answers – for all learners guiding and reflecting questions is more important than providing an answer (see Chapter 6).

One of the most challenging aspects of differentiating a process is that pupils will work at different paces. As a teacher you may differentiate by providing different time-frames to complete a task, but inevitably at some point you will want their learning to converge. This may be an assessment point, moving on to a new topic or just to pause and consolidate the learning. Setting clear timed targets alongside a teacher tracking system is therefore essential.

Differentiation by resource

We may choose to give pupils the same task with the same output, but differentiate by varying their choice of source material. In ICT we are also explicitly teaching the skills of information searching and selection, so as they acquire these skills we should be able to broaden the source base.

The obvious place where resource selection impacts on ICT is in guiding pupils in selecting web-based resources. At one end of the spectrum we may direct them to a single website and at the other they will have free reign to roam the Internet (notwithstanding firewalls, blacklists, restricted search terms and so on). Most often we will direct them to a subset of sites that might be useful. Of course, in teaching them ICT capability we will also use other resources and compare their relative advantages and disadvantages including textbooks, video, audio, websites, magazines, newspapers, posters and teacher written material.

In differentiating our choice of resources we will need to consider, above all, their reading level, trying to find sources which challenge pupils without being demotivating. The degree of complexity in the material is also important (it may be readable, but may not actually aid understanding).

This is an area where teachers have considerable scope in offering variety and choice to pupils (rather than them feeling differentiation is 'done' to them) and asking them to explain why they chose a resource and then evaluating it becomes another route to ICT capability. Clearly you will need to guide pupils outside their comfort zone from time to time. In differentiating resources you can also help pupils find what works best for them for a particular type of learning. For example, some will find watching a video to be more effective, while others prefer reading, another group may find that listening to a narration along with presentation slides is more effective.

Our final goal will be to give children the study skills and methods of inquiry to locate their own resources so that they can answer the questions: 'How do I find out more?' and 'How do I choose between ... ?'

Differentiation by product

This is a very straightforward, but probably underused idea – pupils can produce different outputs to demonstrate the same learning goals. We saw an example of this in Jason's lesson in Chapter 4 where pupils were given the choice of producing a news report/presentation or a sales poster. The challenge in ICT is the range of software that pupils may need to use is quite broad, nevertheless with some skills-based worksheets it is possible to have pupils working on different products. It is important to consider timing issues to ensure that the different products can be completed at the same time. As noted in Chapter 4, the best products relate to appropriate problems which are real (or realistic), relevant to the student and have an audience in mind.

Types of product we might choose include:

- a written report
- a live verbal report or presentation
- a taped verbal report or narrated presentation
- notes in preparation for a debate
- an online chat record
- a flow chart
- a working model
- a user guide
- a mind map/concept map
- a question
- annotated screenshots
- a video

- annotated code
- a summary table
- a website
- an animation
- a quiz

- a screen recording of a set of actions
- a collaborative document
- a diagram, picture or poster
- an advertisement

Even where pupils produce different products there is still an excellent opportunity for them to peer evaluate both the product itself and the process they have undertaken. You can take this a step further and ask if any particular products were more effective at meeting the learning objectives and if they would choose the same product if they were to repeat the task. There are benefits to teachers and pupils in this approach because it refocuses attention on the learning objectives rather than directly comparing pupils against each other.

Grouping arrangements for differentiation

We began considering differentiation by looking at the potential advantages of mixed-ability groups over setted or streamed classes. However, this does not mean that we should not use planned temporary groupings of students for specific tasks. Why are these ideas different? In the former, groupings are fixed and relatively permanent – at least for a year (and probably the whole of an individual's school life). In the latter, the arrangement is flexible and temporary, groups do change and pupils understand this. Generally speaking we will be looking for a balance of skills in a group which provides advantages for all rather than this being purely based upon prior attainment.

There are no hard and fast rules here, it is about using your knowledge of the pupils and of the task to form appropriate groups. For example, in producing a website adventure game we have often found that grouping pupils who are technology oriented, those interested in the narrative and those who have design skills makes for a really good learning mix. This works well where the task requires each to produce a page separately and then link them all together – all have a shared stake in success and they help and teach each other.

Where you are consciously creating groups where a higher-attaining child works with a lower-attaining child it can help to adopt a mentor model. Here the higher-attaining child helps prepare the lower-attaining child to deliver their shared final product, for example a demonstration. This produces large learning gains for both parties because the lower-attaining child receives individual (or small group) attention and the higher-attaining child needs to be able to translate and explain their own skills – it also prevents them from dominating the work.

Pupils whose attainment falls significantly below expected levels

In our discussion of differentiation so far we have considered groups of learners working towards common learning objectives. In some cases there will be pupils working significantly below the level of their peers. It may then be necessary to alter the learning objective itself, perhaps choosing elements from the programme of study preceding their target level. For example, some Key Stage 3 pupils will not yet have attained the level 3 Attainment Target and so it may be appropriate to provide them with objectives based around the Key Stage 2 programme of study. This group of pupils will have faced a barrier to their learning – see 'Overcoming potential barriers' later in this chapter.

Gifted and talented

Pupils who are gifted and talented will typically be exceeding the expectations or attainment of their peers by a considerable extent (or at least have the potential to do this given modest interventions). The Department for Children, Schools and Families (DCSF) further suggest that gifted and talented pupils when compared with their peers tend to:

- show a passion for particular subjects/areas of interest and seek to pursue them
- master the rules of a domain easily and transfer their insights to new problems
- analyse their own behaviour and hence use a greater range of learning strategies than others (self-regulation)
- make connections between past and present learning
- demonstrate intellectual curiosity
- show intellectual maturity and enjoy engaging in-depth with subject material
- actively and enthusiastically engage in debate and discussion on a particular subject
- produce original and creative responses to common problems.

    In addition, gifted and talented students may develop particular characteristics as they progress through the secondary/tertiary phase, such as:

- a tendency to question rules and authority
- a well-developed sense of humour
- growing self-determination, stamina and powers of concentration. (DCSF, 2007: 8)

Schools will have a policy in identifying and supporting gifted and talented children and some ICT departments produce their own guidance in this.

It is interesting to note that being labelled gifted and talented does not confer automatic success in terms of life chances. Professor Joan Freeman has followed three groups of pupils in a longitudinal study since 1974: the first were labelled gifted and talented, the second performed equally well on a measure of intelligence but were not labelled, and the third were a control group randomly selected. Her broad findings were:

The group of labelled gifted were found to have significantly more emotional problems than the non-labelled group, which they mostly grew out of. Now in their forties, a gifted childhood has not always delivered outstanding adult success. Better predictive factors were hard work, emotional support and a positive, open personal outlook. By 2005, the labelled and unlabelled gifted groups are not very different in life outcomes, though both are much more successful than the random ability group. (Freeman, 2006: 384)

We must be mindful therefore that labelling children in this way may have negative effects, including increased pressure from parents and teachers. There may also be an increased sense of social isolation for children who now feel different from their peers. Bear in mind that gifted and talented children often mimic adult language and behaviour, creating an impression of maturity which may mask emotional immaturity.

Creating generic groups for gifted and talented children does not seem to be particularly effective. This should not surprise us as most gifted and talented children have talents in a specific subject domain rather than being polymaths. They therefore need subject-specific mechanisms to make the most of their potential.

A common strategy is to overburden these children by broadening the number of qualifications taken when a deepening of knowledge in a particular area would be more beneficial and appropriate.

There are three broad strategies that we might consider for these children – acceleration, extension and enrichment.

> *Acceleration* – covering the same content in less time than their peers, for example taking A levels in year 11.
>
> *Extension* – increasing the depth of knowledge. Examples include:
>
> - a focus on problems which require critical analysis and evaluation of several possible solutions
> - providing challenging problems, for example in LOGO use recursion to draw a tree
> - using open-ended and extended questions, for example fluid analogies like 'How is a hard disk like a library?'
> - providing access to resources, for example, computer clubs, programming tools, online resources, laptops
> - modelling problem-solving techniques, for example, in computer programming
> - providing information about current issues and research information, for example from news stories and academic journals
> - providing information about relevant professional organizations, for example the British Computer Society
> - a focus on developing reusable systems with robust user interfaces – thinking deeply about how people will realistically use this system.
>
> *Enrichment* – increasing the breadth across which they encounter and apply subject knowledge. Examples include:
>
> - finding out what the child does with ICT outside of the classroom – they may, for example, already have their own website or develop applications
> - extending cross-curricular links, for example work with the science teacher to develop a multiple choice question system or animated concept cartoons
> - peer teaching/mentoring (with careful guidance) – where they become a mentor to other pupils, this requires thinking in different ways to overcome misconceptions
> - offering a choice of learning activities to suit their interests
> - fostering outside school extensions, for example university summer schools, work experience links; for instance there may be a web design agency which would allow pupils to work on a client brief

- designing a web-quest or game for the class
- setting tasks which move them out of their comfort zone, for example technically competent but socially isolated pupils could be asked to solve problems which require social skills such as testing different human computer interfaces
- providing focused roles in specific activities, for example editor on a school newspaper for a day
- entering subject related competitions, for example Lego run regular competitions based around its Mindstorms programmable technology.

RESPONDING TO PUPILS' DIVERSE NEEDS

This element of the statutory inclusion statement requires teachers to focus on the attributes and experiences that pupils bring to the classroom and how we use this information to provide a meaningful learning experience. 'Teachers need to be aware that pupils bring to school different experiences, interests and strengths which will influence the way in which they learn' (QCA, 2007).

In addition, the statement places a statutory obligation upon teachers to 'be aware of the requirements of the equal opportunities legislation that covers race, gender and disability' (QCA, 2007). We should though seek to go beyond the minimum requirements of legislation, to create a classroom where there are opportunities to explore identity, difference and commonality through the work that children do.

Robin Richardson presents a useful non-subject-specific framework for thinking through these issues in *Here, There and Everywhere: Belonging, Identity and Equality in Schools* (2004). The six themes identified follow, together with some ideas of how you might use the contexts within ICT:

Shared humanity – which focuses upon our shared humanity, from shared universal biology through to our basic human rights, shared needs, values and aspirations:

- collaborating with other schools to create a shared artefact which examines commonality and difference, for example a blog or web page (see Chapter 4 for a real-world example of this)
- examining how technology developments such as the growth of mobile phone networks have changed lives across cultures – often in a parallel fashion.

Identity and belonging – which explores the idea that individuals have multiple, overlapping and sometimes contrasting self-identities that change over time and with context. Furthermore there is interplay between self-identity and the individual's sense of belonging and loyalty to any particular group.

- all about me (see Chapter4)
- what does it mean to be … ? Using pupil experiences, Internet research or school to school collaboration to investigate what identity labels (Black, White, Asian, Atheist, Christian, Muslim, Jew and so on) mean to individuals. The product could be a web page, audio or video file which describes what the label means to an individual, and these could then be linked together to illustrate commonalities and differences. The project could also investigate the notion of a 'British' identity.
- exploring online identities – how and why do people choose their online personas?

Local and global – which seeks to make explicit the idea that there is an increasing degree of inter-dependence between cultural groupings. There is a constant cross-pollination of ideas and culture between groups and language, culture and identity are not fixed entities, but intermingle over time. Also, increasingly, 'communities' are not confined by geography; friendships, collaboration and commerce are conducted across international boundaries.

- using mapping software such as Google Earth to illustrate how phenomena have grown and intermingled; examples include language, music traditions, migration, legal and political systems, science and technology
- case study – what are the impacts of outsourcing ICT functions to another country and what are the risks and benefits for both parties?
- social networking – who is your 'community'?
- examining how crossover between cultures in music creates new genres – pupils could find examples and create their own
- using models to investigate how suppliers and consumers are interdependent, for example modelling the impact of fair trade models on suppliers and consumers.

Achievement everywhere – which seeks to avoid the (often implicit and unintentional) assumption that all significant human achievements have arisen in 'western' culture:

- an opportunity for a cross-curricular link with history, music, art, technology, science or mathematics to find parallels between European thinkers and their counterparts in other parts of the world
- examining the historical chain that led to a modern day invention (could be the computer); again this could be plotted on mapping software to illustrate how the idea has developed as it has travelled around the world.

Conflict and justice – which recognizes that disagreements and conflicts of interest arise at all levels from within families to between nations. Therefore there is a need to devise and implement fair and reasonable ways for resolving conflicts of interest through rules, systems and laws:

- examining current debates around technology driven issues such as privacy versus security
- determining how rules are created and policed in online spaces such as through moderated forums. Are there principles that can be applied in the real world?
- using worldwide newspaper reports to examine issues from different perspectives.

Race and racisms – which contrasts the notion of one 'human race' with the false belief that physical appearance (or culture, or religion) is significant in providing a mechanism for excluding or including individuals from a group or society. Consideration is also given to 'institutional racism' where practices, systems and language converge to exclude or marginalize a group:

- using a variety of information sources such as newspaper archives to explore how attitudes and use of language have changed even over recent times
- exploring the use of images in the media and how this can have unintended consequences such as stereotyping
- matching names to faces based only on an online dialogue
- examining how online communication can break down barriers, but can also provide a platform for hatred.

Reflection Point 7.2

How is racism similar and different from other forms of name calling?
Compare your answer with *Aiming High: Understanding the Educational Needs of Minority Ethnic Pupils in Mainly White Schools – A Guide to Good Practice* (DFES, 2004a)

Use appropriate resources, be aware that it is easy to unwittingly select or create resources which may not reflect the diversity of children in your class. Are examples and activities drawn only from white, British, middle-class culture? This is not to say that all resources should reflect all children in a tokenistic fashion, but there should be a mix of people and contexts in our resources. In selecting resources we should always try to present both sides of controversial issues. Images should be selected carefully to avoid stereotyping, and remember that there is diversity within cultures as well as between them. We should seek to provide opportunities for pupils to share and take pride in their own culture and identity.

Language can be a barrier, particularly when pupils unwittingly cause offence or are unsure of whether a term may be offensive (for example, 'coloured'). Our ethos of 'It's OK to make mistakes' needs to extend into this arena also; we need to encourage pupils to ask questions without fear that their phrasing may be incorrect or potentially offensive (provided their intention is clear and the words used are modified in future). Finally, remember that children are individuals with burgeoning identities and ideas. Our role is not to instil in them our particular belief system (or their parents' for that matter), but to give them the tools and the space to make up their own minds.

The QCA's Respect For All website (see companion website, www.sagepub.co.uk/secondary for link) provides many other specific examples of how ICT can be used to help pupils and teachers explore these issues. There is also general guidance on planning.

OVERCOMING POTENTIAL BARRIERS

So far in this chapter we have discussed principles and practices which apply to all children in our class, there may also be children with individual barriers to learning which require additional planning and support. Potential barriers identified specifically in the inclusion statement are special educational needs (SEN), disability and English as an additional language (EAL). Teaching children with one or more additional needs can seem daunting to a beginning teacher, but the very fact that the need has been identified means that plans and resources have already been considered to help overcome the barriers they may face. There are additional professionals to help you in planning, such as SEN/EAL co-ordinators and in class through paraprofessionals such as teaching assistants. Avoid making any assumptions based only on baseline data (class lists) and remember that very often children are well informed and know what works best for them.

Special educational needs and disability in ICT

SEN: A child has 'special educational needs' ... if he has a learning difficulty which calls for special educational provision to be made for him.
(2) ... a child has a 'learning difficulty' ... if –
(a) he has a significantly greater difficulty in learning than the majority of children of his age,
(b) he has a disability which either prevents or hinders him from making use of educational facilities of a kind generally provided for children of his age in schools within the area of the local education authority ... (Great Britain, 1996)

Disability: 'a physical or mental impairment which has a substantial and long-term adverse effect on his ability to carry out normal day-to-day activities' (Great Britain, 1995)

Not all children with an identified special educational need will be identified as having a disability (indeed the majority will not) and similarly not all disabled children will have an identified SEN. Wherever a disability or special educational need presents an obstacle to learning, we need to consider how we can plan to overcome that barrier.

As a teacher of ICT your responsibilities will include working with individuals with a SEN and evaluating and recording their progress. It is also likely that you will from time to time be involved in identifying pupils with an as yet unrecognized SEN. Finally, you may be well placed to offer advice and guidance about how technology can enable access to learning.

Your class lists will identify pupils who have a special educational need. This is based on the school's SEN register. Schools and local authorities differ to some extent in the ways that they record this information (and the way that funding and resources are allocated). Broadly speaking, you will see that pupils are identified as being at one of three stages of need:

- School Action – pupils who have been assessed by the school and have additional resources and interventions in place
- School Action Plus – as above and in order to make progress the pupil is supported or assessed by an external agency, for example a language therapist, educational psychologist or social services
- Statement of SEN – following a statutory assessment the local authority has determined that the child's needs cannot be met within the resources of the school. Additional resources are normally provided by the local authority.

All pupils on the SEN register will have an Individual Education Plan (IEP). The IEP records what is additional or different from the mainstream (differentiated) curriculum provision and will normally focus on three or four areas. It helps classroom teachers by setting out short-term targets for the pupil and suggests teaching strategies to help them learn. The plan is reviewed by the SEN co-ordinator, the child and his/her parents at least twice a year and it is possible that you will be asked to comment on the pupil's progress towards his/her targets, particularly if these are specific to ICT. The IEP is a working, practical document and it is important to secure access to them for those that you teach as early as possible so that you can plan for their needs. An example IEP can be found on the companion website, www.sagepub.co.uk/secondary.

It is impossible to offer a meaningful list of the range of needs you will encounter (though almost certainly you will work with a high number of pupils with a specific learning difficulty). Make good use of the SEN co-ordinator and your own research to best match your plans to pupils' needs. Very broadly, special educational needs are normally classified under one (or more) of four main areas of need:

- cognition and learning
- behavioural, emotional and social development
- communication and interaction
- sensory and/or physical.

The *Special Educational Needs Code of Practice* (DFES, 2001a) defines these areas in detail. It is important to note that pupils may have characteristics which span areas.

We mentioned earlier that identification of special educational needs is also part of your responsibility, in fact very often class teachers are the first to diagnose the need for intervention. If in any doubt it is always worth asking a professional who can then arrange an assessment as necessary. Typically teachers identify specific learning difficulties (SpLD) such as dyslexia or dyspraxia. These conditions can often be seen prominently in ICT where pupils can demonstrate their cognitive ability in forms other than written text, which may then be contrasted against weaker written work.

Being in an ICT suite can help you to make learning accessible by removing many barriers through enabling technologies. Unlike colleagues who may rely on paper-based materials, we have the opportunity to reformat work in an almost limitless way. There is also an enormous amount of enabling software, some built into the operating system, some in applications and other more specialist software. The kinds of technology you are likely to have access to include:

- enlarged icons and cursors
- changing and enlarging fonts
- changing screen display colours
- high-contrast screen themes
- modifications to how the keyboard works, such as toggling modifier keys and turning off key repeat

- allocating specific sounds to events
- text narration software
- screen magnifiers
- spellcheckers
- alternate input devices – for example, overlay keyboards, trackballs and switches

You may also need to be familiar with:

- symbol processors (which use pictures in place of words)
- voice recognition software
- screen readers
- touch screens
- predictive text software
- height adjustable desks to accommodate wheelchair users
- braille printers.

There are many sites and applications which will verify that web pages are accessible (for example, to screen reading software). It is good practice to use these when developing your own sites and you can use them with a class when talking about appropriateness to audience (some will check usability as well as accessibility). They are also a good way to teach that automated processes are not a substitute for common sense.

Of course, ICT offers more than just specific technology solutions. The ability to make mistakes then easily redraft work as often as needed and to work at their own pace are great motivators for all children. Also, the ability to use a variety of media including sound and visual cues makes learning meaningful and interactive.

You can be an invaluable help to the SEN co-ordinator in evaluating enabling technologies and researching alternatives. You will also need to consider when purchasing ICT resources and software whether they will be compatible with any accessibility software your pupils use.

Reflection Point 7.3

Select a specific SEN (example areas are given below).

1. Find out the definition and scope of the SEN. What are the range of needs encompassed?
2. Identify the barriers to learning.
3. Suggest strategies to overcome these.

Cognition and learning needs – specific learning difficulty (SpLD), dyslexia, dyscalculia, dyspraxia, moderate learning difficulty (MLD), severe learning difficulty (SLD), profound and multiple learning difficulty (PMLD)

Behavioural, emotional and social development needs – oppositional defiance disorder (ODD), attention deficit disorder or attention deficit hyperactivity disorder (ADD/ADHD); syndromes such as Tourette's

Communication and interaction needs – speech, language and communication needs (SLCN), stammer/stutter, autistic spectrum disorder (ASD), Asperger's syndrome

Sensory and/or physical needs – visual impairment (VI), hearing impairment (HI), multi-sensory impairment (MSI), physical disability (PD).

English as an additional language (EAL) in ICT

Schools and regions differ widely in the number of children whose first language is not English and those children differ enormously in the scope of their needs. Some schools have large populations of EAL learners and have the corresponding infrastructure to support them. More challenging are situations were there are just a few (or even one) EAL learner and the school does not have an EAL co-ordinator.

English as an additional language is distinct from SEN in that it is a specific communication barrier (rather than cognitive). Some children with EAL will also have a special educational need, but we would not expect the proportion to be very different from the whole school population.

Our goals are for the pupils with EAL to be included in all aspects of our classes and to enable them to function effectively in spoken and written English. Children learning English do catch up with their peers over time. Generally their spoken English will be considerably in advance of their written English.

There is no homogenous group of EAL learners. They will usually have been born outside an English-speaking country. They may be multilingual or speak only one language. They may have had access to schooling (sometimes in advance of their peers in UK schools), or none. English may be spoken at home, or not. In your lessons, they will probably be learning to socialize in English, speak and write academic English and gain ICT capability.

The National Association for Language Development in the Curriculum (NALDIC) produces excellent advice for teachers (see weblinks). Below we examine five principles developed by NALDIC and how they apply to ICT.

1. *Activate prior knowledge.* As with all learners we need to find out what individuals know and can do in ICT. With EAL learners we also need to establish a baseline for spoken and written English (this information is normally provided before they join your class). It is important to know something of their background so that you can ensure contexts are meaningful; many learners will have parallel experiences with their English-speaking peers but do not just assume this. English as an additional language learners can bring an added dimension to the contexts we use in class, for example when considering audience expectations in an advertisement we may want to talk about how a UK audience might differ from say a Turkish audience. This obviously needs to be handled sensitively and we need to be sure our pupils will be comfortable doing this. Also look for opportunities in using music which can be a unifying influence.

2. *Provide a rich contextual background to make input comprehensible.* Teacher talk may be difficult to follow; in ICT we can provide multiple alternatives such as symbols, pictures, video clips, audio clips, graphic organizers, maps, simulations as well as interactive whiteboard and other notes which can be made available through the school intranet. Pupils can also have access during the lesson to bilingual dictionaries and translation tools. Also consider using screenshots and screen recorders to show complex actions – this allows self-paced repetition.

3. *Actively encourage comprehensible output.* Pupils may experience a silent period during the first few weeks in an English-speaking school. Encouraging contributions can be through traditional questioning, beginning with closed questions and moving to more extended questions over time. We can also coach learners in a private moment to later answer a question in public (see Chapter 6). Paired work can help learners practise answers. Finally, we can use ICT tools such as chat rooms, voting systems and collaborative documents to encourage feedback in written form.

4. *Point out and make explicit key grammatical elements.* Engaging all children in the nuts and bolts of language is a worthwhile exercise. There are many opportunities to do this within activities which address the communication element of ICT. For example, in developing a magazine template we may

look at choice of words in headlines and bylines or when drafting emails we may look at how language content affects tone and politeness. Text messaging offers a fruitful area for discussion. Constructing search terms also requires precision in word choice and the subsequent scanning, skimming and selection are all language-based activities. Making links with the child's own language can help them focus on similarities and differences, so for example when labelling elements of a web page we may ask a pupil to help us do this in their first language and this may in turn reveal learning points for the whole class.

5. *Develop learner independence.* As with all pupils we want to move EAL learners up the ladder of cognitive challenge. In order to differentiate the learning experience we may need to select resources with a lower reading age (though not necessarily academic challenge). Our expectation must be that they will bridge the gap to more advanced material within a target time-frame. It is important to have a plan for how long this may take so that the pupil is moved beyond their comfort zone. We could expect them to use worksheets more frequently, to extend written and oral answers, and to tackle material of a higher reading age. Plan graduated expectations of communication with the pupil, for example two weeks listening, two weeks responding pictorially through a notebook, six weeks answer verbally in own language, eight weeks coached verbal answers in English.

Welcoming and including new pupils

Often learners with EAL will arrive part way through the school year, it is important to take time to welcome them. Use the pupils' name accurately whenever they are addressed and check your pronunciation. When you introduce yourself, write your name down.

Allow and encourage the use of their first language especially during the initial period. Incorporating their first language into everyday routines (greetings, yes/no, numbers and so on) helps demonstrate that you are interested in their language. Demonstrate interest in their past experiences, for example through contexts used in presentations, web pages, worksheets and database tasks. Encourage pupils to develop their own bilingual dictionary.

Plan groupings carefully, do not assume automatic friendships with those who share their first language. Be careful of pairing two EAL learners with the same level of English acquisition as they may get little practice in English. Practical ICT-related activities such as conducting a survey help new arrivals get to know their classmates while using a restricted range of language over and over again. Also useful are collaborative tasks that involve purposeful use of language, such as role plays where children have to ask for and share information in order to complete a task.

Allow some time for email and Internet access where pupils want to contact friends and relatives from their previous home country. Be aware that Internet filtering limitations may not work for non-English based sites or search terms, so make expectations clear and keep a watchful eye.

Lesson strategies

In planning lessons request help from your EAL co-ordinator or department. Some local authorities have EAL advisers. Plan how you will work with bilingual assistants or community link assistants and ask for their help in translation of key vocabulary.

Teach pupils how to change regional language settings on computers and allow them to switch between English and first language interfaces. Online dictionaries are a useful resource, with many including pronunciation (ensure the computer they use has sound capabilities). Make translation tools available, for example Babel Fish – be aware and teach the whole class about their limitations. Use ICT to allow recording and playback of pronunciation. The class could also build a database including pronunciation and pictures.

Display key vocabulary including pictures and translations where appropriate. In lessons encourage quantity of response in terms of words used over correct spelling and grammar, initially correcting only key vocabulary. Remember the potential gap between oral and written fluency – do not be surprised if written responses do not demonstrate the cognitive ability seen during verbal responses. Also, encourage feedback either orally or in picture format. Give thinking time in small groups to rehearse answers.

Be aware of any idioms you use such as 'Pull your socks up' – you could get all pupils to compile these as a database task or develop images which illustrate the idiom and meaning in a single digital photograph. Literal translation does not always convey the meaning of a concept such as mouse, cell and laptop.

What the research says: Learning styles

This chapter has discussed how we tailor learning to pupils' different needs. One way that we might choose to do this is by taking, into account the 'learning style' of pupils. Many schools use a learning styles survey and provide the results to teachers and pupils. Most commonly, teachers are provided with information about whether their pupils are predominantly visual, auditory or kinaesthetic learners (or a mixture of two or three of these attributes). Given what we know about the effects of labelling it is worth pausing to consider the research evidence for using learning styles data.

Atherton identifies four assumptions made by proponents of the idea that learning style is important:

1. People do learn in distinctively different ways.
2. It is possible to develop a relatively simple taxonomy of learning styles.
3. Then develop test instruments to ascertain individuals' learning styles.
4. Teach to address them. (Atherton, 2004)

There are some big leaps to be made here and Atherton makes the point that even if the first assumption is uncontested, the second is 'dubious'. Atherton also draws our attention to the debate regarding the malleability of learning styles. If we believe that learning styles are hardwired and cannot be changed, then teachers must adapt their teaching to suit the individual. If learning style is simply a preference for learning in a certain way, then we face a dilemma as to whether we should change our teaching approach or try to stretch the learner to embrace different styles. Atherton believes that if learning styles represent a preference then:

- they are not as clear-cut as the various 'inventories' suggest, and
- motivation over-rides them with no contest.

(Continued)

(Continued)

There are many learning styles models, Coffield et al. (2004) identified 71, and from these categorized 13 'major' models. In their substantial review into whether learning styles were a useful tool in post-16 education they begin by identifying that 'there are very few robust studies which offer, for example, reliable and valid evidence and clear implications for practice, based on empirical findings' (2004: 2). They set out to improve this situation by identifying models which were most influential and examining whether there was evidence which supported the models' claims. Furthermore they sought to examine the implications for pedagogy and whether there was evidence that using the models had a measurable impact upon students' learning. Their results for each of the 13 major models present a very mixed picture, with some tools offering considerable potential, while others are found currently unsound for use in education. None of the models presented robust empirical evidence for pedagogical impact for learners. The cautious optimism for some learning styles models is not reflected in the claims of some practitioners:

> Rita Dunn, for example, ... is quoted by O'Neil (1990: 7) as claiming that 'Within six weeks, I promise you, kids who you think can't learn will be learning well and easily ... The research shows that every single time you use learning styles, children learn better, they achieve better, they like school better.' (2004: 36)

The most promising models identified in the study were Allinson and Hayes' Cognitive Styles Index (for use with adults), Apter's Motivational Style Profile, Herrmann's Brain Dominance Instrument and Jackson's Learning Styles Profiler. It is interesting to note that concerns are raised regarding Dunn and Dunn's Model and Instruments of Learning Styles which includes the visual, auditory and kinaesthetic (VAK) classification; in its current form the authors do not recommend the model for use in the UK. Coffield's findings and recommendations are detailed and we recommend that you read the report. Some of the main findings are summarized below:

1. Use of a reliable, valid tool could improve an individual's understanding of how they learn and how this can be enhanced by choosing an appropriate strategy for a particular situation.
2. Use of a learning styles model can open up a dialogue between teacher and pupil about how they learn best – the teacher needs to fully understand the rationale for their model. While some teachers understand the rationale and research basis for the learning styles model chosen, others do not: 'the use of different inventories of learning styles has acquired an unexamined life of its own, where the notion of learning styles itself and the various means to measure it are accepted without question' (Coffield et al., 2004: 3).
3. A discussion which starts with learning styles could act as a catalyst for wider organizational and particularly pedagogical change.
4. We must be aware of the dangers of labelling in creating a fixed perception of learning style for an individual which becomes a learning handicap, an extreme example might be 'I can't read that, I'm a kinaesthetic learner'.
5. Teachers need to spend their time wisely; other contenders for producing large effects in learning include metacognitive approaches and formative assessment (see Chapter 6).
6. The quality of the models and tools varied greatly – 'some of the best known and widely used instruments have such serious weaknesses (e.g. low reliability, poor validity and negligible impact on pedagogy) that we recommend that their use in research and in practice should be discontinued' (Coffield et al., 2004: 55).

These findings seem at odds with what is happening in schools where versions (often untested) of the VAK methodology are used. Sharp et al. (2006) suggest that the proliferation of the VAK model originated from the work of Alistair Smith on Accelerated Learning. In his (well-received) publications Smith presents VAK as one of a number of tools and is clear in the importance of avoiding labelling children. In later interviews he advises a pragmatic approach, perhaps because of the unquestioning adoption of VAK. 'My position on VAK is that it is one model among many,' he says. 'The brain-based stuff has a value as a metaphor, but we need some honest brokers to let teachers know what is worthwhile and what isn't' (Revell, 2005).

The government have also become more circumspect in their enthusiasm for VAK and their general advice on learning styles:

> The learning styles idea is unhelpful when used to limit pupils' scope as learners, but it can be a helpful reminder to teachers to ensure that pupils are fully engaged in their learning by providing a range of different learning experiences and opportunities in which all pupils are emotionally, physically and intellectually involved. (DfES, 2005c)

Baroness Susan Greenfield (professor of pharmacology at Oxford University and director of the Royal Institute of Great Britain) also makes specific reference to the VAK methodology:

> Unfortunately, from a neuroscientific point of view, it is nonsense. Humans have evolved to build a picture of the world through our senses working in unison, exploiting the immense interconnectivity that exists between the senses in the brain. It is when senses are activated together – the sound of a voice in synchronisation with the movement of a person's lips – that brain cells fire more strongly than when stimuli are received apart.
>
> ... after more than 30 years of educational research into learning styles there is no independent evidence that VAK, or indeed any other learning style inventory, has any direct educational benefits, suggesting valuable time and resources are being wasted. (2007)

Beginning teachers would be wise to critically analyse any learning styles model they consider using.

 Further reading

Department for Education and Skills (DfES) (2004a) *Aiming High: Understanding the Educational Needs of Minority Ethnic Pupils in Mainly White Schools – A Guide to Good Practice.* Nottingham: DfES Publications.
Draws together a range of quality information and case studies to address a number of aspects of the inclusion agenda including EAL, prejudice and racism and education for all principles. For an in-depth examination of the themes outlined under 'Education for All', also see

Department for Education and Skills (DfES) (2004c) *Teaching Strategies and Approaches for Pupils with Special Educational Needs: A Scoping Study.* Nottingham: DfES Publications.

Provides a useful overview of the four main areas of need along with a description of recent research findings and suggested approaches or areas of focus.

Kerry, T. (2002b) *Mastering Teaching Skills Series – Learning Objectives, Task-Setting and Differentiation*. 2nd edn. Cheltenham: Nelson Thornes.

Kerry presents an evaluation of a range of commonly used differentiation strategies, encourages teachers to reflect upon their practical uses and shows how they might be applied in a practical context.

Robin Richardson, R. (2004) *Here, There and Everywhere: Belonging, Identity and Equality in Schools*. Stoke-on-Trent: Trentham Books.

 ## *Weblinks*

Live links to each of these websites can be found on the companion website, www.sagepub.co.uk/secondary.

Multiverse – www.multiverse.ac.uk/. A source of resources and research which focus upon the educational achievement of pupils from diverse backgrounds.

National Association for Language Development in the Curriculum (NALDIC) – www.naldic.org.uk. Contains research and practical advice on all aspects of EAL. See the ITTSEAL section of the site for resources particularly important for beginning (and practising) teachers.

QCA – Respect For All – www.qca.org.uk/qca_6753.aspx. Contains resources, including subject - specific contexts and examples of how all children can be participants in learning.

St Mary's College of Maryland – Differentiation – www.smcm.edu/edstudy/d7Proj/Projects/Research Sites/acbrowning/index.htm. Eloquently makes the case for differentiation and includes an overview of the literature.

8 TEACHING DIFFERENT AGES: KEY STAGE 3 TO POST-16

This chapter covers:

- transition strategies from Key Stage 2 into the secondary phase
- generic issues which apply across age phases and abilities, including questioning, setting the scene for learning, resources, teaching and learning strategies, plus encouraging successful and independent learners
- adapting teaching and learning strategies across the secondary age phases and to suit the changing characteristics of maturing pupils
- the role of induction processes and establishment phases of transition between key stages
- the progression framework for pupils through either academic or vocational education routes.

During Key Stage 3 we are moving pupils from a greater reliance on teacher direction and input towards becoming more independent learners who take greater responsibility for their learning. As pupils move into Key Stage 4, and beyond, this process has to accelerate as they work towards gaining qualifications. The techniques and approaches used, therefore, in a Key Stage 3 classroom will be quite different from those used in a Key Stage 4 and, later, in a post-16 classroom.

Some trainee teachers may believe that Key Stage 4 and post-16 lessons require less planning than Key Stage 3. In reality guiding, monitoring and assessing pupils at these higher levels requires careful planning. You will need a good knowledge of individual pupil capabilities alongside expert knowledge of the subject curriculum. Planning tends to be more focused on individuals than whole classes, so getting tracking systems in place becomes crucial. This chapter will exemplify some of the techniques and processes which are required for effective teaching and learning at each stage and how we can ease the transition between the different stages for pupils.

ICT IN KEY STAGE 2

As part of your training as a teacher you will spend some time investigating Key Stage 2 ICT. This will provide an overview, including: how ICT fits into the primary curriculum;

the ICT resources available; and teaching and learning approaches. The experience you have will largely depend on the primary school which you visit. Some schools are very committed and innovative in their approach to ICT, with excellent resources and proactive and technically proficient teachers. Some schools may prioritize other curriculum areas, have limited access to resources or variable teacher expertise.

There are issues outside of Year 6 teachers' control which can also affect the delivery of ICT in primary school. Many primary schools are disadvantaged by a lack of dedicated technical support on site; this can obviously cause problems for teachers waiting for technicians on a call-out basis. Depending on the turnaround time for a call-out it is likely that at least one day of teaching will have been affected.

The socio-economic background of pupils and their access to ICT outside of the classroom can influence pupils' learning. The *UK Children Go Online* study (Livingstone and Bober, 2005: 13) found that children who use the Internet 'Daily and weekly … have parents who also use the internet more often and are more expert'. The study also found that those teenagers who had been using the Internet since they were younger used the Internet more frequently and had more developed skills online. This helps to exemplify the digital divide and one way in which it may impact on pupils' knowledge of ICT both within primary and secondary education.

KEY STAGE 2 TRANSITION

Year 6 can be a busy and anxious time for pupils. The Primary Review (2007) draws on research findings from a number of sources and reports that primary school pupils are experiencing 'increases in test-induced stress' and anxiety. Also of relevance to secondary teachers is the narrowing of the primary curriculum in response to the perceived requirements of SATs. Our pupils are placed under pressure to do well in tests, with primary pupils displaying knowledge of the purpose of tests, the potential consequences of their results and anxiety about failure (Reay and Wiliam, 1999, cited in Tymms and Merrell, 2007).

This is also when pupils and parents decide on their choice of secondary school and prepare to move into a new phase of their education which will be considerably different from what they have experienced before. Research commissioned by the QCA (2001) examined the dip in performance experienced when pupils enter Year 7. This can be partly attributed to the way in which transition between Key Stage 2 and Key Stage 3 is conducted. The majority of schools had some form of transition support in place, but this was strengthened (and continues to be developed) through recommendations made by the Secondary National Strategy. There is a distinction to be made here between social and academic transition. Social transition – settling in, finding your way around and making friends – tends to be an embedded and effective practice in most schools. Academic transition – receiving attainment data, building upon previous knowledge and setting appropriately challenging work – tends to be less developed, particularly in ICT as there is no requirement for primary schools to share data on pupil progress and attainment (Ofsted, 2005c: 20). In the next section we will look at some of the issues for transition and some of the strategies schools have put in place.

Transition projects

The Secondary National Strategy recommends that transition projects (also called bridging units) are put in place to ease the move from Key Stage 2 to Key Stage 3. Some schools operate transition projects in the three core subjects: English, mathematics and science. However, Galton et al. (2003: 108) found secondary teachers focus on the social aspect of transition projects rather then using them effectively to aid academic progression. In ICT it has been suggested that an effective transition unit would be developing a presentation called 'About Me'. Pupils create the presentation in Year 6 and then use it in Year 7 to explore concepts such as fitness for purpose, audience and evaluation.

The benefits of using a transition project are clear: pupils enter Year 7 with work which is familiar and can see how their prior learning is valued and developed; the foundation work is already completed enabling secondary teachers to focus on new concepts, knowledge and understanding. Despite these advantages there are various reasons why ICT transition projects are not always feasible in schools: it relies on the willingness and capacity of primary and secondary teachers to collaborate; it depends on the number of feeder schools in the area; primary teachers may receive requests from a range of secondary subject areas for transition projects and are not able to accommodate them all; and the logistics of the secondary school receiving the presentation from the primary school or via the pupils. Given these factors, the likelihood is that you will not be involved in a discrete ICT transition project.

Other transition approaches

Other approaches to transition tend to be centrally organized by the schools. Schools will normally have primary pupils to visit during the summer term. During this time they may meet their form tutor, fellow classmates and participate in organized activities to provide a flavour of secondary school life. You may be asked to be involved in this and may need to teach a sample lesson. A sample lesson should be self-contained, introduce pupils to something new and allow them to achieve.

New Year 7 pupils may start school earlier in September than other pupils to give them an opportunity to become familiar with the school. This may include features such as staggered lunchtimes and breaktimes during the first weeks, so that the new intake do not become overwhelmed at these times. You would need to monitor this carefully and ensure that your lessons are planned to take account of these alterations in timetabling.

Some schools manage transition by modelling a primary structure for all or part of Year 7. Pupils will typically be taught some or all subjects within their form group, predominantly by a single teacher. They will often adopt a thematic or topic-based approach, for example 'healthy eating', mirroring the kinds of approaches seen in the primary classroom. This practice could be extended by linking with primary schools so that this work begins in Year 6 with some collaborative teaching.

Secondary schools will often have a transition co-ordinator. This may be a teacher or a learning mentor with specific responsibilities in this area. The transition co-ordinator will regularly visit the feeder primary schools to discuss pupils' profiles with primary teachers and to meet the pupils. This provides a familiar face for pupils when they move to secondary school. Sometimes secondary subject teachers will visit primaries to co-teach their subjects. Again this helps pupils to become familiar with staff and secondary teaching and learning approaches.

Year 7 pupils can also become involved with transition. They are sometimes asked to revisit their primary school to share their experiences with Year 6 pupils. This will usually be based around a Year 7 project in school on the topic of Year 6 to Year 7 transition.

Reflection Point

Reflection Point 8.1

- How do Key Stage 2/3 transition projects and strategies help to support pupils and their teachers as pupils move into Year 7? What are the success factors for transition strategies?

- Create a list of transition strategies. Consider their effectiveness from a costs and benefits point of view. Consider teacher time, pupil time, curriculum coverage and resource implications.

Assessment data

As a teacher with a new Year 7 class you will want information on their prior knowledge of ICT. Practice is variable and you may not receive an ICT level from the primary school. There are sometimes different views between teachers on the assessment of levels. This is mostly due to level descriptors which are open to interpretation. Through the Secondary National Strategies considerable work was done within some local education authorities (LEAs) to reach a common understanding of the level descriptors within the secondary sector. Some LEAs encouraged cross-moderation of Key Stage 3 work between schools to aid this process. There is now a greater level of consensus for interpretation of the secondary levels, but there is still a level of subjectivity in teacher judgements.

The transition approaches we have examined so far have identified ways of supporting and easing pupils into secondary school – social transition. As a secondary ICT teacher you are also focused on academic transition and may be faced with the prospect of starting to teach Year 7 classes with little or no subject-specific data. For effective teaching and learning to take place, the classroom teacher needs to know the prior knowledge and understanding of the pupils in the class. How will you gain knowledge of the pupils in your class? There are four possible strategies which can be used:

1. Make assumptions regarding pupils' ICT capability based on the data provided by the primary school.
2. Conduct an initial test to benchmark pupils' knowledge and understanding and provide data specific to ICT.

3. Use a basic self-assessment audit which can provide a flavour of the ICT capability but without providing any concrete data.
4. Using baseline assessment (usually question and answer) at the start of each new project.

An ICT department will normally have an approach in place which may be a combination of the above.

Reflection Point 8.2

Consider the advantages and disadvantages of each approach for the teacher and for the pupils. How do you think each approach may affect teaching and learning in Year 7?

MOVING INTO THE SECONDARY PHASE

There are a number of issues which need to be considered at all stages of secondary education (and throughout the education system). An overview of these will be provided here and the discussion throughout the rest of the chapter will also provide further examples of these issues in practice.

Questioning techniques

Good questioning techniques help teachers to assess pupils' understanding and develop pupils' thinking skills, their use of language, ability to analyse and to synthesize information. This can be a powerful technique which is frequently not fully exploited. Instead, many teachers use 'surface'-level questioning requiring only recall. Methods of developing higher-level questions is explored in Chapter 6. The way you use questioning and the responses you receive will vary as pupils move through different age phases (Table 8.1).

Project work

ICT lends itself to using project work to explore how ICT can provide solutions and how different aspects of ICT can be integrated to make systems more efficient. Pupils need to understand the systems development life cycle to effectively engage with project work. You should definitely be able to see a systems model in operation in Key Stage 4 when pupils are working on coursework, but there are ample opportunities for introducing this in Key Stage 3 as well.

In Year 7 project work is likely to be strongly guided by the teacher, but can be delivered within the framework of a systems model. It is beneficial to introduce this concept and then return to it as the project passes through each phase thereby making the stages of the system explicit to pupils. In Year 8 and Year 9 the teacher should be transferring

Table 8.1 Questioning techniques for different age phases

Age phase and characteristics	Questioning considerations
Year 6–Year 8 pupils Younger pupils tend to: • be enthusiastic • be keen to respond • want validation and praise • shout out, becoming frustrated by 'hands up'	As a teacher you should: • develop strategies to encourage pupils to spend more time thinking through their answers • encourage all pupils to contribute by directing questions • encourage pupils to justify and explain their response
Year 9–Year 10 pupils Tend to: • be reticent about contributing in class • answer most questions with 'Don't know!' • be self-conscious (image and the views of their peers are extremely important to them) • seek more independence and are developing their own viewpoints on a range of topics	This age group need to refine their thinking skills, ability to justify and evaluate, in preparation for their qualifications. You will need to recognize their anxiety and offset this with strategies like: • paired or group work with feedback from a spokesperson • discussions developed around a written exercise, providing a considered response and a written prompt • examination questions used to practice thinking skills • posing more challenging questions and discussions based on their expanding real-world experience
Year 11–Year 13 students Tend to: • be more confident, self-assured and independent • view their teachers as equals • want teachers to treat them as young adults rather than children and to respect them as individuals • recognize their rights but need reminding of their responsibilities • ask challenging questions to which you may not know the answer	As a teacher you should: • recognize them as young adults • remind them of their responsibilities – their actions can have an affect on their own and others' education • be confident when stating that you do not know an answer but that you will find out for next lesson • encourage debates (where there may not be a correct answer) to develop their own views • challenge biased views and ask them to justify their assertions using evidence

some of the responsibility to pupils for managing projects to solve a teacher-defined problem. The teacher should still provide structure to ensure pupils' learning progresses at a satisfactory pace.

When pupils begin work on their coursework for qualifications, they are expected to work independently. The likelihood is that many pupils will still need to be guided through this process, but this should be through general guidance which is provided to the class and the pupils are then expected to apply this to their own project work. The projects which pupils complete in Key Stage 4 will usually be on a similar topic and will utilize the same software which makes it easier to provide generic guidance.

In post-16, students will be taught the knowledge, skills and techniques required for a project using specific software. They then work independently on their individually designed coursework with bespoke, interim support from their teacher.

Personal development and aspirations

As a teacher, you are responsible not just for teaching your subject, but also for the pastoral care and development of pupils. A significant minority of children have low self-esteem, limited aspirations and little or no control over their impulses. Part of your role is to try to develop their confidence, provide inspiration and to help them to develop control over their emotions. A number of these factors are encompassed within research on emotional intelligence (EI): it has been found that people with high levels of emotional intelligence tend to achieve their goals and be happier (Qualter et al., 2007). Research with disadvantaged pupils with low emotional intelligence has helped raise their EI. These pupils exhibit more control and have raised aspirations. This links strongly with Chapter 5 and the behaviour management strategies you use to help pupils to control their own behaviour.

In this section, we have looked at issues which have relevance across the key stages and into post-16 education. In the rest of the chapter we examine the teaching and learning strategies you will adopt with different age phases. You will be able to see how using different strategies promotes more effective and age-appropriate learning.

KEY STAGE 3

During Key Stage 3 pupils gradually move from hand-holding through tasks towards greater independence and self-reliance. In Year 7 pupils may be uncertain and anxious about this new phase of their education. The first half-term tends to be a settling in period for new classes and the new Year 7 pupils. This is when you should be establishing your rules and routines, and when pupils' own expectations of your lessons will be established.

Introducing Year 7 to ICT

At the start of any new academic year there is an establishment phase for all classes, regardless of year group. Year 8 onwards will settle relatively quickly into the normal routines of the secondary school, because they have at least one year of experience to guide them. Year 7 will take longer to settle, a few examples of how this may impact on your first half-term are discussed below:

- They have to become orientated to a new school environment, meaning that pupils will arrive late to your class (you may also have pupils in your class who should not be there!).
- They may also be using a network for the first time. It can take a considerable length of time for some pupils to remember their user ID and password (keep a record of these to minimize disruption to your lessons). Pupils need to be taught that work is stored in and retrieved from different network areas.
- They will need to understand your rules and routines, including how their work is stored, whether it is electronically stored and marked, printed and put in folders or a combination of these.

Reflection Point 8.3

Consider the issues and practicalities which you will need to cover in your first lesson with a new Year 7 class. What systems do you need to have in place to ease the transition for pupils and to overcome potential problems?

It is essential that Year 7 pupils are given a general introduction to ICT within the school. This will normally include the administration of setting up user names and passwords, as well as helping them to find their way around the network: it is useful to demonstrate how to set up folders in their network area and to cover naming conventions (calling files 'Bob1', 'Bob2' and so on will seem like a good idea to some pupils!).

Most schools will also have an Acceptable Use Policy which is usually signed by pupils and sometimes by parents too. This sets out the expectations for use of ICT within the school both during ICT lessons and at other times. It is good practice to read through this with pupils and to discuss important issues. Internet safety is a growing concern and schools have a responsibility to educate children in the best use of the Internet, including how they can remain safe. It is not good enough to control software in school and adopt the attitude that parents should monitor their child's Internet use at home. Research demonstrates that many parents do not possess the necessary knowledge and skills to do this, particularly as Internet access is now available through a range of portable and wireless technologies to which children have ready access. Pupils can gain access to inappropriate content without adult knowledge or authority, it is our responsibility to teach them to manage this access safely.

Key Stage 3 teaching and learning

At the beginning of Key Stage 3, pupils will need a great deal of support and guidance as they develop their knowledge of ICT concepts, theory, practical skills and using new hardware and software. As they progress through the key stage, the teacher needs to gradually step back and allow pupils greater independence and responsibility for their learning.

Older pupils tend to regulate their behaviour and are quicker to respond to a teacher's calling for attention. At Key Stage 3, teachers have to work harder to get and maintain pupils' attention. The following extract gives examples of strategies which can be used with this age group.

Scenario

Teacher welcomes the class at the door, 'Good morning Year 8, lets get logged on, then join me at the front ready to start'. His tone of voice and attitude is enthusiastic and welcoming.

The class enter the room and follow the instructions, this routine is well established.
'While I'm taking the register, write down the objectives for today's lesson in your exercise books, please ...'
Following the register, the teacher visually checks that pupils are starting to finish writing and says, 'Right, you've got one minute to identify with the person next to you three things we did last lesson'.

The use of established routines results in minimal instruction to pupils, freeing up time to complete any administrative tasks before starting to teach. The tasks which are set occupy the pupils from the moment they enter the classroom thereby reducing the opportunity for disruptions. The pupils are immediately focused on the learning objectives and in recalling their previous learning: they are given thinking and discussion time to consider their response and have the prompt from today's learning objectives to help them.

Reflection Point 8.4

Consider the reasons for making explicit the links between prior and future learning. How might this help pupils to focus on the learning activities?

There are other techniques, too, which focus pupils' attention and start to prepare their minds for the lesson. The use of starters is well recognized for preparing pupils for learning and providing a strong and focused start to a lesson. A company called Independent Thinking takes this a step further by suggesting the use of pre-starter activities. These help to mentally warm up pupils ready to start learning. The activities are brief, but stimulate thinking and creativity and reduce the opportunity for disengagement with the lesson at an early stage. They recommend using lateral thinking puzzles, such as giving an answer and asking pupils for the question. You could also use puzzles such as trackwords, dingbats or anagrams displayed on the board for pupils to decipher. These activities should last only a couple of minutes and should have a controllable end point. It should also be fun to encourage a positive start to the lesson.

These types of activities could be used with older pupils as warm-up activities, however, these pupils are usually easier to settle and tend to be more focused on their future qualifications.

In the scenario peer discussion is used to give pupils thinking time. Allowing pupils time to discuss an answer tends to enrich the discussion: pupils have thinking time, they prompt each other's ideas and they have added security from sharing their ideas. It is important that pupils see how the different lessons fit together and the progression from one lesson to the next: everyone likes to see how their activity fits into the whole picture, no matter what they are doing. At Key Stage 3 pupils may only have one lesson of ICT per week. If schools operate a two-week timetable it can sometimes be nearly two weeks since their last ICT lesson. They need the opportunity to recall what they did last time.

Scenario continued

The class is creating mini-adverts for the school for parents evening. They have created their storyboards and are ready to start using the software.

Teacher: 'Right, everyone should have completed their storyboard for homework and should have them ready now. Last week we decided on some criteria we could use to evaluate our storyboards ...' The saved file is displayed on the interactive whiteboard (IWB). 'We are going to use this criteria to evaluate our partner's storyboard and to constructively suggest improvements. Can anyone give me an example of how we don't do this? Yes, Mina?'

'We don't say "That's rubbish", Sir.'

'Thanks, Mina. So what do we say, Jack?'

'You could say "You can make it better it by using different colours", Sir.'

'Excellent. You have four minutes to identify three things you like about each others' storyboard and two things you would like to see improved, does anyone have any questions? Right, off you go ...'

These lessons are clearly linked by reintroducing criteria agreed by the class last lesson. The IWB enables the teacher to take notes on class discussions, to save them and then reuse them at a later date. Pupils appreciate that their contributions are valued, recorded and used.

The discussion on constructive criticism is obviously building on prior experience from other units, but it is still important to remind pupils of expectations. It is clear what is required and the duration of the task. As the teacher moves around the room, he gives the pupils reminders about the length of time left until the end of the task which helps to maintain pace and focus.

Using peer-evaluation helps pupils to develop the skills needed for effective self-evaluation and to acquire a more critical eye for their own work. If pupils are to become self-regulated, independent learners then they must be able to formulate evaluation criteria, evaluate their work objectively and identify how their work can be improved. These are essential skills for pupils to develop in order to move successfully into Key Stage 4 and beyond.

Scenario continued

'Okay, has anyone used Moviemaker before?' Three pupils raise their hands. 'Right, you can help me as we go along.'

The teacher shows where the software is using the IWB. 'Now, we've already got the photographs we need in our shared drive, so the first thing we need to do is import them. Can anyone show me how to do this?' Sarah puts her hand up and is asked to come to the front to demonstrate how to import the photographs.

'Once we have imported the photographs we can start to arrange them on the storyboard by dragging and dropping them ...' The teacher commentates during the demonstration.

'Then we can apply different effects, timings and transitions. Can anyone show us how to add effects and transitions? Great, Salim, come and show us ...'

After demonstrating the techniques for today's lesson, a volunteer is asked to run through the whole process again from the start.

'Right, Kate is going to remind us all of what we need to do, but we may need to help her as we go along. Okay, Kate, you start off with importing the photographs ...' As Kate demonstrates, the teacher commentates, asks questions and requests help from the rest of the pupils until the demonstration is completed.

'Thank you, Kate. Right, when I tell you, I want you to start building your movie, using your storyboard for reference. I expect you to have completed at least five frames using the techniques we've covered. You have got 20 minutes ... any questions? ... Right, off you go.'

As the pupils move to the computers and log on, 'Today's Tasks' are displayed on the board as a reminder.

In the first part of the scenario pupils' prior experience is recognized, even though this was acquired outside school. This recognition can help to build rapport with the pupils you teach.

The use of peer discussion, pupil demonstrations and question and answer sessions help to make this an interactive lesson helping to maintain pupils' interest. Research (McIntyre et al., 2005) has shown that levels of engagement rise and learning improves when interactive activities are used.

The second demonstration helps to consolidate pupils' understanding. The demonstration is carefully controlled through the commentary, targeting questions to the class and requesting help for Kate when she forgets how to do something. Without this two-way interaction involving the whole class it is easy for pupils' attention to wander and disruption to occur. Inattention at this stage will impact later during the on-task phase of the lesson, manifesting itself as pupils who do not know what they should be doing and increasing the potential for off-task behaviour and disruption.

Even though the task has been clearly discussed and demonstrated, an additional visual prompt is displayed giving pupils a clearly structured reminder of what they should be doing during the lesson. Help sheets can be useful, but consider having these available either in a central location for pupils to help themselves or on request to encourage pupils to 'have a go' and to become more independent. We should then direct pupils to the help sheet rather than providing the answer, again to help foster independence.

The resources we use to support teaching and learning can be crucial to success. This will normally mean adapting resources or creating your own. An important consideration is the readability of resources. There are various tools which can be used to determine the reading age of a resource, but there are general principles which help. Guidelines include keeping your language simple, using short sentences, using diagrams and pictures to aid understanding and using good design principles, such as clear font, font size and breaking up text with white space.

It sounds obvious but the scenarios and resources we use should be of interest to pupils. This may mean giving pupils an element of choice about the scenario they use: whichever scenario you choose will only engage a proportion of the class. It is possible to provide a framework within which they work, but also for pupils to develop their project on different topics; for instance, creating a website on their hobby or using a drawing package to develop a logo for an organization of their choice. Giving pupils a choice is more likely to engage and sustain their interest in the project over a period of weeks.

BRIDGING KEY STAGE 3 TO KEY STAGE 4

The transition from Key Stage 3 to Key Stage 4 is not as disconcerting as the transition from Key Stage 2, but it still involves a step-change for pupils. This transition can be eased with careful planning, helping pupils to understand what will be expected of them and the content of their future studies.

Research conducted by Rudduck et al. (2003) highlighted four areas where teachers and schools can help pupils' transition to Key Stage 4:

1. Making the importance of and nature of work in Year 10 clear at the start of the year, perhaps using induction sessions or subject teachers reviewing course content across Key Stage 4.
2. Clarifying the term independence and how this will impact on pupils.
3. Sharing the relevance of the learning.
4. Making time for pupils to reflect on their learning.

These can be fairly easy to achieve and some draw on the good practice we have examined in Key Stage 3 pedagogy.

MOVING TO EXAMINATION SUBJECTS

Traditionally we perceive Key Stage 4 as being the start of the examination years, however some schools have decided to deliver vocational ICT examination courses from Year 9. It can be difficult to provide sufficient curriculum time in Year 10 and 11 to enable pupils to attain the full level 2 qualification for courses such as DiDA or OCR Nationals. Some schools have also opted to deliver a discrete short-course vocational qualification, such as AiDA (part of the DiDA suite), in Year 9 which is equivalent to one GCSE. In these schools it is not always expected that pupils will continue the qualification in Year 10 and 11. In Year 9 pupils choose their option subjects for the next two years of study. Pupils will not only choose their subjects, but also the nature of the qualifications they will study: academic or vocational.

The academic qualifications route (GCSEs progressing to A levels) is generally seen as the gold standard. Employers, universities, parents, pupils and the general public all know and understand what these are and have a perception of the standard of education which is enshrined within these qualifications. All other qualifications which are delivered through education (specific vocational or industry training is viewed separately and is generally well regarded) are naturally compared against these established qualifications, which are widely understood. Unfortunately, this can lead to the devaluation of vocational qualifications in some circles.

Vocational education and training are frequently offered as an alternative to GCSEs for pupils who struggle with academic content, but thrive in a more practical, hands-on context. Vocational courses offer an excellent alternative for these pupils, though not necessarily an easier route. Unfortunately, it is a widely held view that vocational courses are easier than academic routes, rather than that the practical content is more accessible to certain types of learners. It is important that you understand the nature, value and probable progression routes for qualifications so that you are able to discuss options with pupils in Year 9 (and again in future years). You should give this advice having viewed the options critically and without personal bias towards a particular route: we are advising pupils about what is best for *their* future. Over recent years the menu of vocational qualifications on offer to pupils in school or via further education (FE) partners has expanded. Where this is done well, schools can be deemed to be providing a personalized curriculum benefiting all pupils.

You will also be aware that vocational qualifications can also offer benefits to schools in terms of league table results. This first became apparent when GNVQs were delivered in schools, with each GNVQ being equivalent to four GCSEs. The full level 2 DiDA and OCR National qualifications are also equivalent to four GCSEs.

Reflection Point 8.5

- What are the advantages and disadvantages of delivering vocational qualifications in Year 9? Consider both higher and lower ability pupils.
- Review the specification for a vocational level 1/2 course. Do you think that pupils in Year 9 are able to work with sufficient independence to succeed with these qualifications?
- How might delivery in Year 9 affect a pupil's perception of ICT?

Routes for progression

The National Qualifications Framework (NQF) provides a structure for qualifications and assigns every qualification to a specific level to aid comparison between them. Pupils need careful and informed guidance from their teachers when selecting their optional subjects, as these will determine the probable progression routes open to them from Key Stage 4 into post-16 and beyond. You should be able to advise pupils on the best options for them in Year 9 and again in Years 11, 12 and 13, in order for them to achieve their goals, or if these are unknown, to provide suitable routes for progression through which they will be able to achieve. Figure 8.1 shows some of the ICT qualifications which are available at different levels of the NQF. The levels shown are those with which you should be most familiar, but be aware that the NQF extends beyond level 4.

NQF level	Examples of ICT qualifications
Entry	Entry Level Certificates in Using ICT Entry Level Certificate in ICT Skills for Life
Level 1	GSCE (grades D–G) Level 1 Certificate for ICT practitioners NewCLAiT Level 1 NVQ for IT Practitioners DiDA suite of qualifications at Level 1 OCR Nationals Level 1 iMedia Level 1 Foundation Diploma in IT
Level 2	GCSE (grades A* – C) Level 2 Certificate for ICT practitioners DiDA suite of qualifications at Level 2 OCR Nationals Level 2 iMedia Level 2 Higher Diploma in IT
Level 3	AS & A2 ICT AS & A2 Applied ICT iMedia Level 3 Level 3 BTEC National Diploma for ICT practitioners Advanced Diploma in IT
Level 4	Level 4 NVQ for IT Professionals Year 1 of undergraduate degree programmes

Figure 8.1   Examples of ICT qualifications on National Qualifications Framework (NQF)

STARTING YEAR 10

As pupils move into Year 10, focus centres on the qualifications which they are now working towards. The learning is assessment-driven from the outset, with the curriculum designed around the qualification's specification to maximize opportunities for all pupils to do their best. Pupils, though, must not only possess the required knowledge and skills in ICT as dictated by the qualification, but must also hone their study skills, revision and examination techniques, if they are to be successful.

The pedagogical principles employed at Key Stage 3 including use of the three-part lesson structure, sharing objectives target-setting, enabling thinking time for pupils to extend their answers, peer and self assessment, and so on, should all be continued throughout Key Stage 4 and beyond. This includes lessons where coursework development is the focus. The pedagogic practices employed at Key Stage 3 are good practice and should not be abandoned because pupils are now 'independent learners'. We have a responsibility for using the best tools and strategies at our disposal. Unfortunately, these principles are sometimes discarded when pupils begin to engage with coursework.

The change at Key Stage 4 is not the pedagogic practice, but rather in the interaction with the pupils, the focus on a different curriculum and different teaching and learning approaches. This is what we will explore in the next section.

In the following lesson transcript, we see a Year 10 class who are completing their coursework. The teacher is delivering both theory and practical work in a blend over the duration of the course, using the coursework as a vehicle for delivering the theoretical aspects of the qualification. Other aspects of the theory which cannot be covered in this way will be studied later.

Scenario

The Year 10 class are waiting outside, the teacher says, 'Right, folks, can you come in, get your files out and complete your self-review checklist, please. You'll need to go through your coursework and tick off what you've done so far.' The class enter and carry out the instructions, reviewing their coursework and completing the checklist. They then write down a target in the space provided on the checklist for today's lesson. This is a routine and while they do this the register is taken.

'Right, has everyone completed the checklist and your target for today? Great, Sam – what's your target?'

'I want to finish my design, Miss.'

'Great! It would be really good if you could do that as we need to be moving on to implementation next week. Anyone else got that as their target? Remind me: what do we need to include in the design? Maria?' ...

The established routines work well for the teacher and the class. The self-review document is used regularly and helps pupils to self-evaluate and monitor their progress. Pupils also routinely set their own targets helping to develop independence and making them accept responsibility for their own progress. This activity then leads into the starter providing the basis for the teacher to review (through question and answer) prior learning and look forward to what they will be studying later.

During the main part of the lesson new concepts are explained and pupils complete activities to develop their understanding. The pupils will have to apply the theoretical knowledge to their coursework later. Pupils are encouraged to take notes which they will be able to use when completing their coursework and for revision later on.

Scenario

'Today we're going to look at validation and verification and how we can use this in our systems. This is something you need to use for your coursework and it may come up in your exams, so you need to take notes.' The objectives are on the board and are discussed.

(Continued)

(Continued)

The teacher then explains validation and verification methods and rationale. She asks the pupils to read the relevant section in the class set of textbooks.

'Okay, now that we've looked at the definitions and you've read about it in your textbooks, I want you to spend two minutes jotting down one example of validation and one example of verification. Think about when you've seen it used. Then I want you to give one example for each of how you could use it in the system you're creating. Any questions? Right, start work.' She displays the activities on the board as a reminder for the pupils of what they need to do. When the time is up, she asks some of the pupils to share what they have written and discusses the results.

'I'm going to show you how to set up validation and verification in our database. You need to take notes on this, because you won't remember how to do it when you get to it next week, but you need to know how it works so you can include it in your design today.' A quick demonstration follows and pupils are prompted to write down the different stages. 'Right, let's run through it again, this time you guys telling me how to do it ...' Pupils give instructions to the teacher for a second demonstration.

'Okay, all designs are to be completed this week and I'll be collecting them in for marking on Friday. There's an extra lesson on Thursday after school, so if you're behind you'll have to attend. I'll be coming round to check your files and checklists and make a note of where you're up to, then I'll see how many of you I'll have here on Thursday. Can you make sure your files are on your desk for me? Any questions? Right, lets get started.'

The pupils move to the computers and start work. The teacher circulates around the room with her mark-book, checking the contents of the files, the checklists and making a note of where pupils are up to. She discusses progress briefly with each pupil.

A number of approaches have been used in this scenario to help pupils learn successfully about the topic:

- The teacher explains what validation and verification are and when they are used.
- She reinforces this through a reading activity.
- Pupils are asked to give examples based on their experience.
- The technique is applied to individual projects followed up through question and answer.
- A practical demonstration.

The next extract will show this knowledge being further consolidated through plenary and homework activities.

Clear deadlines are given and additional support is provided to help them to achieve by these dates. Although pupils have more independence through self-evaluation and target-setting, the lesson is structured to keep the pupils on target for completion dates and their progress is closely monitored and assessed, both formatively and summatively.

Extra lessons, either after school or at lunchtime are a useful strategy for supporting weaker or borderline pupils. It provides them with additional time and the pupil-to-teacher ratios are generally more favourable, thereby giving pupils more opportunity to ask questions and receive formative feedback on their work. Setting interim deadlines for each section of coursework means that even if pupils have not completed all aspects of their design that they will have to hand it in for marking. Generally, teachers will tell pupils that this is final marking, but then give additional opportunities to either work in their own time (through, for example, extra lessons) or will plan additional time into the curriculum for 'coursework catch-up' once all of the coursework has been 'completed'.

Even when pupils are completing coursework, it is still good practice to have a three-part lesson to enable pupils to review and consolidate what they have learnt. Plenary time can be used to develop pupils' examination techniques and practice examination questions on the topic covered in the lesson. This also helps to reinforce that the theoretical knowledge covered may be needed for examinations.

Scenario continued

Ten minutes before the end of the lesson, the pupils are asked to finish what they are doing, save their work and log off. Pupils put their files away and sit at the central desks. Already laid out on the desks are sample examination questions on validation and verification.

'Okay, folks, can you pop your name on the sheet in front of you and answer the questions. We'll go over them together in a minute.' The teacher moves around the desks checking that pupils are completing the questions.

As the pupils finish, the questions are displayed on the board.

'Okay, the first question then is "'Presence checks' and 'Range checks' are two validation checks used in a database. For each of them, explain how they are used to detect errors when entering data (2 marks)." Right, in the exam, what's the first thing we do after reading the question? Neil?'

'Re-read the question, Miss, and check how many marks it's got.'

'Good, Neil! Reshma, what have you got for "Presence checks"?'

Reshma responds, 'A presence check makes sure that the field isn't left empty'.

'Okay, does everyone agree with that?' Pupils nod. 'Yep, that's right Reshma, and that response would get you one of the two marks, so even if you can't remember what a range check is, you still answer what you can. But, of course, we all know what a range check is, don't we, Alison? Can you give me your answer for that.' Alison gives her answer which is briefly discussed.

'Right, I want you to mark your own work; the answers for the rest are … If you've got any wrong, I want you to look up the correct answers for homework and note them down. I'll be collecting these in next lesson to check through and I expect you all to get full marks.'

The lesson is brought to a close and the pupils are dismissed.

Two objectives are achieved here: first, pupils' examination techniques are developed through practice and discussion and, second, pupils knowledge from the lesson is reviewed and consolidated. Responsibility for having the correct information in their files is given to the pupils, by setting research of the correct answers for homework. The teacher does recognize, though, that some pupils will shirk this responsibility unless it is monitored, so she states that the work will be marked

Reflection Point 8.6

Consider the ways in which a teacher can give greater responsibility to pupils in Key Stage 4. How might you use these strategies in your own lessons?

Boosting attainment

At Key Stage 4 you will have pupils in your class who are on the C/D borderline. In many cases it is possible to boost the attainment of these pupils to help them achieve a C grade. We have already discussed the importance of setting targets with pupils to provide focus and to clarify expectations. All your pupils should be aware of their target grade, their current attainment and how best to achieve (or exceed) their target. For those pupils who are borderline C/D you should set short-term targets and provide frequent, good quality formative feedback to help them to improve. These pupils frequently benefit from booster classes, which can be held at lunchtime, after school or during holiday periods. These classes tend to have smaller numbers of pupils, who will normally be working at a similar level and need more intensive support and additional time to reach their potential. It is vital that you regularly assess pupils' progress against their targets and share this data with them: pupils must understand what they need to do to succeed.

Other strategies we have previously mentioned is the role of a good induction into Key Stage 4, making clear our expectations and those of the course of study, introducing project work in Year 9 as an introduction to Key Stage 4 ICT, and providing time for pupils to reflect on and consolidate their learning. Many of the strategies to help boost attainment require additional time and effort from the teacher. The majority of pupils appreciate the extra efforts you make to support them. Teachers want their pupils to do well, but ensure that you are supporting them appropriately by enabling them to work independently using the guidelines and formative support you provide.

During Key Stage 4 pupils should work more independently and should be given greater responsibility for their own learning. The teacher's role moves towards a facilitator of learning but also retains many elements of active teaching. You will be guiding and supporting pupils and ensuring that they know the best way to proceed in order to fulfil their goals.

POST-16 EDUCATION

When students enter post-16 education, they need to take a significant step up in terms of independent learning. Many students do not realize at the beginning of their post-16 studies that they need to spend approximately the same amount of time in independent study as they do in the classroom. Some students require convincing about this requirement, particularly as this phase of education tends to coincide with students obtaining part-time jobs and social lives featuring greater freedom.

Your school should have transition and induction arrangements in place for new Year 12 students. This may commence at the end of Year 11 or may start in September, depending on the school. It will probably include expectations while on a course, developing study skills and introduction to the courses they have elected to study. No matter what the school has put in place to ease the transition to post-16 study, you will also need to make clear your expectations and the requirements of studying at level 3 in your subject. Students will normally have a good knowledge of their rights, you will need to clarify their responsibilities to their course of study, to their peers and to you.

For you as a teacher, there will be a shift too; the students have opted to stay on and study your subject. Your focus will shift to developing the students as independent learners and facilitating their studies. Part of teaching this age group is preparing them for either work or higher education. Once more we would like to reinforce that the shifting role of the teacher and change to teaching and learning approaches does not mean that the pedagogic good practice employed at Key Stage 3 should be abandoned. You will still need to carefully plan your lessons to incorporate the good practice we have previously covered.

The following extracts from a lesson demonstrate some of the techniques which can be used to develop the skills of independent learning at post-16. The class is looking at ICT and society.

Scenario

'Right, I asked you last lesson to read through Chapter 9 in your textbooks, ready for today. So using that knowledge, I want us to create a class mind map on ICT and Society. You will need to write this down yourselves and take notes. Who can start us off?'

The teacher takes contributions from the class, gradually developing a mind map. When students cannot think of any more points, he asks prompt questions to stimulate further discussion as well as to check understanding. He refers to a teacher resource to ensure that all points have been identified.

'Remember your numbers, 1, 2, 3, 4, 5. 1, 2, 3 ...' Each student is pointed to in turn, giving each a number. '... right, get into your groups please: all the 1s together; 2s together, etcetera.' The students move into their groups. 'Each group is going to research an aspect of ICT and society and then create a presentation which will be given to the rest of the class. A copy of each presentation will be uploaded to the VLE for you all to access and use for revision. On the board is a list of topics numbered one to five, Group 1, take topic one, Group 2 topic two and so on down the list. You can go to the library, use the Internet and your textbooks, but I do expect to see more than what is in your textbooks in your presentation.'

The criteria for the presentations is displayed. 'Remember, slides should use bullet points which you then talk around, not whole paragraphs. Each presentation should be no more than 10 minutes and please cite your sources. You've got until 2.00 p.m. to complete the presentation and get back here all ready to present your research. Any questions?' There are some questions about the logistics of presenting, then, 'OK, let's start work!'

(Continued)

(Continued)

The students move off into their groups to discuss how to manage the project between them. The teacher circulates to check understanding and discusses strategies with each group. He also gives some ideas about possible sources of information which they need to explore.

At 2.00 p.m. the students are adding the finishing touches to their slides and preparing to present. The teacher says, 'You've got three minutes to finish off, then we'll start with Group 1. If you're ready Natasha, do you want to come and set up?' Natasha moves to the front and sets up her group's presentation.

Although, teachers explain the requirement for extensive independent study outside class time, it helps to guide students as to what they should be researching. Here homework is used to support the work they are completing in class, setting them reading material, as well as work to finish and extend (see following extract). The students are supported in developing skills such as note-taking, teamwork, project management, working to tight deadlines and delivering presentations. When the students progress to higher education or employment, these skills will be developed further, but they are being given a good foundation by their teacher here.

The style of teaching is quite different to that at Key Stage 3 and 4 when the teacher imparts information and knowledge. In these extracts, discussion is encouraged and the teacher uses notes to ensure that all aspects are covered. He is transferring ownership of learning to the students and giving them greater responsibility for developing their own knowledge, as well as contributing to the knowledge of their peers. This can also be seen through the development of resources which are then shared via the virtual learning environment (VLE).

After giving the class the details about the task, the teacher circulates ensuring understanding and giving hints regarding topics and sources of information. Not all the students will have the necessary skill-set for this task. For some of the students additional guidance is needed if they are to successfully engage with it. The approach here is 'light-touch' and provides additional guidance where appropriate, rather than to all the students.

Scenario continued

As the presentations are given, the teacher makes notes against his checklist of areas to be covered by each one. Following each presentation, he gives feedback and encourages a discussion of any areas which were not covered in sufficient depth. The students take notes on the areas which he raises.

When the presentations have finished the teacher says, 'Thanks to all of you for your hard work on that. I know it's pretty tough having to research and present quickly on a topic – but sometimes that's the way it happens in work. I'm impressed by how well most of you have covered the topics.' He knows that some aspects have not been covered enough. 'We discussed some areas which needed a bit more work, so I want your groups to amend the presentations and submit them to me for next lesson. Then I can upload them to the VLE for us all to use. OK? ...'

'Right, for homework ...' The task is displayed. 'Next lesson we are going to have a trial! On the VLE you will find a number of case histories for various computer crimes and you have been allocated to a group and a role within that group. Your task is to read the case history, investigate the relevant laws and prepare to either defend your client or develop a case against them, depending on your job. The rest of the class will be the jury and we will make a ruling, based on the law, and pass sentence. Have a look on the VLE, if you have any questions, come and see me *before* next lesson. OK?'

In this extract, teacher resources are used to provide prompts for extending the discussion. Responsibility for ensuring that accurate and complete information is included in the presentation for uploading to the VLE is retained by the students, not by the teacher. Students' note-taking skills are developed by requiring them to take notes on discussions for developing their work further. This is an important skill for the students to develop and one which will not always come naturally to them.

In this lesson, the students worked well and developed good presentations. The teacher recognizes this and gives them appropriate praise and encouragement. This is not always the case: you should be prepared early on in the year to have to repeat your expectations for the quality of work.

The lesson finishes with an outline of the following lesson. He introduces the topic and is utilizing the VLE to encourage independent work. It is possible to see from the two activities described in the scenario that interactive, interesting activities are possible which will engage students and help them to learn. It should not be assumed that teachers give lectures at this level: this is not the case. These activities help students to develop a deeper and more thorough understanding of the topic by requiring them to work through the material independently. This is then explored in more detail in class when differing viewpoints can be discussed to enhance understanding further.

THE LEARNING JOURNEY

You should be able to see through this chapter that the way in which pupils learn and our teaching approaches change over time. During your wider reading you have probably encountered the theories of Piaget, Vygotsky and Kolb, among others. These well-known theories offer ways to conceptualize pupils' learning, providing a framework to help direct our teaching and pupils' learning. We learn from these theories that a child must understand certain concepts to be able to build on them and understand new concepts. We need to remember this as we move through the spiral curriculum (see Chapter 3). Pupils can only progress if we provide a suitable framework in which they can learn.

As a teacher it is very easy to spoon-feed the required information to pupils, but this does not allow them to develop their ICT capability or to learn how to learn. The young people we teach have a thirst for knowledge (although in some this can appear latent until re-awoken by an inspiring teacher). We should be teaching our pupils to be independent learners capable of lifelong learning. This involves a flexible approach and hard work to adapt your teaching across different ages and abilities from hour to hour, but the resulting success is what makes teaching our pupils so rewarding.

What the research says: learning theories

During your reading, you will encounter different theories of learning. The differences between these theories can often be blurred and it can be difficult for beginning teachers to identify where one theory ends and another starts. Many of these theories have been developed based on earlier theories which can lead to this confusion (Mergel, 1998). Below, we provide a very brief synopsis of some common theories.

Behaviourism: reinforcing a particular stimulus will result in a change in behaviour. You may recall Pavlov's experiments involving dogs trained to expect food when a bell rang. The stimulus was the ringing bell followed by food. This resulted in the dogs salivating when they heard the bell rather than when food arrived – behaviour change. The principles of behaviourism can be found in school with positive discipline systems which seek to modify behaviour through rewards and sanctions. In ICT games can create a similar result when players are rewarded for correct answers.

Cognitivism: developed when researchers identified limitations in the behaviourist model. Piaget identified cognitive development structures whereby individuals create their own internal knowledge structure (*schema*) and then attempt to classify new information into our existing schema (*assimilation*) or we develop new schema if it does not fit within our existing structures (*accommodation*). There needs to be *equilibrium* between assimilation and accommodation. The schema affects how individuals process and internally organize new information (Parsons et al., 2001). Cognitivists believe that we need to provide feedback to facilitate learners in organizing new information into their internal schema. Techniques which are grounded in this tradition are those which help to categorize relatively meaningless sets of data or lists, such as the use of mnemonics or creating stories to help make lists more memorable.

Constructivism: individuals construct their own knowledge. A person's interpretation of knowledge is influenced by their experiences, environment and beliefs. Learning can occur consciously or not, for instance pupils may alter their behaviour or beliefs based on a role model. Social constructivism theorizes that people construct knowledge together through discussions or joint activities. This is a key theory in online learning where learners contribute to online discussion boards in order to develop the knowledge of the group as well as their own knowledge as an individual (Mergel, 1998).

Further reading

Galton, M., Gray, J. and Rudduck, J. (eds) (2003) *Transfer and Transitions in the Middle Years of Schooling (7–14): Continuities and Discontinuities in Learning*. Research Report RR443. London: DfES. (www.dfes.gov.uk/research/data/uploadfiles/RR443.pdf).

McIntyre, D., Pedder, D. and Rudduck, J. (2005) 'Pupil voice: comfortable and uncomfortable learnings for teachers', *Research Papers in Education*, 20(2): 149–68.

Qualter, P., Gardner, K. and Whiteley, H. (2007) 'Emotional intelligence: review of research and educational implications', *Pastoral Care in Education*, March: 11–20.

 # *Weblinks*

Live links to each of these websites can be found on the companion website, www.sagepub.co.uk/secondary.

Independent Thinking Ltd provide ideas on creativity in education and pre-starters – www.independentthinking.co.uk/default.aspx

James Atherton's website on teaching and learning theory – www.learningandteaching.info/

Mergel, B. (1998) *Instructional Design and Learning Technology*. Canada: University of Saskatchewan. www.usask.ca/education/coursework/802papers/mergel/brenda.htm

TEACHING OUTSIDE THE CLASSROOM

This chapter covers:

- the benefits of educational visits for pupils
- possible contexts for educational visits
- recommendations for the organization of educational visits following the Glenridding Beck tragedy
- some of the practicalities of organizing an educational visit which are explored through a scenario.

ICT is an exciting subject: it is one which offers a huge range of possibilities to pupils. It is also an area with which many pupils naturally engage on a day-to-day basis – via social networking, mobile phones, podcasts, music downloads, gaming, digital photography – integrating the technology seamlessly into their world. The average computer suite has 20–30 computers, printers, a scanner, some digital cameras and a curriculum and school rules which can limit pupils' use of technology. How, then, can we create opportunities for pupils to engage with some of the more innovative approaches to ICT and to learn about how ICT is now embedded in and shapes the world around us?

Educational visits provide good opportunities for pupils to learn and develop. In Figure 9.1, we have divided these benefits into two main areas to show that the learning is not only connected with the subject area, but also is about the broader development of individual pupils.

In addition to the benefits in Figure 9.1, for some disadvantaged pupils this may be their only opportunity to visit a foreign country, to go to a top tourist attraction or to visit a skating rink: all trips which dedicated teachers organize and take their pupils on every year. They can help to foster good relationships between pupils and staff which can be continued into the classroom.

Reflection Point 9.1

Review the topics you have taught or are going to teach on placement. What opportunities exist for pupils to learn in an out-of-school context?

You may wish to make note of these opportunities in your scheme of work.

Subject learning	Self-development
• Learn about subject area • Opportunity to explore new approaches • Real-life experiences (see, hear and do) • Consider possible future applications of learning • Learning from experts	• Works towards a long-term goal • Behaves appropriately • Works with others, developing team-working and collaborative skills • Motivation • Respect for self and for others • Problem-solving • Enjoy new experiences • Sense of achievement • Making a positive contribution • Building positive relationships with others (peers and adults)

Figure 9.1   Benefits of educational visits

CHOOSING A CONTEXT

Learning outside the classroom can take place in a number of ways and it does not always involve a visit off site. Pupils can also learn from a visiting speaker, video conferencing, using the school's VLE or going out of the classroom to take photographs or video around the school grounds. Learning outside the classroom can be achieved through creative use of the resources and facilities around you. Projects such as the National Space Centre (see weblinks) provide opportunities for pupils to learn how ICT is applied in a real context. Through video conferencing the experts can visit your classroom remotely, speaking to the pupils and answering their questions. This could be combined with a physical visit to the National Space Centre.

ICT is used by all organizations to a lesser or greater extent, however, it tends to be overlooked as a subject for school visits. You will need to discuss your requirements carefully with the organization and will probably have to supplement any activities on the day with your own resources (for use either on site or in the classroom, prior to or following the visit). Larger organizations offering school visits for ICT sometimes combine ICT with business studies. Check resources and the content of any talks offered to ensure that they do meet your requirements. Often business studies is the principal focus which will result in limited learning for ICT.

Beginning teachers tend to picture educational visits as full-day excursions which require months of planning, but this is not always the case. Significant learning opportunities exist in local organizations which will provide familiar contexts for pupils. Examples include the police, local banks, supermarkets or a local library. The benefit of these local organizations is that pupils will already be familiar with some of the ways ICT is used by them. It is advantageous to complete some work in class prior to the visit as preparation and then extend this through the visit. A local organization is also easier to discuss requirements with informally and they will normally have a connection with the school already – even if this is only as part of the same community.

Further opportunities exist for visiting ICT-specific businesses, such as design agencies, telecoms or media industries. These visits may involve travelling further and will therefore require additional planning. Larger organizations (including businesses) may have education outreach departments which will liaise with you regarding your requirements. You will need to be clear if you require specific learning outcomes from your visit and to check that they are able to address these and how they will do so. Organizations with education outreach departments usually have a website with contact details and the types of activities and programmes they offer. We would advise phoning them as this allows you to fully explore the possibilities with them and to assess the educational value of what they are offering (some organizations may have a vested interest in presenting a particular picture and you should be alert to the impact of this for learning). Organizations which have a strong educational focus, such as museums, can be very useful for extended visits. They will already have documentation including risk assessments in place and they offer a good level of support for planning the learning opportunities you need.

Residential visits for ICT are offered through educational tour operators. Sometimes it is possible to combine a residential visit across different subject areas. This is particularly beneficial for visits abroad and where pupils are studying both subjects. This results in economies of scale for costs, staffing, travel and so on. If you organize the visit using an intermediary company then larger pupil numbers often result in decreased costs per person. You should also be aware that some organizations offer free teacher places for particular teacher:pupil ratios. As with any educational activity you need to assess the learning which will take place and this can become more complex when it involves a visit abroad. Careful liaison with the organizations to be visited and creation of appropriate resources for use prior to and following the visit will be necessary. This type of educational visit can provide a stimulating and engaging context for learning back in the classroom.

PRACTICALITIES OF ORGANIZING AN EDUCATIONAL VISIT

In 2002 a 10-year-old pupil drowned while on an educational visit to Glenridding Beck in Cumbria. The investigation concluded that the accident could have been avoided if proper assessment of risks had been conducted and safety guidelines followed. The teaching unions advise members to exercise caution when participating in or leading educational visits and to ensure all local authority guidance is followed. The safety of pupils should always be paramount when organizing educational visits. As a beginning teacher your role should be in identifying appropriate opportunities and then seek advice and support from more experienced colleagues.

The Health and Safety Executive conducted a thorough investigation into the Glenridding tragedy. They published a report and website (HSE, 2005a) following the investigation, which included lessons for future educational visits. These are summarized below:

- Pupils should be involved in the planning of the visit. They should be made 'risk aware' by discussing possible risks with them and involving them in the identification of how those risks can be minimized. This helps to share responsibility for managing risks with pupils.

- The group leader should provide good quality leadership through responsible attitude and behaviour. They should hold any relevant qualifications or accreditation which demonstrate their competence in the activities to be undertaken.
- All other group leaders should be prepared to challenge the group leader if they are concerned about risks. This may include where they feel the group leader is being careless or reckless regarding safety.
- Pupils and parents should be made aware of any risks involved in the activity so that they can give informed consent.
- As with all learning activities, the educational visit should be well planned with clear learning objectives which are shared with relevant people.
- Alternative activities need to planned at the same time as the original activity in case of unforeseen circumstances. The details of both the original activities and the planned alternative activities should be simultaneously shared with pupils and parents. All necessary consents for both sets of planned activities should be sought together.
- A risk assessment should be carried out using a structured document. Local education authorities and schools will have their own guidance and pro formas for this, including guidance on when an educational visit would need to be cancelled due to unacceptable risk.
- Emergency plans need to be in place and understood by all leaders (not just the principal leader). These should include evacuation procedures, emergency contacts and knowledge of the equipment to deal with an accident or emergency situation efficiently.

We are going to explore the process of planning learning in an out-of-school context through a scenario. This is not intended to be a comprehensive guide to planning educational visits, but rather an illustration of some of the steps you might take. Each LEA and many schools will have their own forms and procedures which you will be expected to use rather than the generic examples provided here. It is vital that you seek local advice and support before you start to plan any learning in an out-of-school context.

Scenario

Elaine is an NQT and is keen to organize an educational visit to enhance pupils' learning. Elaine feels that the ICT facilities in the school do not allow her to teach pupils some of the creative projects she would like. She has decided that pupils in her Year 8 class would benefit from an animation project to reinvigorate their interest in ICT and to explore some newer technologies than those available in the school. She knows that the local city learning centre (CLC) supports these types of projects.

During Elaine's training she shadowed teachers who were organizing educational visits, but did not organize one by herself. Although she wants to organize the visit herself, the head teacher asks her to seek support from a more experienced member of staff. Elaine decides that this could be a good cross-curricular project and she seeks support from an art and design teacher. Salim has worked as a teacher for five years and is a group leader for the Duke of Edinburgh Awards in the school: he is ideally placed to support Elaine's development in this area.

Seeking initial approval

The head teacher is responsible for overseeing all educational visits for the school. Their responsibilities include ensuring the staff are competent, experienced and appropriately qualified to lead the visit; that all necessary paperwork has been completed (including any returns to the LEA and parental consents obtained); that adequate child protection measures are in place; that insurance cover is adequate; that emergency procedures and information are in place and held by group leaders and a school-based contact. This list is not comprehensive but aims to provide a flavour of the responsibilities. Many of these responsibilities will be delegated to the group leader. As can be seen from this list of responsibilities, seeking initial approval for the visit is only the first stage of planning. The head teacher will expect to be informed of progress throughout.

Scenario continued

Salim explains that they need to complete an internal form with the initial plans for the educational visit. This will be submitted to the head teacher and may also be used to seek approval from the governors or the LEA. Elaine completes a first draft of the form and shares it with Salim for feedback. Following some minor corrections the form (Figure 9.2) is submitted to the head teacher for consideration.

Planning the project

Planning the educational visit is more than the logistics of the visit. Equally important is how the visit enhances pupils' learning through integration into the curriculum. The educational visit should seek to consolidate and extend learning through visiting a different setting. 'Activities have to be carefully planned. Well taught, they should extend learning before and after the event. Just as important as the quality of individual activities, is planning learning outside the classroom into the curriculum' (DfES, 2006: 13). Just as with any learning activity, the teaching and learning approaches need to be carefully considered in relation to the learning objectives which have been set.

Scenario continued

Following approval from the head teacher, Elaine and Salim need to work through the details of the project and the educational visit. The project involves cross-curricular collaboration so they need to be clear who will be teaching which elements of the project. Elaine drafts a scheme of work which covers five activities. During the first two activities she will introduce the project, analyse the brief with the pupils and the pupils will create storyboards. The third activity is for creating the clay models with support from Salim. The educational visit where pupils will experience stop-frame animation using their own models will be the fourth activity. Evaluation of the project will be the final activity.

Salim does not teach the same group of pupils, so they discuss options for teaching activity three. After looking at timetables and room availability they decide that one of the ICT lessons will be held in an art and design room where Salim and Elaine will jointly teach clay-modelling techniques. The clay models created by the pupils will be delivered to the CLC prior to the educational visit. Elaine will teach activities one, two and five. Both Elaine and Salim will teach on the educational visit with support from a learning mentor and CLC staff.

Educational Visits: Proposal Form

Lead teacher:............ Salim Kibaki ....
Other staff: .... Elaine Johnson (Deputy Group Leader) ....

Purpose of visit: To explore creativity in ICT curriculum through a cross-curricular project with Art & Design ....

Learning objectives: Pupils will:

1. engage with the systems life cycle to meet a customer's requirements for a multimedia project
2. design a storyboard based on their analysis of the brief
3. use appropriate materials and technology to animate their storyboard
4. peer and self evaluate project work ....

Start date: 9 February .... time: 9.00am ....
End date: 9 February .... time: 4.00pm ....
Place(s) to be visited: Grebesend CLC ....

Year group: ....8............ ~~boys~~ / ~~girls~~ / mixed* (*delete as appropriate)
Approximate numbers:..........25..............

Transport: Coach hire...

Proposed arrangements for informing:
Pupils: Discuss during lessons: there will be engagement with project before and after educational visit in ICT and Art & Design lessons. ....
Parents: Letter home with all details. Consent forms required from parents.
Approved ☐   Not approved ☐   Date ....
Head teacher signature..

Figure 9.2   Example of an initial proposal form

When planning the educational visit you need to ensure adequate pupil:teacher ratios. These will depend on the type of activity which is taking place. Some organizations will request certain ratios, the school and LEA will certainly have policies which reflect current government guidance. Not all staff on the visit need to be teachers. Learning mentors or teaching assistants are often eager to be involved and this can bring an enriched skill-set to the visit.

When planning staffing levels you should also consider emergency situations. Provision should be made for a person with knowledge of first aid to be on the visit, in our scenario the CLC will have a first aider on site. The head teacher or group leader may decide (particularly for residential visits) that a qualified first aider will need to go on the visit. It is a requirement to have a school-based contact (normally the head teacher or a deputy) who will be available for the duration of the educational visit. You will need to provide the nominated person with information to enable them to carry out the school's emergency procedures. For residential visits this role may be divided between a number of people, but there should be a clear schedule showing who is the contact for which days and nights.

RISK ASSESSMENT

Once the details of the project have been drawn together, Salim and Elaine book a visit to the CLC to discuss their requirements and to conduct a risk assessment (usually educational organizations will have an up-to-date risk assessment which can be used). If a risk assessment is not already in place, then one needs to be completed well in advance of the visit. The school or LEA should offer additional support for this process.

A risk assessment should be regularly reviewed. It forms part of a continuous process of evaluation and management of risk. It is important that staff involved in educational visits are aware of changes to the site (which may even occur on the day of the visit) and respond to these changes through the risk assessment process.

Scenario continued

Salim and Elaine visit the CLC to conduct a risk assessment (see Figure 9.3). The CLC provide a copy of their own risk assessment which Salim uses to help identify possible hazards and actions already being taken to minimize the risks. He also uses it to identify any areas where the pupils in the group may be at particular risk. Most of the additional control measures he identifies are related to continual monitoring during the visit, but he makes note of these, who will be responsible and when the action needs to take place.

They also meet with the CLC's ICT consultant to discuss their ideas for the project. The consultant shows them the facilities available in the CLC, identifies some additional software which could be used in the project and discusses his role. Elaine has not used the software before, so arranges some sessions when she can visit the CLC to familiarize herself with it before the visit.

When Salim and Elaine return to school they submit a copy of the risk assessment to the head teacher for the central file. They review their plans for the educational visit to ensure that the action points from the risk assessment are incorporated into their project planning. Elaine reviews her scheme of work to incorporate the relevant suggestions made by the ICT consultant.

Educational Visit Risk Assessment

Risk assessment date: _____
Conducted by: _____

Potential hazards	People at risk	Existing risk management controls	Additional controls/action required	Person responsible and when	Additional controls in place?	Continual monitoring required
Walking across the car park between CLC and the coach	Pupils and staff	Speed restrictions apply	Visit timings to be after school day starts and ends to minimize exposure to moving traffic. Staff to monitor traffic flow	Group leader – communication with pupils/ parents. All staff		Yes
Trips due to trailing wires when pupils are using video cameras	Pupils and staff	Work benches and sockets positioned to minimize trailing wires	Monitor wires and cover trailing wires with rubber floor covers where appropriate	All staff during visit		Yes

Figure 9.3 Risk assessment

The pro forma (Figure 9.3) is adapted from DfES (1998) *Health and Safety of Pupils on Educational Visits* and HSE (2006a) *Five Steps to Risk Assessment*.

FINAL APPROVAL

Once the internal planning and documentation is completed then final approval from the head teacher and, if appropriate, from the governors and LEA is needed. The head teacher will want confirmation that all the necessary arrangements are in place to ensure the safety of the children and staff on the educational visit.

It is vital that sufficient time is spent planning the visit and thinking through any accidents, emergencies or delays which may occur. It is always hoped that emergency procedures or contingencies will not be needed. If something does go wrong, though, careful planning makes it easier to deal with the situation. The head teacher will want to ensure that all eventualities have been considered.

INVOLVING PUPILS

Once the details of the educational visit have been established, the next stage is to inform pupils and parents. Pupils need to be clear about the purpose of the educational visit and how this will contribute to their learning. They should be informed of any risks and how they are to be managed, including the expectation that rules, procedures and instructions are followed and that they are expected to behave in an appropriate way. It is valid to withdraw a pupil from the educational visit if their behaviour could endanger themselves or others: pupils should be made aware of this.

Health and Safety Executive guidance following the investigation of the Glenridding Beck accident states that pupils should be made aware of the risks and become actively involved in planning to manage those risks. This makes pupils 'risk aware' and more able to predict and respond appropriately to risks, not just on the educational visit but also in other contexts. This can be seen as an important lesson in itself which can only be learnt through out-of-school contexts (HSE, 2005b).

Reflection Point 9.2

Consider how pupils could become involved in the planning for risk management through the scenario provided in this chapter. What opportunities are there to build this into the context provided for the pupils' work?

INFORMING PARENTS

When communicating with parents (or guardians) we are seeking to achieve two objectives: first, to inform them of the arrangements for the visit so they can make an informed decision regarding their child's participation and, secondly, to obtain permission and

Giving information	Seeking consent or information
The date and purpose of the visit including how it contributes to pupils' learning	Permission for pupil to participate
The place to be visited and the travel arrangements, including arrangements for departure and return	Agreement that parents will collect pupils on return from the educational visit
Details of supervision, including names of the group leaders and other staff on the visit. Also a school-based contact for parents in the event of an emergency	SEN or medical information held by the school being correct and up to date
Procedures for pupils who become ill	Confirmation that current contact details are correct
The standard of behaviour expected and arrangements if this expectation is not met	Agreement that the pupil must maintain the required standard of behaviour
Arrangements for risk management	
Insurance cover arrangements	
Items pupils will need to take, including appropriate clothing, food, equipment and spending money	

Figure 9.4 Considerations when communicating with parents

information from the parents to ensure the educational visit is successful. Figure 9.4 gives details of some of the areas you need to consider when drafting a letter seeking consent from parents. You should include all of the information in the 'Giving information' column and provide opportunities for parents to provide information or agreement for all issues in the 'Seeking consent or information' column.

Your school or LEA will have draft letters which you should adapt for your educational visit. Pupil misbehaviour can have a detrimental effect on the learning experience of other pupils. In the context of an educational visit, it can also put other people at risk. It should be made clear that the intention is to exclude pupils from the educational visit if their behaviour does not conform to the required standard (usually set out in a written code of conduct). You may then be obliged to provide alternative arrangements for any excluded pupils to meet the learning objectives through other means. Provision for this should be made during the planning stages.

Scenario continued

At the start of the project Elaine tells the pupils what the project will involve, the cross-curricular links and about the proposed visit to the CLC. She gives out letters (see Figure 9.5) with reply

(Continued)

(Continued)

slips (see Figure 9.6) to the pupils for them to pass to their parents or guardians. She explains that she must receive the completed reply slips in the next two weeks; if she has not received the reply from pupils then those pupils will be unable to attend. Elaine goes on to remind pupils of the school's code of conduct and that pupils who do not behave appropriately may be excluded from the visit. Elaine then starts work with the pupils on the project.

Figure 9.5 and Figure 9.6 provide examples of the possible content of a letter and permission reply slip for an educational visit taking place during school time (as per our

---

Dear Parent/Guardian,

It is proposed that your son's/daughter's ICT class will visit Grebesend CLC on Tuesday 9th February. They will leave the school at 8.45 a.m. and return at 4.15 p.m. The school has arranged for a coach to transport pupils and staff to the venue.

The educational visit will help pupils to

1. engage with the systems life cycle to meet a customer's requirements for a multimedia project
2. design a storyboard based on their analysis of the brief
3. use appropriate materials and technology to animate their storyboard
4. peer and self evaluate project work

The CLC has specialist hardware and software to help pupils gain a greater understanding of multimedia use of ICT.

The group leaders are Mr Kibaki and Miss Johnson. In the event of an emergency during the visit please contact Mrs Pearce on 01234 567890.

Pupils will be covered by the Local Authorities Public Liability insurance during the visit. Details of the scope of the insurance is attached.

Risk assessments have been carried out by the school and measures taken to minimize risks. A copy of the risk assessment is available on request. To help minimize risks all pupils will be expected to comply with the school's code of conduct both before and during the visit. Any pupils who do not follow the code of conduct may be excluded from the visit.

Pupils who wish to participate in the visit will need to:

1. Return a reply slip signed by a parent/guardian indicating consent by 2nd February
2. Follow the code of conduct for the school
3. Wear school uniform during the visit
4. Bring a packed lunch and drink on the visit

If you have any questions regarding the visit please contact a group leader to discuss.

Yours faithfully,

Group Leader

Figure 9.5 Sample letter to parents

Currwhistle School

Proposed visit to Grebesend CLC on Tuesday 9ᵗʰ February

Name of pupil: ⋯⋯⋯⋯⋯⋯⋯⋯⋯⋯⋯⋯⋯⋯⋯⋯⋯⋯⋯⋯⋯⋯⋯⋯⋯

I give/ do not give* permission for my son/ daughter to participate in the educational visit. (*delete as appropriate)

I will collect my son/daughter from the school at 4.15 p.m. on the 9th February.

I agree that my son/daughter will follow the school's code of conduct and instructions given during the educational visit by staff. If they do not follow the code of conduct I understand that they may be excluded from the visit.

I confirm that I have read the insurance details and understand the extent and limitations of this insurance policy.

The contact details held by the school to contact me are correct ❏
My contact details have changed and are now: ❏
Address: ⋯⋯⋯⋯⋯⋯⋯⋯⋯⋯⋯⋯⋯⋯⋯⋯⋯⋯⋯⋯⋯⋯⋯⋯⋯

Home phone ⋯⋯⋯⋯ Work phone ⋯⋯⋯⋯ Mobile ⋯⋯⋯

My son/daughter has special educational needs and/or medical needs which need to be taken into consideration during the visit:

⋯⋯⋯⋯⋯⋯⋯⋯⋯⋯⋯⋯⋯⋯⋯⋯⋯⋯⋯⋯⋯⋯⋯⋯⋯
⋯⋯⋯⋯⋯⋯⋯⋯⋯⋯⋯⋯⋯⋯⋯⋯⋯⋯⋯⋯⋯⋯⋯⋯⋯
⋯⋯⋯⋯⋯⋯⋯⋯⋯⋯⋯⋯⋯⋯⋯⋯⋯⋯⋯⋯⋯⋯⋯⋯⋯

Signed: ⋯⋯⋯⋯⋯⋯⋯⋯⋯ Date: ⋯⋯⋯⋯⋯
(Parent or guardian)
Name (please print): ⋯⋯⋯⋯⋯⋯⋯

Figure 9.6 Sample permission slip for educational visit

scenario). If the educational visit involved adventure activities, swimming or a residential stay, then further information and permissions would be needed. You need to seek specific local advice from school on this.

BUDGETS

The school will have procedures which need to be carefully followed if you need to collect money for your visit. The procedures will include details on setting up a separate account for the educational visit, security arrangements for the money collected and how any surplus will be handled following the visit.

Whether you need to collect money or not, you will need to prepare a budget to submit to the head teacher detailing all the proposed costs (and any income) of the educational visit. Following the visit, you will need to update this to reflect the actual costs. The school will be able to advise you on local budgeting arrangements.

ON THE DAY

Provided the educational visit has been well planned, the visit should run smoothly. All staff will need to be alert and continuously monitoring potential hazards which may occur, but you should also aim to enjoy the visit. Both staff and pupils should benefit from the experience.

Before leaving the school you should ensure that the school-based contact has a copy of all the documentation for the visit. In the event of an emergency the school-based contact will need to liaise with relevant people. The school policy will provide details on the documents to be left with the school-based contact. Group leaders also need to take all necessary documentation with them which will be detailed in the school's or LEA's procedures. In addition, a first aid box should be available on the trip.

Scenario continued

The day before the educational visit Elaine meets with the deputy head (school-based contact) to discuss the educational visit. She gives the deputy the pack of information and talks through the emergency and contingency plans. At the end of the school day Salim and Elaine meet to talk through the process for the following day. They check that they have all of the documentation they will need and that the first aid box is adequately stocked.

At 8.30 a.m. Salim and Elaine meet the pupils in the school hall. They take a register and remind pupils of expected behaviour on the visit. Salim goes to the meet the coach, leaving Elaine to supervise the pupils. Once the coach has arrived Salim leads the pupils to the coach. Elaine leaves the hall last, ensuring that all pupils are making their way to the coach. When they arrive at the coach, pupils are asked to line up and they are counted onto the coach. Pupils choose their own seats and are instructed to fasten their seat belts and to remain seated for the whole journey. When the pupils are settled, Elaine moves down the aisle checking seat belts and doing a final headcount while Salim checks he has all the documentation and the first aid box. Salim and Elaine then tell the driver they are ready to leave.

Before they arrive at the CLC Salim gives the pupils clear instructions not to leave their seats until instructed, that they are to walk to the CLC and to be aware of any traffic in the car park, they will line up along the wall of the CLC not blocking the entrance. As the coach pulls up, Salim reminds pupils to remain seated. Elaine goes into the CLC to tell them of their arrival and then waits outside to manage pupils across the car park and lining up ready to enter the CLC. Salim gradually allows pupils to leave the coach one row at a time.

The pupils are escorted into the CLC and to the room they will be using. Once pupils are in their seats Elaine does another head count. Pupils are introduced to the CLC teacher and the learning mentor who will be assisting during the day, and their project work starts. Pupils work well during the day, producing animations with their clay models based on the storyboards they had created.

At the end of the day, the pupils are escorted back to the coach, again with clear instructions and with staff performing headcounts to ensure all pupils are accounted for. They arrive back at the school at 4.00 p.m. where the majority of parents are waiting to collect the pupils. Elaine and Salim wait with the remaining pupils until they are collected.

Reflection Point 9.3

What measures have Salim and Elaine put in place to manage risks during the educational visit? Discuss with your mentor the procedures used in the school and how these ensure pupil safety. Investigate how these procedures would need to be adapted for remote supervision for older pupils.

AFTER THE VISIT

All educational visits should be evaluated to identify good practice and areas for improvement. The evaluation may be used by other teachers who organize visits to the same (or a similar) venue in the future, so it should contain sufficient detail to enable them to improve on or use your good practice. Your school is likely to have an evaluation form to complete which will capture the necessary information.

You will also be required to report on any incidents that occurred which did result or may have resulted in an accident or emergency. These reports should be rigorously completed to enable yourself and others to learn from the situation. These may also be used in the event that any questions arise regarding how the incident was managed. Carefully completed documentation is vital to enable you to respond appropriately weeks or months following the event. Needless to say this reporting should take place as soon as possible after the incident while events are still fresh in your mind.

The school will hold central copies of your evaluation and reports. The LEA may also require copies of any incident reports for their records. We would advise you to retain a copy of all documentation in your own records, this can make it easier to access and use to plan future events.

CONCLUSION

Educational visits offer terrific benefits to pupils – and to staff. As a beginning teacher you will probably be keen to organize an educational visit and should seek support and guidance from more experienced staff in your school. The aim of this chapter was to discuss some of the practicalities from a generic viewpoint. It should not be seen as a set of instructions for organizing a visit as the processes (including the documentation, permissions and levels of experience required as a group leader) will vary between schools and LEAs. We hope that from reading this chapter you will have increased confidence for approaching experienced staff to discuss organizing an educational visit or that you will consider an innovative approach to bringing the outside world into your classroom through use of technologies.

What the research says: learning outside the classroom

In 2006 the government published the *Learning Outside the Classroom* (LOtC) *Manifesto* (DfES). The aim of the manifesto was to draw together those involved (or with the potential to become involved) with LOtC through a common statement of intent and to encourage more widespread use of this form of learning. The manifesto invites signatories to the manifesto to support the aims and to pledge tangible support through initiatives for LOtC.

A recent report (Malone, 2008: 13) found 'evidence from a number of significant research studies that children and young people benefit substantially and in a variety of ways from LOtC'. This takes LOtC in the broadest context, including visits to museums, galleries, zoos, residential visits and so on, as well as projects undertaken within the school grounds. Research into LOtC has shown positive effects on behaviour and attitudes. It also impacts on children's values and the decisions they make now and into adulthood (DfES, 2006; Malone, 2008).

Learning Outside the Classroom provides a number of benefits: academic performance; development of critical thinking skills; risk-taking and problem-solving skills; creativity; improving attitudes, attendance and behavioural issues; motivates pupils and inspires a love of learning (DfES, 2006).

Learning Outside the Classroom projects take many forms and ones which are within the school grounds can be just as effective as others venturing further afield. Creative Partnerships, established in 2002, bring creative professionals, teachers and pupils together. These projects run in a variety of settings including on school grounds. They link project work to creative industries in some projects getting pupils to design and create new school uniforms, redesign the school reception or designing and creating a wildlife habitat (Ofsted, 2006). Mobile technology is increasingly being used in creative ways across the curriculum and has the potential to be extremely powerful in LOtC contexts. For example, WildKnowledge enable pupils to capture data about their environment using branching databases and forms or add multimedia content to geographical information system (GIS) maps (Teachernet, 2008; www.wildknowledge.co.uk/). Meanwhile Learning through Landscapes have used PDAs and GIS systems to map school grounds to enable pupils to design and project manage landscape improvements. The projects provided opportunities for pupils to see how GIS is used in other contexts, such as local government (Learning through Landscapes, 2007).

The National Curriculum (QCA, 2007) and the vision for the implementation of the curriculum in schools (Waters, 2008) is for pupils to experience a richer, broader curriculum which will harness the potential of cross-curricular delivery. Many of the projects outlined above and through the pledges made to the *Learning Outside the Classroom Manifesto* (DfES, 2006) demonstrate creative, authentic projects which could fulfil this vision.

Further reading

Department for Education and Skills (DfES) (1998) *Health and Safety of Pupils on Educational Visits*. London: DfES.

Department for Education and Skills (DfES) (2006) *Learning Outside the Classroom Manifesto*. Nottingham: DfES.

Weblinks

Live links to each of these websites can be found on the companion website, www.sagepub. co.uk/secondary.

Health and Safety Executive guidance on educational visits – www.hse.gov.uk/schooltrips/index.htm

National Space Centre – www.spacecentre.co.uk/

TeacherNet resources on educational visits including current government guidance – www. teachernet.gov.uk/wholeschool/healthandsafety/visits/

10 WHAT NEXT?

> ## This chapter covers:
>
> - the role of your Career Entry Development Profile and considerations when writing it
> - making applications for teaching positions
> - how to answer typical interview questions
> - support during your newly qualified teacher year
> - continuing professional development and career development opportunities
> - how you can contribute to the profession as your career progresses.

CAREER ENTRY AND DEVELOPMENT PROFILE

Towards the end of your Initial Teacher Training course you will be asked to complete Transition Point 1 of your Career Entry and Development Profile (CEDP). This will be completed in conjunction with your tutor, but you will retain ownership of it.

Completing your CEDP should give you an opportunity to think back and reflect on what you have learnt and achieved during your course. The CEDP will be used during your newly qualified teacher (NQT) year as the basis of discussions, action plans and target-setting between yourself and your induction tutor in school. It is, therefore, an important document and one which you should spend time carefully considering.

The CEDP contains questions which are intended to guide you in completing Transition Point 1, they are not prescriptive questions, but if you base your text around them, you will have covered most aspects required. We would suggest that you use the following headings, which are based on the questions, and write using paragraphs with continuous prose:

1. *Aspects of teaching I have found interesting and rewarding.* In this section you should identify two or three areas which you found to be particularly interesting during your training. These may be areas with which you want to have more involvement through your induction year, but which may not normally fall within the remit of a NQT. Examples may include a form tutor role, involvement in Young Enterprise

co-ordination or Duke of Edinburgh Awards. This provides the opportunity for you to discuss these areas with your induction mentor and to identify ways in which you could become involved.

2. *My strengths and achievements.* You should reflect not only on the areas which you have identified as strengths and achievements, but also those which are supported through evidence from your placements and assignment work. Consider areas which your tutors and mentors in school have identified as your strengths using the documentation from your course to help you. Mentors and tutors will often identify areas which beginning teachers overlook or do not consider important. This section is used to sell yourself to your new employer and to help create a good impression from the outset: take advantage of it.

3. *Aspects of teaching in which I would value additional experience.* You should avoid any negative comments in here regarding your level of experience. Instead, you should focus on these as areas for development. It may be that you have only had limited opportunities to explore issues around particular groups of pupils, such as EAL, SEN or gifted and talented; or you may want the experience of organizing out-of-class learning for yourself with limited support from experienced staff. Again, the areas identified here can form the basis of discussions and an action plan for your development, so you should include them here in a positive way, for instance 'I would benefit from additional experience of … '.

4. *My future aspirations and goals.* It can be difficult at the end of a demanding course of study to look beyond the summer holiday, but you should try to think approximately five years into the future and imagine the position you would like to have in education at that point. Again, this is an opportunity for you to market yourself to your new employer as an ambitious, up-and-coming teacher who they should be investing in and developing. Your aspirations may focus on your subject area, such as a key stage co-ordinator, head of department, advanced skills teacher, or may be elsewhere in the school, such as a year group leader, SEN co-ordinator examinations co-ordinator.

While you are writing your CEDP Transition Point 1, you should always try to focus on the positive: remember that your new employer will be reading the document; do not write anything which you may be uncomfortable with later on. You should also consider it the discussion document for establishing your action plan for training, development and support through your induction year. If you want to be able to do something, or think you need additional support in a particular area, make sure that it is raised in the document: the school has a responsibility to provide you with the necessary support for issues raised in the CEDP.

FINDING A POST

You should start applying for teaching posts from the autumn term of your final year of study. Although this may seem to be very early days for those who have just started a PGCE, some posts for September will be advertised at this stage.

Teaching posts are advertised through various media including local authorities' websites or vacancy bulletins; school's own websites; the *Times Educational Supplement* (*TES*) jobs section (these are also advertised through their website and daily alert service); and the Eteach website. The primary source is the *TES* and it is well worth using their job alert service. Even before your final year, it may be worthwhile registering with the *TES* job alert so you can become familiar with the employment situation.

When you make an initial enquiry regarding a post, you will be sent an information pack and application form. Read through the essential and desirable requirements. Ensure that you have addressed as many of these qualities as possible, preferably supported with examples, through your application form and covering letter or personal statement. By matching your skills and experience against the school's list of essential and desirable requirements, you will be tailoring your application: this is always necessary. Try, also, to be discriminating: do not apply for a job if you feel that you will be unhappy there. The NQT year is hard enough, without adding the extra pressure of a school you are not happy in.

When you receive an invitation for an interview, you should prepare thoroughly. First, do some background reading on the school. If you have not already looked at their Ofsted report, do so now. This will help you identify strengths and weaknesses of the school: consider if there are any areas which you feel you could help to develop, or you may want to ask them what they are doing to remedy any identified areas of weakness within ICT. Most schools also have a website which you should visit. This will normally give you an overview of the curriculum, extra-curricular activities and some of the policies and procedures within the school. This background reading enables you to speak authoritatively about the school, to anticipate questions they may ask you, to ask relevant and informed questions yourself and to tailor your responses to their needs.

An interview at a school normally lasts all day and you will spend much of the day with the other candidates. You will usually be expected to arrive for the start of school, when you will probably meet with key staff. You will probably have a tour of the school. Normally, you will have been asked to prepare a lesson and you will have a formal interview.

The interview process is as much about you finding out about the school as the school selecting you for a post. You may decide during the day that there is not a good fit between your skill-set and the school's needs. In these circumstances it is better to withdraw prior to the formal interview by informing the organizer.

The aspect of the interview process which concerns most beginning teachers is the sample lesson. Depending on the school, this may be a whole lesson or an abbreviated one, perhaps lasting 30 minutes. During this time try to retain the three-part lesson structure, make sure that the pupils have done some learning and make sure that you use engaging and, hopefully, new activities. We would not recommend using materials which the school will have seen multiple times before, or that other candidates are likely to use: try to come up with something yourself which will showcase your talents and creativity.

The formal interview is likely to be the final stage of the interview process. Depending on the position you are applying for the questions will vary, so if you are applying for an NQT position you will be asked questions such as:

- *Can you tell us a little about yourself?* This question is designed to help you relax. In response you should provide a bit of your history, explaining how you've reached this point and why.
- *Why do you want to work in our school?* You should have researched the school before applying and again before attending for interview. Consider what the strengths of the school are from their

latest Ofsted report, but also ways you could contribute to any areas which need to be developed. Also read the school's website and any newsletters or bulletins which may be online (you should also keep your eyes open for these while you are waiting for your interview in the school). Think about what is happening at the school now, the positive aspects of this and how you can contribute. If you are finding it difficult to access specific information on the school, focus on current educational issues and your experiences from the day. You may have had the chance to talk to pupils or have had a tour of the school. Look at the work pupils produce, the pupils' attitude to you and to learning and comment on these.

- *Can you tell us about your two main strengths and two weaknesses?* This question is loathed by people in general. Your strengths are usually easy enough to identify – do not be coy! You do need to be positive about your strengths – and about your weaknesses. Everyone has weaknesses, so do not try to bluff this one by claiming you do not. Before your interview identify a couple of weaknesses which you can turn to your advantage. For instance, 'I'm very stubborn, which I realise can be very frustrating to other people, but it also means when I decide to do something that I always see it through'.

- *What can you bring to the life of the school?* This again can be informed by the research you do before the interview. What extra-curricular activities does the school offer to which you could contribute? These do not have to be ICT related, they could be sporting activities, Duke of Edinburgh Awards, reading groups, or your experience from industry could contribute to Enterprise events. It is worthwhile knowing a little about what is currently offered as well as suggesting new activities.

  Another facet of this question is linked to extended schools and the school's role in the community. You may be keen to become involved in community education schemes, perhaps helping to educate and inform parents about Internet safety for their children. The school may offer courses of an evening and may be seeking support from staff to help run these. Even if your research has not identified these as current issues for the school it could be worthwhile raising these as potential areas for development with which you could be involved.

- *If a pupil in your class was behaving badly, what would you do?* This question sounds as if it is targeting your classroom management, but the focus is actually on your relationship with the pupils and your pastoral care. Your response to this question should include that you would assess whether this was normal behaviour for this particular pupil. If it is normal behaviour then you would follow the school policy for positive discipline. However, if the pupil was behaving out of character then you would give them some form of time out, speak to them quietly and try to find out what was wrong and try to deal with this appropriately. You would seek to mend the pupil: teacher relationship and refocus their attention on the lesson.

- *What are the current challenges facing schools?* To answer this question you will need to keep abreast of current developments in education. Ensure that you read the *TES* regularly, check education-related websites and keep up to date with the news on educational matters.

- *Where do you see yourself in five years time?* When answering this question you will need to strike a balance between staying in post long enough for the school to benefit, but also to demonstrate that you are keen to progress and develop. A typical answer may be 'I'm keen to develop and consolidate my skills as a teacher over the next few years, but in five years time I would like to be a head of department'. This shows the school that they will have a dynamic member of staff, but one which will enhance the school for a few years to come.

If the position you are applying for has a responsibility attached to it, then the questions will be designed to test your suitability for that position. So a key stage co-ordinator may be asked questions around their ability to plan imaginatively and innovatively. A role involving ICT co-ordination may ask about use of new technologies and your ability to build relationships, persuade others and put in place suitable training tools. A year group leader will focus on your pastoral care and relationships with parents and guardians.

If you are having difficulty securing a post you may need to review your strategies. It may be worthwhile asking someone else to look over your applications with a critical eye. Seek advice from your tutors or careers service regarding interview techniques and your sample lessons. If the summer is fast approaching and you have yet to find a post, register with supply agencies and be proactive in asking them for work. Sometimes NQTs find their first post through supply work and meanwhile you are gaining valuable experience which helps when applying for other positions. If the supply agency finds you long-term contracts then you would be able to complete your NQT year through these: make sure you speak to the school about this possibility.

NQT YEAR

The NQT year is an exciting as well as a nerve-racking time. During this year you will work hard to consolidate your knowledge and skills and to develop your role as an independent, autonomous classroom teacher (see companiaon website, www.sagepub.co.uk/secondary video clip, *Rewarding career*, for an NQT's view on his first year).

As an NQT, you are entitled to support from your school and the local authority to help you to succeed in your first year. Your induction tutor is responsible for overseeing the induction process for all the NQTs in the school. You will share your CEDP (discussed earlier in the chapter) with the induction mentor and possibly your head teacher. This provides the foundation for discussions between you and your induction mentor for establishing your objectives for development and how the school will support you in achieving these aims. Your induction mentor, or other staff, will observe you twice per term to assess your progress and give you feedback to aid your development.

As an NQT, your attendance at induction-related events are facilitated by having a 90 per cent timetable (as compared with a normal classroom teacher). You should use this time to attend training; for observations of experienced staff and for induction meetings. The local authority may have a programme of events for all NQTs in the area. These events go beyond just providing you with training, by giving you the opportunity to meet other NQTs from other schools and to start to develop your own network of contacts for support.

You will now be expected to fulfil all the usual duties of a classroom teacher. This can be quite a daunting prospect when previously you may have only produced sample reports, observed at parents evenings and assisted at open events. It is important to be open with your head of department or other staff when you are struggling, and ask them for ideas and tips to try to make life easier. The first year is always hard work, but it becomes easier after this. It is important that you have support networks in place, through colleagues, family and friends. It is very easy in your first year to allow your job to become all consuming, so try to create a sensible work–life balance which gives you time for yourself: you will feel more relaxed, have greater perspective and feel happier too.

CONTINUING PROFESSIONAL DEVELOPMENT

Once you are qualified you are responsible for your continuing professional development (CPD). The CEDP structure can be used to provide a framework for your records and reflections on CPD. The General Teaching Council for England (GTCE) provides an overview document with suggestions for CPD activities and how schools could support teachers' CPD activities.

There will be a number of opportunities for your continuing professional development within your school. All schools will have In-Service Education and Training (INSET) during the school year. Some of these will be used for planning and preparation for particular aspects of the school year, such as in September for preparing for the start of the new academic year, or for moderation purposes later in the year. These can be good opportunities, particularly as a new teacher, to learn from your colleagues and to share good practice. Other INSET days will be used to help staff development for all staff, identified as priority areas by the school. You will be expected to attend all INSET days.

The LEA may provide training on new or ongoing initiatives, such as the Secondary National Strategy. These will normally be targeted at specific groups of teachers, and are a good way of staying up to date and for developing your own network of peers. Other organizations such as the Specialist Schools and Academies Trust also have a programme of events and training which members can attend for minimal costs.

You may be able to take advantage of training offered by one of the teaching unions. The unions will normally offer targeted training, particularly for new or developing teachers. For instance, the National Union of Teachers offers training on behaviour management, young teachers' conferences and moving into management courses, or the National Association of Schoolmasters and Union of Women Teachers (NASUWT) offers training and seminars on behaviour management and career development. These events may be free or subsidized making it affordable to attend, although your school would need to arrange cover for your classes.

The award boards hold meetings and training events for delivery and marking of their courses at Key Stage 4 and post-16. It is advantageous to attend these events as it provides you with hints and tips for delivery of the course and how the marking will be conducted. This is information which you can use when planning delivery of the course and to help maximize pupil grades. Again, it is also a way of networking and sharing good practice with teachers outside of your own school.

As a professional you also have to take responsibility for keeping your subject knowledge up to date – particularly important in an ever-changing subject such as ICT. Local further education colleges often have programmes of evening courses which can be used to update and refresh your ICT knowledge and skills. The Open University offer modules which can be studied as stand alone and at a distance, again which can be used to develop your subject knowledge. The award boards may offer training in the future to help teachers to deliver their courses which have significantly new content: this will be important with the advent of diplomas. As an ICT specialist you will also be used to independently learning about new hardware and software. You should regularly read around your specialist area using the Internet, computing magazines and the press.

MOVING ON

Trainee and new teachers tend to focus on subject-related progression, usually identifying a head of department role as their next step on the career ladder, but there are other roles which a new teacher may want to consider too.

Pastoral

It is advantageous for an NQT to have form tutor responsibilities: a form tutor is immediately seen as being an integral part of the school with an important role to play. If you are fortunate enough to have your own tutor group you will quickly become involved in the pastoral side of school life. There are promotion prospects through pastoral leadership roles, like year group leadership, or working as a transition co-ordinator. These areas are usually overlooked initially by new teachers, but can prove very rewarding as you work closely with pupils, their parents or carers and other professionals to help develop the pupils in your care as individuals and to ensure their safety and well-being.

Subject specific

The obvious route for career progression for new teachers is that of head of department. There are steps towards this which you may want to consider, if this is the career path you want. Larger ICT departments will have co-ordinator roles for different key stages which enables you to develop the curriculum, resources and additional activities, not just within your classroom, but across the department. This is a good intermediate step as you are able to develop your leadership skills and knowledge with the support of your head of department. Many heads of department will encourage (or expect) all teachers to be involved in curriculum planning for use by the department. This is a good opportunity for your development and provides enhanced experiences to include in future job applications.

Advanced skills teachers

Some teachers feel that their passion and commitment remains in the classroom and they have no desire to move up through the hierarchy. This, though, is not necessarily a bar to progression. Advanced skills teachers (ASTs) are officially recognized for their exemplary classroom practice. They have the opportunity to share their good practice both within their own school and in other schools too. For those who are passionate about staying in the classroom, this is a positive route forward, providing you with recognition and rewards for your exemplary skills and giving you the chance to help develop other teacher skills.

Examiner

The award boards recruit teachers as examiners for marking and moderating for all the qualifications they offer. Teachers are paid for the work they do, but it also provides added benefits for your own practice and for your pupils. Examiners tend to have a more in-depth understanding of the qualifications they are teaching and marking, which enhances their delivery of the curriculum. They also understand the marking criteria and are better able to interpret the specification. Examiners will mark work from centres across the country and will therefore see examples of good and bad practice, it is possible to pick out and develop good practice for use in your own classroom and to advise delivery throughout your department. Schools often value the added insight which examiners bring to the school, not just for a specific subject, but knowledge which can be applied across the school. This is also a method of progressing in your career outside your own school.

CONTRIBUTING TO THE PROFESSION

During your teacher training you will have been encouraged to reflect on incidents or episodes of importance which occurred during your time in university and on your placements. You should continue to reflect throughout your career in order to improve your own practice and to help identify issues for CPD. There are roles within the profession which explicitly form part of the reflective cycle (Figure 10.1) or help us to continue to reflect on our own (and others') practice. Alongside this, these roles also enable us to contribute to the continuing success and growth of the profession.

Involvement in professional associations

There are a number of organizations with which you could become involved to contribute to the teaching profession in general. These include the unions, the General Teaching Council and forums such as TeacherNet, BECTA and the *TES* online forums. Naace is the current professional association for promoting ICT in education and provides a forum for member ICT specialists. It organizes events and conferences which can help you to stay up to date but it also enables members to share good practice and collaborate through their online forums, newsletters and Sharing Success e-zines.

Active membership of a professional association is a good way of developing your professional profile, of staying up to date, finding like-minded people to collaborate with and telling other people of the good work you yourself are doing.

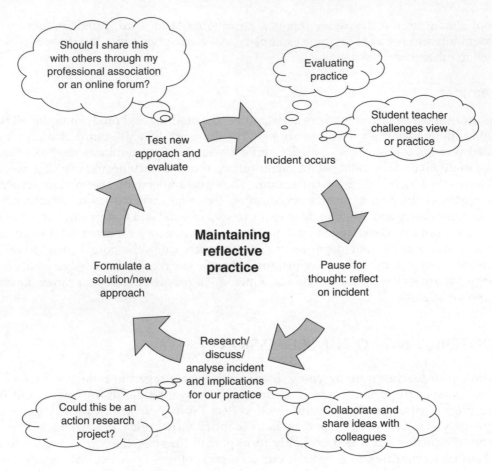

Figure 10.1 Reflective cycle

Mentoring

Mentoring can take place at different stages of a person's career: as a trainee teacher, an NQT, moving into management or changing roles. Good mentors are highly valued by the people they mentor and the profession in general. They contribute by passing on their knowledge and experience to new or developing colleagues. Whatever your own experience of mentoring has been (and hopefully it has been a good and positive experience) once you have consolidated your experience and feel confident, you could consider mentoring a trainee teacher.

Mentoring a trainee can help to keep fresh your own perspective on teaching and learning. It forces you to constantly re-evaluate your own practice and justify the choices you make. The mentoring should have two-way benefits, though, as trainees will normally have new ideas and should be abreast of the current research in education.

A symbiotic relationship between the mentor and mentored, whereby both benefit is the best situation.

Action research

During your training you will probably have engaged with some research for either a dissertation or other assignment work and will be familiar with some of the terminology associated with research. Action research may be of use to you if you are starting work on an area of research for your training or if you are mentoring a trainee who is involved with research.

Action research is the name given to practical research which you may undertake in your own classroom or school in order to investigate and improve an aspect of your current practice. Many successful action research projects later feature in journals, so this is a positive way in which you can contribute to the teaching profession, as well as to your own professional practice. See the companion website, www.sagepub.co.uk/secondary for an action research model.

Action research differs from other forms of research which you may consider because it is immediately useful in improving classroom practice.

As you complete your training, you are entering a new and exciting phase of your career. You have worked hard to complete your course of study and will now need to refocus your energy on consolidating and developing your career. There are many opportunities available for your career progression and for you to contribute to the profession you have chosen too.

Further reading

Cowley, S. (2007) *Guerrilla Guide to Teaching: The Definitive Resource for New Teachers*. 2nd edn. London: Continuum.

TES 1st Appointments – this is published annually providing help and advice for trainee teachers and NQTs seeking their first teaching post. Your careers office will normally have this available or you can download it from the *TES* website (www.tes.co.uk).

Weblinks

Links to each of these websites can be found on the companion website, www.sagepub.co.uk/secondary.

General Teaching Council for England CPD publications – www.gtce.org.uk/cpd_page
NAACE: a professional association for the advancement of education through appropriate ICT use – www.naace.co.uk/
TeacherNet advice on CPD – www.teachernet.gov.uk/professionaldevelopment/
TES job search facility – http://jobs.tes.co.uk/home

REFERENCES

Anderson, L.W. and Krathwohl, D.R. (eds) (2001) *A Taxonomy for Learning, Teaching, and Assessing: A Revision of Bloom's Taxonomy of Educational Objectives.* New York: Longman.

Assessment Reform Group (2002) *Assessment for Learning: 10 principles.* ARG. http://k1.ioe.ac.uk/tlrp/arg/CIE3.PDF.

Atherton, J.S. (2004) *Teaching and Learning: Authority and Learning.* www.learningandteaching.info/learning/authority.htm.

Barnes, D. (1976) *From Communication to Curriculum.* Harmondsworth: Penguin Books.

Barrow, R. and Woods, R. (2006) *An Introduction to Philosophy of Education.* London: Routledge.

Batho, R. (2005) 'Teaching literacy across the curriculum', in V. Ellis (ed.), *Learning and Teaching in Secondary Schools.* Exeter: Learning Matters.

Bell, J. (2005) *Doing your Research Project: A Guide for First-time Researchers in Education, Health and Social Science.* 4th edn. Maidenhead: Open University Press.

Black, P. and Wiliam, D. (1998) 'Inside the black box: raising standards through classroom assessment', *Phi Delta Kappan,* 80(2): 139–48.

Black, P., Harrison, C., Lee, C., Marshall, B. and Wiliam, D. (2003) *Assessment for Learning: Putting it into Practice.* Maidenhead: Open University Press.

Bloom, B.S. (ed.) (1956) *Taxonomy of Educational Objectives: The Classification of Educational Goals – Handbook I: The Cognitive Domain.* New York: McKay.

British Educational Communications and Technology Agency (BECTA) (2007) *Signposts to Safety – Teaching E-safety at Key Stages 3 and 4.* Coventry: BECTA.

Bruner, J. (1977) *The Process of Education.* London: Harvard University Press.

Butler, R. (1987) 'Task-involving and ego-involving properties of evaluation', *Journal of Educational Psychology,* 79(4): 474–82.

Byron, T. (2008) *Safer Children in a Digital World: The Report of the Byron Review.* London: Department for Children, Schools and Families, and the Department for Culture, Media and Sport. www.dfes.gov.uk/byronreview/.

Coffield, F., Moseley, D., Hall, E. and Ecclestone, K. (2004) *Should We Be Using Learning Styles?* London: Learning and Skills Research Centre.

Cohen, L., Manion, L. and Morrison, K. (2004) *A Guide to Teaching Practice.* London: RoutledgeFalmer.

Cohen, L., Manion, L. and Morrison, K. (2007) *Research Methods in Education.* 6th edn. London: Routledge.

Cotton, K. (1988) *Classroom Questioning.* Northwest Regional Educational Laboratory. www.nwrel.org/scpd/sirs/3/cu5.html.

Cowley, S. (2007) *Guerrilla Guide to Teaching: The Definitive Resource for New Teachers.* 2nd edn. London: Continuum.

Daniels, H. (2001) *Vygotsky and Pedagogy.* London: RoutledgeFalmer.

de Freitas, S. (2007) *Learning in Immersive Worlds: A Review of Game-based Learning.* London: JISC. www.jisc.ac.uk/media/documents/programmes/elearninginnovation/gamingreport_v3.pdf.

Department for Children, Schools and Families (DCSF) (2007) *Effective Provision for Gifted and Talented Students in Secondary Education.* Nottingham: DCSF Publications.

Department for Children, Schools and Families (DCSF) (2008a) *Being the Best for Our Children: Releasing Talent for Teaching and Learning.* London DCSF DCSF-00246-2008.

Department for Children, Schools and Families (DCSF) (2008b) *Framework for Secondary ICT.* London: DCSF. www.standards.dcsf.gov.uk/secondary/framework/ict/fwsict/.

Department for Education and Employment (DfEE) (1999) *The National Curriculum: Handbook for Secondary Teachers in England.* London: The Stationery Office.

Department for Education and Science (DES) (1989) *Discipline in Schools: Report of the Committee of Enquiry Chaired by Lord Elton*. London: The Stationery Office.

Department for Education and Skills (DfES) (1998) *Health and Safety of Pupils on Educational Visits*. London: DfES.

Department for Education and Skills (DfES) (2001a) *Special Educational Needs Code of Practice*. Nottingham: DFES Publications.

Department for Education and Skills (DfES) (2001b) *Framework for Teaching English: Years 7, 8 and 9*. Nottingham: DfES Publications.

Department for Education and Skills (DfES) (2002) *Framework for Teaching ICT Capability: Years 7, 8 & 9*. DfES 0321/2002. Nottingham: DfES Publications.

Department for Education and Skills (DfES) (2004a) *Aiming High: Understanding the Educational Needs of Minority Ethnic Pupils in Mainly White Schools – A Guide to Good Practice*. Nottingham: DfES Publications.

Department for Education and Skills (DfES) (2004b) *Every Child Matters: Change for Children*. DfES/1081/2004. Nottingham: DfES.

Department for Education and Skills (DfES) (2004c) *Teaching Strategies and Approaches for Pupils with Special Educational Needs: A Scoping Study*. Nottingham: DfES Publications.

Department for Education and Skills (DfES) (2005a) *14–19 Education and Skills*. White Paper. Cm 6476. London: HMSO.

Department for Education and Skills (DfES) (2005b) *Harnessing Technology: Transforming Learning and Children's Services*. DFES/1296/2005. Nottingham: DfES.

Department for Education and Skills (DfES) (2005c) *Personalised Learning: FAQs*. DFES standards website, www.standards.dfes.gov.uk/personalisedlearning/faq/#140.

Department for Education and Skills (DfES) (2006) *Learning Outside the Classroom Manifesto*. Nottingham: DfES. www.teachernet.gov.uk/teachingandlearning/resourcematerials/outsideclassroom/.

Evans, C. (1979) *The Mighty Micro: The Impact of the Computer Revolution*. London: Gollancz.

Festinger, L. and Carlsmith, J. (1959) 'Cognitive consequences of forced compliance', first published in *Journal of Abnormal and Social Psychology*, 58: 203–10. See also http://psychclassics.yorku.ca/Festinger/.

Fildes, J. (2008) 'Robot glider harvests ocean heat', BBC News. http://news.bbc.co.uk/1/hi/technology/7234544.stm.

Freeman, J. (2006) 'Giftedness in the long term', *Journal for the Education of the Gifted*, 29: 384–403.

Galton, M., Gray, J. and Rudduck, J. (eds) (2003) *Transfer and Transitions in the Middle Years of Schooling (7–14): Continuities and Discontinuities in Learning*. Research Report RR443. London: DfES. www.dfes.gov.uk/research/data/uploadfiles/RR443.pdf.

Gibbs, G. (1988) *Learning by Doing: A Guide to Teaching and Learning Methods*. Oxford: Oxford Polytechnic Further Education Unit.

Glass, G. (2000) *Meta-Analysis at 25*. College of Education, Arizona State University, Phoenix. http://glass.ed.asu.edu/gene/papers/meta25.html.

Great Britain (1995) *Discrimination Act 1995* (c.50). London: HMSO.

Great Britain (1996) *Education Act 1996* (c.56). London: HMSO.

Greenfield, S. (2007) 'Brain & behaviour: the scientific basis for learning styles', *Times Educational Supplement*, 27 July. www.tes.co.uk/2412193.

Gutherson, P., Pickard, L., Turner, R., Akoh, J., Daszkiewicz, T., Davies, H. and Barton, E. (2006) *Behaviour Management and Pastoral Skills Training for Initial Teacher Trainees: Trainees' Confidence and Preparedness, Reading TAC*. The Centre for British Teachers, www.cfbt.com/PDF/91094./pdf.

Hall, S. (1997) 'The problem with differentiation', *School Science Review*, 78: 95–8.

Hattie, J.A. (1999) 'Influences on students' 'learning, inaugural lecture'. University of Auckland, Auckland.

Hattie, J. and Timperley, H. (2007) 'The power of feedback', *Review of Educational Research*, 77(1): 81–112.

Health and Safety Executive (HSE) (2005a) *Glenridding Beck – Investigation Report: Drowning of Max Palmer in Glenridding Beck, 26 May 2002*. London: HSE. www.hse.gov.uk/schooltrips/pdf/investigation.pdf.

Health and Safety Executive (HSE) (2005b) *Glenridding Beck – Conclusions: Drowning of Max Palmer in Glenridding Beck, 26 May 2002*. London: HSE. www.hse.gov.uk/schooltrips/pdf/conclusions.pdf.

Health and Safety Executive (HSE) (2006a) *Five Steps to Risk Assessment*. London: HSE.

Health and Safety Executive (HSE) (2006b) *Working with VDUs*. London: HSE Books.

James, M., McCormick, R., Black, P., Carmichael, P., Drummond, M., Fox, A., MacBeath, J., Marshall, B., Pedder, D., Procter, R., Swaffield, S., Swann, J. and Wiliam, D. (2007) *Improving Learning How to Learn: Classrooms, Schools and Networks*. London: Routledge.

Jarvis, P. (2006) *Towards a Comprehensive Theory of Human Learning: Lifelong Learning and the Learning Society, Volume 1*. Oxford: Routledge.

Kerry, T. (2002a) *Explaining and Questioning*. Cheltenham: Nelson Thornes.

Kerry, T. (2002b) *Mastering Teaching Skills Series – Learning Objectives, Task-Setting and Differentiation*. 2nd edn. Cheltenham: Nelson Thornes.

Kiili, K. (2007) 'Foundation for problem-based gaming', *British Journal of Educational Technology*, 38(3): 394–404.

Kounin, J.S. (1970) *Discipline and Group Management in Classrooms*. New York: Holt, Rinehart and Winston.

Lambert, D. and Lines, D. (2000) *Understanding Assessment: Purposes, Perceptions, Practice*. London: Routledge Falmer.

Learning through Landscapes (2007) *DfES School Grounds of the Future: Final Evaluation Report*. London: Learning through Landscapes. www.ltl.org.uk/schools_and_settings/research/research-downloads.htm.

Livingstone, S. and Bober, M. (2005) *UK Children Go Online: Final Report of Key Project Findings*. London: London School of Economics and Political Science. www.children-go-online.net.

Malone, K. (2008) *Every Experience Matters: An Evidence Based Research Report on the Role of Learning Outside the Classroom for Children's Whole Development from Birth to Eighteen Years*. London: Farming and Countryside Education and Department for Children, Schools and Families. www.face-online.org.uk/index.php?option=com_content&task=view&id=1308&Itemid=850.

McInnerney, J. and Roberts, T. (2004) 'Online learning: social interaction and the creation of a sense of community', *Educational Technology & Society*, 7(3): 73–81.

McIntyre, D., Pedder, D. and Rudduck, J. (2005) 'Pupil voice: comfortable and uncomfortable learnings for teachers', *Research Papers in Education*, 20(2): 149–68.

Mergel, B. (1998) *Instructional Design and Learning Technology*. Saskatchewan: University of Saskatchewan. www.usask.ca/education/coursework/802papers/mergel/brenda.htm.

Milgram, S. (1963) 'Behavioral study of obedience', *Journal of Abnormal and Social Psychology*, 67(4): 371–78.

Mortimore, P. (ed.) (1999) *Understanding Pedagogy and its Impact on Learning*. London: Paul Chapman Publishing.

Office for Standards in Education (Ofsted) (2002) *Information and Communication Technology in Secondary Schools: Ofsted Subject Reports Series 2001/02*. HMI 819. London: Ofsted.

Office for Standards in Education (Ofsted) (2004) *The Key Stage 3 Strategy: Evaluation of the Third Year*. HMI 2090. London: Ofsted.

Office for Standards in Education (Ofsted) (2005a) *Embedding ICT in Schools – a Dual Evaluation Exercise*. HMI 2391. London: Ofsted.

Office for Standards in Education (Ofsted) (2005b) *English 2000–05: A Review of Inspection Evidence*. HMI 2351. London: Ofsted.

Office for Standards in Education (Ofsted) (2005c) *The Secondary National Strategy: An Evaluation of the Fifth Year*. HMI 2612. London: Ofsted.

Office for Standards in Education (Ofsted) (2005d) *Managing Challenging Behaviour*. London: Ofsted.

Office for Standards in Education (Ofsted) (2006) *Creative Partnerships: Initiative and Impact*. HMI 2517. London: Ofsted.

O'Neil, J. (1990) 'Findings of styles research: murky at best', *Educational Leadership*, 48(2) 7.

Parsons, R., Hinson, S. and Sardo-Brown, D. (2001) *Educational Psychology: A Practitioner-researcher Model of Teaching*. London: Thomson Learning.

Petty, G. (2004) *Teaching Today – A Practical Guide*. 3rd edn. Cheltenham: Nelson Thornes.

Qualifications and Curriculum Authority (QCA) (2000) *A Scheme of Work for Key Stage 3 Information and Communication Technology*. QCA/00/446. London: QCA Publications.

Qualifications and Curriculum Authority (QCA) (2001) *Do Pupils Get Better at Reading and Writing English as They Progress?* www.qca.org.uk/qca_5630.aspx.

Qualifications and Curriculum Authority (QCA) (2007) *National Curriculum.* London: QCA. http://curriculum.qca.org.uk/index.aspx.

Qualifications and Curriculum Authority (QCA) (2008) *Report on the 2007 Key Stage 3 ICT Test Pilot.* QCA/08/3513. London: QCA.

Qualter, P., Gardner, K. and Whiteley, H. (2007) 'Emotional intelligence: review of research and educational implications', *Pastoral Care in Education*, March: 11–20.

Revell, P. (2005) 'Each to their own', *Guardian,* 31 May, www.guardian.co.uk/education/2005/may/31/schools.uk3.

Robin Richardson, R. (2004) *Here, There and Everywhere: Belonging, Identity and Equality in Schools.* Stoke-on-Trent: Trentham Books.

Rogers, B. (2002) *Classroom Behaviour.* London: Paul Chapman Publishing.

Rogers, B. (2006) *Classroom Behaviour.* 2nd edn. London: Paul Chapman Publishing.

Rudduck, J., Berry, M., Demetriou, H. and Goalen, P. (2003) 'Managing institutional and personal transitions – developing the work in schools', in M. Galton, J. Gray and J. Rudduck (eds), *Transfer and Transitions in the Middle Years of Schooling (7–14): Continuities and Discontinuities in Learning.* Research Report RR443. London: DfES. www.dfes.gov.uk/research/data/uploadfiles/RR443.pdf.

Savage, A. (2007a) *Personalised Data* CommunICTy. www.learnblog.net/ict/2007/04/25/personalised-data/.

Savage, A. (2007b) *School Life Blogs* CommunICTy. http://communicty.edublogs.org/2007/10/15/school-life-blogs/.

Sharp, J.G., Byrne, J. and Bowker, R. (2006) 'The trouble with VAK', *Educational Futures* (BESA), 1: 76–93. www.besajournal.org.uk/journals/200706/sharp.pdf.

Slavin, R. (2003) *Educational Psychology: Theory and Practice.* Boston, MA: Allyn and Bacon.

St Mary's College of Maryland (2005) Differentiation web pages, www.smcm.edu/edstudy/d7-Proj/Projects/ResearchSites/acbrowning/index.htm.

Stefani, L., Mason, R. and Pegler, C. (2007) *The Educational Potential of E-portfolios: Supporting Personal Development and Reflective Learning.* Oxford: Routledge.

Steinkuehler, C. (2008) 'Massively multiplayer online games as an educational technology: an outline for research', *Educational Technology*, January–February: 10–21.

TeacherNet (2008) *Learning Outside the Classroom Newsletter,* April, www.teachernet.gov.uk/teachingandlearning/resourcematerials/outsideclassroom/newsletters/april2008/.

Teaching and Learning in 2020 Review Group (2006) *2020 Vision: Report of the Teaching and Learning in 2020 Review Group.* Ref: 04255-2006DOM-EN. London: DfES. http://publications.teachernet.gov.uk/default.aspx?PageFunction=productdetails&PageMode=publications&ProductId=DFES-04255-2006.

The Primary Review (2007) *Primary Review Research Briefings Overview of 3/4, 4/1 & 4/2. How Well Are We Doing? Research on Standards, Quality and Assessment in English Primary Education.* Cambridge: University of Cambridge. www.primaryreview.org.uk/Publications/Interimreports.html.

Training and Development Agency (2007) *Professional Standards for Teachers: Why Sit Still in your Career.* London: TDA. www.tda.gov.uk/upload/resources/pdf/s/standards_a4.pdf.

Tymms, P. and Merrell, C. (2007) *The Primary Review: Interim Report. Standards and Quality in English Primary Schools Over Time: The National Evidence.* Research survey 4/1. Cambridge: University of Cambridge. www.primaryreview.org.uk/Publications/Interimreports.html.

Waters, M. (2007) 'Interview', in Teachers TV: *Estelle Morris meets Mick Waters.* 14 November. www.teachers.tv/video/23258.

Waters, M. (2008) 'Curriculum and the learner', *Annual Review 2007.* Qualifications and Curriculum Authority, British Museum, London, 12 February.

White, B.Y. and Frederiksen, J.R. (1998) 'Inquiry, modeling, and metacognition: making science accessible to all students', *Cognition and Instruction*, 16(1): 3–118.

Williams, R. (2008) *The Non-Designer's Design Book.* 3rd edn. Berkeley, CA: Peachpit Press.

Williamson, B. and Morgan, J. (2007) *Enquiring Minds: Year 2 Research Report.* Bristol: Futurelab.

Working Group on 14–19 Reform (2004) *14–19 Curriculum and Qualifications Reform: Final Report of the Working Group on 14–19 Reform.* London: DfES.

INDEX